The Cognitive Psychology of Proper Names

The 'tip-of-the-tongue' state is something most people have, at some time, experienced when recalling proper names, especially people's names. *The Cognitive Psychology of Proper Names* addresses the issue of why recall of proper names is so difficult.

Tim Valentine, Tim Brennen and Serge Brédart critically examine current thinking on the creation and retrieval of proper names and challenge the view that proper names are meaningless labels. They use evidence from speech production, face recognition and word recognition to develop a new functional model of the production and recognition of people's names. They also consider the relationship between processing proper names and common names. Evidence is drawn from experimental studies, everyday memory difficulties and case studies of patients with brain damage. These highlight some startling dissociations, but also some important similarities between processing of common names and proper names.

The Cognitive Psychology of Proper Names will appeal to researchers and students interested in the psychological and cognitive neuropsychological aspects of picture naming, face recognition, speech production and word recognition.

Tim Valentine is a lecturer in Psychology at the University of Durham. His previous publications include *The Cognitive and Computational Aspects of Face Recognition* (Routledge 1995).
Tim Brennen is a senior lecturer in Psychology at the University of Tromsø.
Serge Brédart is a research associate of the Belgian National Fund for Scientific Research at the University of Liège, Belgium.

The Cognitive Psychology of Proper Names

On the importance of being Ernest

Tim Valentine, Tim Brennen and
Serge Brédart

London and New York

First published 1996
by Routledge
11 New Fetter Lane, London EC4P 4EE

Simultaneously published in the USA and Canada
by Routledge
29 West 35th Street, New York, NY 10001

Typeset in Palatino by Keystroke, Jacaranda Lodge,
Wolverhampton
Printed and bound in Great Britain by Mackays of
Chatham PLC, Chatham, Kent

British Library Cataloguing in Publication Data
A catalogue record for this book is available from the
British Library

Library of Congress Cataloguing in Publication Data
A catalogue record for this book has been requested

ISBN 0-415-13545-1 (hbk)
ISBN 0-415-13546-X (pbk)

'I cannot at the present moment recall what the General's Christian name was. Your poor dear mother always addressed him as "General". That I remember perfectly.'

Lady Bracknell in *The Importance of Being Earnest* by Oscar Wilde.

For Viv, Ragnhild and Catherine

Contents

Illustrations

FIGURES

TABLE

Preface

Proper names form a linguistic class that is of considerable practical and theoretical importance. The failure to recall a person's name at the right moment can be embarrassing and inconvenient and yet it is a common difficulty observed in our everyday lives. Despite the social significance of proper names, and in particular people's names, cognitive psychologists have shown little interest in developing a cognitive psychology of proper names until very recently. However, some fascinating data on proper names have been reported in the last few years. Proper names are *the* linguistic category most likely to provoke retrieval difficulties in normal healthy adults, and for some brain-injured patients proper name recall is their only linguistic problem. Why should this be? We believe that the attempt to answer such questions will reveal much of practical significance on memory for proper names and will also prove a powerful approach to develop our understanding of human cognition.

The aim of this book is to draw together a wide range of evidence which bears on the cognitive processes involved in recognising and recalling proper names. Our work has been guided by the literature on familiar face processing. This literature emphasises the special status of people's names in comparison to other information we know about them. The status of proper names is an issue which we consider from a number of different perspectives. Our aim is to make the issues as accessible as possible to readers without specialist knowledge of cognitive psychology.

We begin with a multi-disciplinary look at proper names, and then focus on information processing models of proper names. Throughout the book we present theories of proper name processing in the form of box-and-arrow models. We believe that such paper-and-pencil modelling is, and will remain, a useful way of structuring ways of thinking about cognitive processes and of generating empirical predictions.

In this paragraph, we wish to clarify what we intend to imply by drawing such box and arrow models. Our comments are addressed primarily to some cognitive psychologists who may consider this approach to be rather old-fashioned. This discussion might appear technical to readers who are not familiar with either information-processing models of cognition or connectionist models and can easily be skipped. It is aimed at avoiding mis-interpretation of our approach among cognitive psychologists. By drawing box-and-arrow models we do *not* intend to imply a strict hierarchy of processes to be interpreted in terms of the logic of additive factors. It is clear from the content of the following chapters that we have no objection to the suggestion that information (or activation) is passed between 'boxes' operating in cascade or in full interaction, passing activation rapidly both up and down the hierarchy. Thus we do not believe that processing at an earlier level must be completed before processing at a subsequent level can begin. In short, we have no objection to implementation of the models we propose in terms of connectionist models and indeed have considerable enthusiasm for such an approach. We believe our box-and-arrow models provide guidelines for the design of the architecture of the macro-structure of such models.

What we intend to imply by drawing a box-and-arrow model is to identify the function of the representations necessary to perform a given task and the relationship between these representations. Thus if two boxes are shown in a serial hierarchy, we mean to imply that the first representation must be activated before the second, and that a factor affecting the first representation will have some knock-on effect for the activation of the second (although this will not necessarily always be observable). In contrast two boxes receiving inputs in parallel will operate largely independently of each other; however, the possibility that gross impairment to one can influence the activation of the other cannot be ruled out entirely (see Chapter 5 for an example).

Many people laid the foundations for this book. Vicki Bruce deserves particular mention, not only because of her crucial role in face recognition research but also because she was an inspirational supervisor for two of the authors. Tim Valentine and Serge Brédart began working together on processing of people's names following a summer school organised by the European Society for Cognitive Psychology at Bernried, Germany in 1987. The original idea that we should write a book on proper names emerged from a period when Serge Brédart met Tim Brennen while visiting the University of Grenoble, France. The three authors have made equal contributions to the writing of the book. Our ideas have benefited greatly from discussions with many people. In particular we would like to thank Mike Burton, Danielle David, Rick Hanley, Jacques Pellat and Andy Young. Special thanks are due to Rick Hanley for reading an earlier draft of the entire manuscript.

Some of the original research reported here and the writing of this book has been supported by funding from the following sources. Two grants were awarded to Tim Valentine from the Economic and Social Research Council (nos. R000232836 and R000234612). Tim Brennen was supported by an ATIPE grant from the CNRS Région Rhône-Alpes, and a stipend from the Norwegian Research Council (Norges Forskningråd, no. 101152/330). Serge Brédart is a research associate of the National Fund for Scientific Research of Belgium, and his work was supported by a grant (no. 1.5.115.93F) from the National Fund for Scientific Research of Belgium.

Chapter 1

Approaches to proper names

Proper names, particularly the act of naming, is a well-established research topic in disciplines as diverse as anthropology, history, law, linguistics, philosophy, social psychology and sociology. There is even a series of International Congresses of Onomastic Sciences where researchers from various disciplines meet to discuss their work on proper names. For instance, the XVIIIth International Congress (held in April 1993 at the University of Trier, Germany) was mainly devoted to the study of one category of proper names: family names. The programme of this congress mentions no less than ten different colloquia which were scheduled to provide a panorama of the current trends in research on proper names. These colloquia dealt with topics like the interdependence of naming and social structure in various cultures (socio-onomastics); intercultural comparison of proper name systems; the relations between cultural history and the choice of a name; the poetics of name-giving or the logical status of literary names (literary onomastics); proper names, and lexicography, legal aspects of naming, or 'deonomastics', i.e. the study of words which have been formed on the basis of proper names (for instance, the French word 'poubelle' (dustbin) is derived from the name of Eugène René Poubelle, a prefect who ordered the use of dustbins in 1884).

There was no colloquium devoted to the cognitive approach to proper names during this meeting. The reason is surely that cognitive psychologists' interest in proper names is very recent. In this introductory chapter, we will briefly present questions that were discussed in some of the aforementioned disciplines. We have deliberately chosen not to report work on the etymology of proper names since this kind of work is probably known to various extent by most people. Dictionaries of proper names providing the etymology of family names and place names are available in all good bookshops. Rather, we have chosen to present work that is less well known to cognitive psychologists, namely the judicial, anthropological, socio-psychological and philosophical approaches to proper names. We do not claim to present an extensive, or even a representative, review of this enormous literature. Our aim is to show the diversity of the literature on proper names outside cognitive science. We will show later in the book how some of this research, particularly work by philosophers of language, may provide intuitions for cognitive psychologists. After this overview, we will describe the topics that a cognitive approach to proper names deals with.

First of all, we will define what will be taken as a proper name in this book.

WHAT IS A PROPER NAME?

Webster's Third New International Dictionary of the English Language (1976) defined a proper noun (or proper name) as 'a noun that designates a particular being or thing, does not take a limiting modifier, and is usually capitalised in English'. The famous French *Grand dictionnaire encyclopédique Larousse* (1984) defined a proper noun as a sub-category of nouns, that designate a being or an object considered as unique. These two definitions constitute fair summaries of the way linguists define proper names. Let us consider some definitions of 'proper name' from dictionaries of linguistics or grammar:

- 'The name of an individual person, place or object, as opposed to a common noun which refers to any one of all things denoted by the noun. Thus, *John, Eiffel Tower, The Tyrol, London* are proper nouns. . . . In English, proper nouns are usually written with an initial capital letter' (Hartmann and Stork, 1972).
- 'The name of an individual, place, etc. . . . Proper nouns cannot be used with determiners in the way common nouns can' (Crystal, 1980).
- 'Proper nouns are basically names of specific people (Shakespeare), places (Milwaukee), months (September), days (Thursday), festivals (Christmas), magazines (Vogue) and so forth. Proper nouns do not generally share the formal characteristics of common nouns. In particular they lack articles, or rather article contrast. . . . Proper nouns generally have unique denotation, and are usually written with initial capital letters' (Quirk *et al.*, 1985).
- 'The proper name has no real meaning, no definition; it is not linked to what it designates by a semantic link but by a particular convention. . . . Proper names have an initial capital letter, they lack number contrast and are often used without determiner' (our translation from Goose, 1986).

Most of these definitions share a number of features:

1 A proper name designates a particular being or thing. Typically, authors cite names of persons and names of places as examples of proper names.
2 Proper names have a capital initial letter.

3 Proper names are not used with determiners in the same way as common names are (see also Dubois *et al.*, 1973; Allerton, 1990).

However, each of these features deserves more comment. Note that while the expressions 'proper noun' and 'proper name' are generally used as alternative terms, some authors do draw a distinction between these two expressions (see for instance Quirk *et al.*, 1985). A proper noun is then seen as a single word while a proper name may consist of more than one word (e.g. Oxford Road, Good Friday); proper names normally function as a single unit with respect to grammar. Following this distinction will not be necessary for our purpose.

Names of people and names of places are the most typically cited kinds of proper names. Names of people include family names, first names, pseudonyms and nicknames, while names of places include names of cities, villages, monuments, districts, countries, islands, mountains, rivers, seas and stars (Goose, 1986). But linguists have identified other kinds of proper names: for instance, temporal names, animal names and titles. In English, temporal proper names include names of festivals and religious periods (Christmas, Ramadan, Easter, Independence Day), names of months (January, February...) and days (Monday, Tuesday ...). Animals may also receive a proper name (e.g. Bucephalus, the horse of Alexander the Great). Some objects like ships commonly receive a proper name (Jules Verne gave the name 'Nautilus' to a famous submarine). Some people give a proper name to their computer. Goose (1986) also noted that a set of meaningful words can become a proper name when it is used to designate a particular entity. This is the case with titles of books or musical pieces.

Proper names are written with a capital initial letter. This property does not perfectly distinguish proper nouns from common nouns, since not all nouns beginning with a capital letter are proper nouns. For instance, in English, ethnic or national adjectives (African, Canadian) are written with a capital initial letter but they are not proper names (see Quirk *et al.*, 1985).

Finally, authors agree that determiners and number contrast are not used in the same way with proper nouns and common nouns. But this does not mean that proper names always lack number contrast, and that proper names are always used without determiners. According to Quirk *et al.*, proper names normally lack number contrast. Proper names are singular and do not have a plural, or they have a plural but no singular (e.g. the Netherlands, the Pyrenees). In some circumstances, proper names may be made plural. By saying the 'John Smiths' one may designate people who bear a high frequency name like 'John Smith'. But in such a case the 'John Smiths' is no longer a proper name since it denotes a category and not a particular entity. However, other cases are less obvious. A surname can also be made plural to refer to members of a family. For instance, 'the Fondas' can be used to designate the family called 'Fonda'. It is not easy to decide whether the 'the Fondas' denote a particular entity or not. In some sense it does: it designates a particular family; but this family is composed of a number of individuals sharing properties (Henry Fonda, Jane Fonda, Peter Fonda and Bridget Fonda). The question of whether the proper noun has to be reclassified as a common noun is not easy to answer in such cases.

In English, personal names and temporal names have no article. But several kinds of proper names are preceded by the definite article. Classes of proper names typically preceded by 'the' are plural proper names in general (the Netherlands), and more particularly groups of islands (the Bahamas, the Shetlands) and ranges of mountains (the Himalayas, the Alps). Names of rivers (the Danube), seas (the Atlantic, the Baltic), canals (the Suez Canal) and other geographical features of coastline (the Gulf of Mexico, the Cape of Good Hope, the Isle of Wight) are also preceded by the definite article. It is also the case for names of public institutions (museums, libraries or hospitals); hotels, restaurants, theatres or cinemas; ships (the Titanic), or famous aeroplanes (the Spirit of St Louis). However, Quirk *et al.* (1985) argued that proper names, unless they are reclassified as common names, lack article contrast. This means that the article preceding the proper name cannot be varied to give expressions like 'a Netherland' or 'some Netherlands'. In contrast, proper names, when reclassified as common names, may have their meaning modified by determiners. For instance, 'an Einstein' can mean 'somebody as clever as Albert Einstein', or 'the French Bob Dylan' means 'a French singer whose songs sound like those by Bob Dylan' (see Clark and Gerrig (1983) for an investigation of how people understand proper nouns when they are preceded by an article). For further information on the grammar of proper names the reader may refer to Quirk *et al.*'s (1985) comprehensive discussion of the problem which we have briefly summarised here.

What will be considered to be a proper name in this book? Following linguists' definitions we will take proper names as names of unique beings or things. These include:

- personal names (surnames, first names, nicknames and pseudonyms);
- geographical names (names of cities, countries, islands, lakes, mountains, rivers and so forth);
- names of unique objects (monuments, buildings, ships or any other unique object, e.g. Excalibur – the sword);
- names of unique animals (e.g. Benji or Bugs Bunny);
- names of institutions and facilities (cinemas, hospitals, hotels, libraries, museums or restaurants);

- names of newspapers and magazines;
- titles of books, musical pieces, paintings or sculptures;
- names of single events (e.g. Kristallnacht).

Temporal names like names of days of the week, months or recurrent festive days will not be seen as true proper names. The fact that there is one Monday each week, one month of June and one Good Friday each year suggests that 'Monday', 'June' and 'Good Friday' do not really designate unique temporal events but rather categories of events, and therefore are not true proper names. This contrasts with the 'Kristallnacht' which refers to one unique event that happened on 9 November 1938. In agreement with this, note that, in French, names of the days of the week and names of months are not considered proper names and are not capitalised.

Some authors take brand names as proper names (e.g. Cohen and Faulkner, 1986). Although brand names are generally capitalised, they are an unclear case of pure proper names because they do not designate a unique object. It could be argued that in fact a brand name designates a unique object that is simply replicated in a number of identical exemplars. This can be the case, for instance, of drugs (Perdolan, Haldol) or beers (Orval, Jupiler) where each exemplar designated by the label is a perfect clone. But this is not true of all brand names. For example, we know a lot of different cars called 'Volkswagen' or even 'Golf' and the different exemplars of Golf we know are not pure clones. They differ from each other in colour, power of the engine, year of the model and so on. In fact, brand names like 'Golf' and 'Volkswagen' designate categories of objects rather than unique objects. The use of brand names, and the entities to which they refer, is extremely diverse. Therefore, it is difficult to place the category of 'brand names' definitively within any taxonomy of proper names. However, at least some brand names do appear to share the properties of proper names and therefore brand names are included in some of the topics discussed in this book.

Finally, if denotation of unique entities is the key criterion, this criterion would lead one to not consider a surname as being a proper name if this name designates two (or more) individuals. The proper name 'Moore' is shared by many people (Roger Moore, Dudley Moore, Demi Moore, Viviene Moore, etc.) but it is not a label for a particular category of individuals called 'Moore'.

PROPER NAMES AND LAW

Human rights

The right to a name is one of the most basic rights of human beings. The right to a name is not written in the Universal Declaration of Human

Rights adopted by the General Assembly of the United Nations on 10 December 1948. However, this right is mentioned in one of the international pacts that were elaborated to provide the Declaration with mandatory judicial power. Article 24-2 of the International Covenant on Civil and Political Rights which was adopted in 1966 states that 'Every child shall be registered immediately after birth and shall have a name.'

The Declaration of the Rights of the Child, adopted by the United Nations (20 November 1959), stated the right to a name in Principle 3. More recently, the right to a name has been clearly stated in Article 7-1 of the Convention of the Rights of the Child which was adopted by the General Assembly of the United Nations on 20 November 1989:

> The child shall be registered immediately after birth and shall have the right from birth to a name, the right to acquire a nationality and, as far as possible, the right to know and to be cared for by his or her parents.

The background note nº2 of the Convention recalls that

> The simple act of registering births and deaths, and giving a child a name and a nationality, is taken for granted in most places today. However, some developing nations still do not keep written records, and furthermore, children of indigenous or migrant populations as well as refugees and internally displaced groups are not always properly registered. Sometimes, children are even treated as possessions or commodities to be bargained with or traded. In its more extreme forms, the denial of an identity to children has led to slavery, prostitution, discrimination against ethnic minorities, and forced separation from parents.

Finally, the Interamerican Convention on Human Rights (adopted on 22 November 1969) explicitly mentions the right to a name in Article 18 which states that everyone has the right to a first name and to the names of both parents, or to the name of one of them.

Attribution and protection of names

Specialists of comparative law have shown that the rules for the attribution of a patronym vary considerably from one country to the other. The following three systems of patronym attribution are commonly used in western countries:

1 The name of the husband is attributed to his wife and to his children.
2 Spouses bear a double name (the husband's name followed by the wife's name or vice versa) which is transmitted to children. This is the case in Spain and in Portugal.
3 At marriage, spouses choose a family name that they will bear and

transmit to their children. In Germany, this name may be either the husband's name or the wife's name, or both.

However, lawyers observe an evolution of laws ruling the attribution of patronyms. In the United States, for instance, according to the traditional Common Law, a child receives his or her father's name and a married woman receives her husband's name. But in some states like Florida or Hawaii, parents may attribute to their child a name which is neither the father's name nor the mother's name. In Florida, parents may choose to use, for instance, the three first letters of the mother's name and the three last of the father's name to compose a new name for their child. In Hawaii, parents may even give their child a name which is completely different from their own names (Boucaud, 1990). In North Carolina, Tennessee or Virginia the Common Law is no longer used as far as the attribution of the married woman's name is concerned. A woman may choose to keep her own name instead of taking her husband's name. Complicated judicial problems may arise when spouses who originate from countries which do not apply the same law for the attribution of personal names do not agree on the family name to be given to a child.

Another kind of problem that lawyers have to face concerns the attribution of first names. Children must sometimes be protected against facetious parents who choose names that lead easily to mockery. Rubellin-Devichi (1990) reported the following example. Mr and Mrs Vaissel had chosen the first name 'Aude' for their daughter. 'Aude' is certainly a beautiful first name, but in French 'Aude Vaissel' is pronounced in the same way as 'eau de vaisselle' (dishwater).

Apart from the attribution of names, lawyers are also concerned with the protection of names. Names are not protected in all countries. For instance, in the United Kingdom names are not protected so that a British person may not initiate a prosecution if his or her name has been usurped. However, in all other countries belonging to the Council of Europe the protection of names is a judicial matter. In all of these countries the protection of personal names is relatively efficient if a name is usurped for commercial purposes. For instance, in the ex-Federal Republic of Germany, Douglas Fairbanks has been protected against the use of his name as a brand name for cigarettes. The motivation for instituting a prosecution is sometimes less obvious. For instance, in Liège (Belgium), two people restored an old family mansion. From this house, they made a small hotel in which each room is decorated to recall one novel by Simenon (the famous Liège-born author of detective stories). This hotel was named 'Hôtel Simenon'. Simenon's heirs swiftly issued a writ against the owners of the hotel. According to the heirs, the name 'Simenon' was used for commercial purposes in a way that undermined the rights of the novelist (Anonymous, 1991). At the time of writing, the affair is not over. The controversial judicial point is to determine whether suggesting to guests that rooms evoke the atmosphere of Simenon's novels is prejudicial to the author's rights (Anonymous, 1992). In such a case, there is a good chance that an agreement will finally be found between the hotel keepers and the heirs satisfying both parties.

Personal names are well protected against commercial use in most European countries. However, jurisprudence on the protection of names differs from one country to another as far as the use of personal names for literary or artistic purposes is concerned (Boucaud, 1990) but it is generally more flexible than protection against commercial use.

Another legal aspect of proper names arises when brand names become so frequent and widespread that they enter languages as words in their own right, e.g. Hoover and Durex. From one point of view, if one of your company's trade marks passes into use as a generic term, then this can be seen as an unambiguous sign of success. It is thus paradoxical that this process is referred to in the trade as 'genericide', because a brand name is deemed to be 'murdered' by becoming a generic name. Large corporations spend large quantities of time and money preventing, tracking down, scolding, and occasionally punishing generic uses of trademarks. A slogan used by a well-known photocopier equipment firm was once apparently 'Use our name as the good law intended', thereby indicating the seriousness with which such matters are taken.

Since genericide can, by definition, occur only to very well-known names, it might seem that the phenomenon would be merely a trapping of success. The negative consequences however are not psychological but legal. A name that becomes genericised can be declared public property and no longer the exclusive property of the creators of the name.

PROPER NAMES AND SOCIAL PSYCHOLOGY

Social psychologists have described an intriguing phenomenon that has been called the 'name letter effect': letters occurring in one's own name are found to be more attractive than letters that are not part of this name (Nuttin, 1985). One plausible account of this effect is that mere ownership of a compound object is a sufficient condition for the enhancement of the attractiveness of the constituent elements of the owned object. The mere ownership of a name (the most unique attribute of the self, according to Nuttin) enhances the attractiveness of the letters included in that name.

To test this hypothesis, Nuttin (1985) presented elementary school children and undergraduate students with two lists of letter pairs and asked them to choose the more attractive letter in each pair. In one list, the pair consisted of one letter found in the subject's name (own name letter) and one randomly chosen letter which was not part of the subject's name (not own name letter). The other list consisted of pairs including one own name letter and a not own name letter of another subject, who was also presented with the same two stimulus lists. This means that subjects were yoked two by two, and that the same two lists of pairs of letters were seen by the two matched subjects. A given letter was indeed more often selected by subjects whose names included this letter than by their yoked partners whose names did not include the letter.

In a second series of experiments, Nuttin's (1987) subjects were asked to select their six most preferred letters from a random presentation of the alphabet and then to write down their full name. For each letter of the alphabet, the proportion of subjects who selected it from among the six preferred letters was calculated when the letter was an own name letter and when it was not an own name letter. Results showed that letters were seen as more attractive to subjects for whom they were own name letters than for the other subjects. Nuttin's paradigm eliminated artefactual explanations for the name letter effect based on the visual or the acoustic characteristics of letters, or on their relative frequencies.

The name letter effect is not restricted to a specific linguistic or ethnographic community, as Nuttin (1987) found this effect across twelve European languages (Dutch, English, Finnish, French, German, Greek, Hungarian, Italian, Norwegian, Polish, Portuguese and Spanish). For Nuttin, the name letter effect is an experimental demonstration of the more general principle that entities that are owned by a person are deemed more attractive by that person, and that this also extends to the elements composing the entities. Hoorens and Todorova (1988) tested an alternative explanation for the name letter effect. Their hypothesis was that this effect was a remainder of the positive mastery affect that people experienced when first succeeding in reading and writing their own name. In other words, according to this 'mastery pleasure hypothesis', the name letter effect is due to the fact that their own first and family name are typically the very first items that children can read and write. This achievement in valued abilities like reading and writing would be accompanied by such an intense positive mastery effect that letters associated with this experience keep an enhanced attractiveness throughout life.

According to their hypothesis, the acquisition of a second alphabet in the context of foreign language studies should be less likely to elicit a comparable mastery experience. In addition, the acquisition of a second alphabet does not typically start with writing or reading the own name. They therefore predicted a name letter effect only in the very first learnt alphabet. They presented a Cyrillic and a Roman letter preference task to Bulgarian students who became familiar with the Roman alphabet through their foreign language courses. They found a name letter effect in both alphabets. This result did not support their 'mastery pleasure hypothesis' but was consistent with Nuttin's 'mere ownership hypothesis'.

Hoorens *et al.* (1990) tested the 'mastery pleasure hypothesis' further. If the hypothesis is correct, the name letter effect should be maximal shortly after the experience of mastering writing skills. Then one would predict a decreasing name letter effect over elementary school years. In fact the authors did not find such a decrease over school years in Flemish, Hungarian and Thai children of three different grades. The authors also tested a 'mitigated' version of the mastery pleasure hypothesis. This version states that mastery pleasure contributes to the genesis of the name letter effect but is not its main determinant. If this was correct, the name letter effect should be stronger in one's first alphabet than in one's second alphabet only when there is a considerable interval of time between the acquisition of the two alphabets. Hoorens *et al.* found that this prediction was not supported by data. The mere ownership hypothesis remains the better explanation to name letter effect, a remarkably robust effect obtained across languages and alphabetic systems.

Another issue studied by social psychologists is the effect of name attractiveness on social judgements: judgements of person attractiveness (Hensley and Spencer, 1985) and judgements of performance (Seraydarian and Busse, 1981). In particular, social psychologists have produced a great deal of research on the consequences of first name stereotyping. First names vary in attractiveness. Some authors think that people with unfavourable names may be negatively affected by a stereotype associated with those names (Ellis and Beechley, 1954). There is a positive correlation between the attractiveness of a first name and its frequency of occurrence (McDavid and Harari, 1966; Colman *et al.*, 1981; Erwin and Calev, 1984; Mehrabian, 1992). Several studies have shown that the attractiveness of first names may affect school grading (Harari and McDavid, 1973; Harris, 1975; Erwin and Calev, 1984). Harari and McDavid (1973) presented inexperienced college sophomores and experienced teachers with short essays. The purported author of each essay was identified only by a first name and a randomly selected initial. The authorship of the essays was randomly associated with frequent and attractive names (Karen, Lisa, David) versus unusual and unattractive names (Bertha, Elmer, Hubert). Each essay was graded on a scale from 50 to 100. Results showed that the attributed quality of each essay was higher when the purported author had an attractive/frequent name than when the author had an unattractive/unusual name. Moreover, the authors showed that this bias was stronger for experienced teachers than for inexperienced college sophomores.

More recently, Erwin and Calev (1984) confirmed that attractiveness of the first name of the hypothetical author exerts a significant influence on the marks awarded to essays. But they also showed that the attractiveness of the teacher's name influences the grading of pupils: teachers with attractive names rated essays more highly than teachers with unattractive names. No interaction between the pupils' names attractiveness and the teachers' names attractiveness occurred.

At first sight, it may seem that it is not a good idea to give a rare name to a child. However, Zweigenhaft (1977) stressed that such a generalisation should be approached with extreme caution. Indeed, most studies use the terms 'unusual', 'rare' and 'peculiar' synonymously. Infrequent names tend to be lumped into one large 'undesirable' category. Zweigenhaft argued that many studies did not consider the possibility that different kinds of unusual names might have different kinds of psychological impact, or might be associated with different kinds of stereotypes: 'sports fans and movie fans have long realised the charm and desirability of an unusual name' (p. 293). He cited Jim Murray, a sports writer on the *Los Angeles Times* who wrote,

> When I was a kid back in Connecticut, I used to love U.S.C. backfields. You had to be fascinated. I remember rolling the names off my tongue. Morley Drury, Homer Griffith, Grenville Landsdell, Gaius Shaver, Irvine Warbyton, Orville Mohler. You read them and felt like going out and throwing rocks at your mother and father for naming you Jim.
>
> (Zweigenhaft, 1977, p. 293)

Information about name and sex stereotyping may be found in Kasof (1993).

Name attractiveness may even influence the act of voting (Kamin, 1958). Some political analysts think that candidates' surnames can affect their electability, especially when voters are called upon to choose between candidates about whom they have little information. O'Sullivan *et al.* (1988) reported the case of the 1986 Illinois Democratic primary, the outcome of which was widely attributed to voters' surname preferences. The candidates who won the nominations for Lieutenant Governor and Secretary of State were adherents of Lyndon LaRouche, a presidential candidate known for his unconventional views. After the highly unexpected victory of these candidates, the question was raised whether the outcome should be interpreted as an endorsement of Lyndon LaRouche's political views. But political analysts found another reason for that victory. In fact, the primary campaign had generated very little public interest. Neither party endorsed candidates, perhaps because they took their nominations for granted; nor did the LaRouche candidates call much attention to themselves. Political analysts assumed that, in fact, voters did not know much about the candidates in general, and they did not know about the LaRouchian connections of the candidates they elected. According to analysts, voters would not have nominated followers of a political figure about whom unfavourable opinion outran favourable opinion by a ratio of 20 to 1. Finally, the explanation favoured by journalists and the officials of the Democratic Party was that the victory of LaRouche's candidates was attributable to their names. The names of LaRouche's candidates (Mark Fairchild and Janice Hart) were attractive and familiar Anglo-Saxon names, while the names of their opponents (George Sangmeister and Aurelia Pucinski) were 'ethnic' names that might appeal to voters of German and Polish heritage only. Gailey (1986) cited a voter: 'I voted for them [Fairchild and Hart] because they had smooth-sounding names.'

From this affair, O'Sullivan *et al.* (1988) undertook further exploration of the political potency of names. They approached this issue through simulated voting experiments. It was shown that the attractiveness of candidates' names influenced voters' preferences only when no relevant political information about candidates was known to subjects. When voters had information, however little, about the candidates' political views, their preferences were not influenced by candidates' names. This is surely encouraging.

PROPER NAMES AND PHILOSOPHY

What is the semantic status of proper names? This question has drawn the attention of many linguists and philosophers of language since the last century.

Roughly speaking, there are two main classes of theories about the semantic status of proper names: the *description theories of reference* (or descriptivist theories) and the *theory of direct reference*. According to description theories of reference, a proper name can designate a person (or another unique entity) only via intermediate descriptive properties. By contrast, the theory of direct reference prescribes that proper names are directly linked to their bearer without intermediate descriptive properties.

One of the most famous description theories of names is due to Russell (1905). For Russell, the meaning of a name is given by a definite description of the individual it names. Russell does not accept Mill's (1843) idea that a proper name has no meaning and is just a kind of logical constant without an internal semantic structure. One important, and controversial, point of Russell's theory is that the definite description giving the meaning of a proper name is seen as unique. For instance, the meaning of 'Mikhaïl Gorbachev' might be 'the man who introduced pereïstroika to the USSR'.

Frege (1892) also refuted the position that proper names have no meaning other than their external referent. He considered a unique object that can be identified by using two distinct labels; for instance, the planet Venus can be referred to as the 'morning star' or the 'evening star'. According to Frege, if the meaning of a proper name was confined to its external referent, the statement 'the morning star is the evening star' should be as trivial as 'the morning star is the morning star', and this is obviously not the case. Some information is imparted in the former sentence, while the latter sentence conveys no information at all. According to Frege, this difference reflects the fact that the proper names 'the morning star' and 'the evening star' do not have the same meaning. For Frege, the two expressions 'morning star' and 'evening star' have the same referent but they do not have the same sense. Unfortunately, the meaning of a proper name is not clearly defined in Frege's work. In some texts Frege suggested that this sense might be a definite description (see Carroll, 1985; Engel, 1990).

Several philosophers and linguists have found the idea that one unique description exists which forms the meaning of a proper name unsatisfactory. Authors like Searle (1958) and Strawson (1959) suggest that the meaning of a proper name is given by a conjunction of descriptions which defines one particular individual. The meaning of Mikhaïl Gorbachev would be something like 'the man who introduced pereïstroika to the USSR', 'the man with a birthmark on his forehead', 'the man who received the Nobel prize for peace in 1990'. A cluster of such descriptions that can be regarded as a criterion that uniquely picks out Mikhaïl Gorbachev is seen as a plausible candidate for being the meaning of 'Mikhaïl Gorbachev' (Chierchia and McConnell-Ginet, 1990). Similarly, Jespersen (1965) suggested that the meaning of a proper name is 'the complex of qualities characteristic of the bearer of the name' (p. 67).

In another kind of description theory of names (the 'nominal description theory'), proper names have a minimal meaning consisting of a definite description which specifies that the name designates its bearer. Thus 'Gorbachev' would mean 'the individual called "Gorbachev"' (Loar, 1978).

The notion that proper names have definite descriptions as their meaning has been challenged and is nowadays considered as mistaken by many philosophers who adhere to the theory of direct reference (see Martin, 1987). Recall that according to this theory, a name designates directly an individual without intermediate descriptive properties. For Kripke (1980), proper names are rigid designators in the sense that they refer to the same individual in all possible worlds. The referent of this kind of rigid designator 'is stipulated to be a single object whether we are speaking of the actual world or a counterfactual situation' (Kripke, 1980, p. 21). In contrast, definite descriptions are not rigid designators because they can refer to different individuals as a function of circumstances. Thus names cannot be seen as semantically equivalent to definite descriptions. A famous example given by Kripke is as follows. Suppose that the only description you associate with the name 'Gödel' is 'the one who proved the incompleteness of arithmetic'. Suppose that you find out that a certain Mr Schmidt rather than Gödel proved the aforementioned theorem. If the name 'Gödel' is semantically equivalent to the definite description 'the one who proved the incompleteness of arithmetic', then you are committed to the following striking statement: the name 'Gödel' actually refers to Mr Schmidt. Of course this statement is false.

If the meaning of proper names cannot consist of a definite description, or a cluster of definite descriptions, what is the meaning of a proper name? According to the theory of direct reference, the answer is that proper names have no meaning. A proper name has one referent (the person or the unique object it designates) but no meaning.

One important point to notice is that Kripke's theory addresses the semantic status of names but not the mental representation of meaning. Like Putnam (1975), Kripke sees meaning as something which is different from semantic representation in human brains. The fact that humans first thought that dolphins were a kind of fish and then realised that dolphins were mammals did not change the meaning of the word 'dolphin' but changed humans beings' semantic representations of dolphins. The following paragraph from Chierchia and McConnell-Ginet (1990) illustrates this view:

> We certainly must cognitively represent concepts of tigers and of Pavarotti and somehow use these representations in processing the words *tiger* and *Pavarotti*. But it is unclear whether these concepts play any semantic role. On the causal theory of reference, such cognitive representations do not enter into determining truth conditions. What is crucial for truth is the referential link itself, and that is a matter of the causal history of the world (which baby it was whose parents named it *Lucciano Pavarotti*, for example) rather than of conceptual structure (the concept a speaker has of Pavarotti).
>
> (p. 85)

In summary, according to such a thesis meanings are not in the mind. We have presented in a few lines what has been (and is still) a long debate between psychologism and realism. For a deeper and fuller discussion of this topic, the reader can turn for instance to Putnam (1975) or Johnson-Laird (1983).

Strictly speaking, Kripke's theory on the semantic status of proper names is not directly relevant to the cognitive modelling of proper names processing since this theory does not deal with mental representation of meanings. Yet we will see that philosophical theories on names, even Kripke's realist theory, have more or less explicitly influenced cognitive psychologists and neuropsychologists. In cognitive psychology there is also a debate on whether a proper name is directly linked to the individual it designates or if biographical properties mediate between the name and the individual. But this debate refers to mental representations of individuals, mental representations of describing properties and mental representations of names within the information processing system.

PROPER NAMES AND ANTHROPOLOGY

One issue addressed by anthropological work on proper names and naming lies in the fact that there is striking intercultural diversity in the use of proper names. One aspect of diversity deals with the moment of name giving. In industrialised countries, an infant receives a name at birth. In several traditional African cultures, giving a name at birth is unusual. Adults may wait a few weeks, a few months or even a whole year before giving a name to a child. The reasons for this delay seem to be linked to the high rate of infant mortality in some areas of Africa. Anthropologists have explained this delay by taking into account the way the infant is represented in some traditional African cultures. The identity of this 'being' (the baby) is uncertain (Journet, 1990). There is doubt about the human nature of the infant. Is this the incarnation of a spirit that will leave soon, or is this an indecisive ancestor who is unsure about settling back into the world of living beings? So, adults will wait for the occurrence of some signs that will prove the human nature of the baby before giving him or her a personal name. Name giving is a very important act which anchors the child in the human society. Before this moment infants are identified by generic names like 'water baby' (in Bantoo tribes), 'new stranger', or 'white man' (in Mossi tribes) (Lallemand, 1978).

Another reason why new-born babies do not receive a name at birth is that divulging the name of a person may be dangerous. Indeed, knowledge of a person's name makes him or her more vulnerable to attack through magic or sorcery. Consequently, people are particularly discreet about the names of vulnerable people like pregnant women or newly initiated adolescents. Since uttering the name of a person is necessary to attack this person through sorcery, not giving a name to a baby protects him or her against sorcery.

One may sometimes protect infants against bad spirits by giving him or her a derisive name. For instance, if a mother loses several new-born babies in succession, the first baby to be born after this painful series might be attributed a derisive name. The aim of this procedure is to try to ward off fate by feigning absolute detachment from the child (Journet, 1990). In the Mossi tribes such names may be Kida (he is going to die), Kunevi (dead thing), Jinaku (born to die), Kügba (stone) or even Kayure (without name). This practice is used in other tribes. In Joola tribes (living in the south of Senegal and Guinea-Bissau) names like Holobahan (already buried) or Ukop (dump) may be used. Names like Yegul Con (he will not live until the night), Sagar (rag) or Ken Bugul (nobody wants him) have the same function in Wolof tribes who live in the north of Senegal. Journet (1990) neatly expressed the essence of this naming practice: the name is sacrificed in order that the child lives.

Another feature of cultural diversity deals with the continuity of naming. We are used to thinking that a person's name is a permanent property. Mr John Smith received his name at birth and will keep it all his life. This continuity is not present in all cultures. The example of American Indians is often cited. In some Indian tribes a person receives a new name at important moments of change in the person's life (for instance, puberty). What is probably less well known is that this discontinuity in naming also exists in some rural areas of industrialised countries. The case of Minot-en-Châtillonais, a French village, has been well documented (Zonabend, 1977, 1980).

In fact, the work of anthropologists shows that there are many features of naming practices that differ across cultures. Another feature is the plurality of names. We have already mentioned that the name was not necessarily a constant property of persons. Anthropologists have also shown that a person may have several different current names in some cultures. In some African tribes people have a whistled name or even a drummed name in addition to the spoken name. Moreover, people may have several current spoken names. Journet (1990) gives the example of a Mossi girl called 'Sweet head' by her parents, 'Luck' by her grandfather, 'Who does not contradict religion' by her grandmother, and 'Ramata' (her Muslim name) by the young adults of the family; thus each uses one particular label. This level of diversity of names is unusual in western countries. However, anthropologists have shown that, in rural areas of our countries again, people may also bear several names that are not used indifferently across naming contexts (see Collier (1970) for Mexico; Dorian (1970) for Scotland; Zonabend (1977) for France; Severi (1980) for Italy, and Breen (1982) for Ireland). Using a particular label to name a given person denotes something about the nature of the relationship between the speaker and the referred person. For instance, the same person will not be called by the same name by members of his or her age group, or by younger and older people. Yet another name may be used by people living outside the village. Curiously, in some cases care is taken never to utter the real patronym of the person. The name is kept 'hidden'.

Anthropologists have extracted some pervasive principles of naming practices from this apparent heterogeneity. A name is a social classifying device; it enables people (either the speaker or the referent person) to be classified in terms of parental, social, ethnic or geographical group. But simultaneously, a name should *identify* the bearer (Levi-Strauss, 1962). Similarly, Alford (1988) argued that people's names serve two principal functions – categorisation and differentiation.

These will often be in conflict, as the more a name differentiates its bearer from other people, the less category information it carries regarding its bearer. In an attempt to study the ways in which these two functions are achieved, Alford used the Human Relations Area Files database to explore naming practices in sixty cultures around the world. There were large variations in the degree of uniqueness of a given name in different cultures. For instance, it is reported that in a study of some villages in the Scottish Highlands, three surnames were shared by over three-quarters of villagers, and furthermore, that first names were often drawn from a small set of biblical names. Thus, from their names, people were readily identified as coming from the area and as being Christians: the categorisation function is largely fulfilled within a naming system such as this one; it was observed that the differentiation function was fulfilled by a system of 'by-names' that described an individual, such as 'Lame Sandy' or 'Robber John'.

Vernier (1977, 1980) showed that in Karpathos (Greece), rich farmers bear patronyms that evoke a prestigious ecclesiastic function, members of the middle class bear patronyms formed from masculine first names, and poor countrymen and shepherds bear names formed from ludicrous nicknames. It is thus possible to place a person in one of these socio-economic categories simply by hearing his or her name.

In contrast, other societies use names that are always unique to a person – in some, one may not even take the name of a dead person. Yuman Indians, according to Kendall (1980), are attributed a name related to circumstances at the time of birth, and one which is unique to each individual. Thus the differentiation function of names is fulfilled. Categorisation is achieved, in practice, by addressing people by a term of kin. Indeed, among the Yuman Indians the given name is only used as reference, and never directly when speaking to the person.

Even these examples of extremes along the scale of name uniqueness demonstrate both functions of names as conceptualised by Alford (1988), in both cases by using another name in order to compensate for the inadequacy of the given name to perform one of the functions. As Goodenough (1965) pointed out, in some communities the classificatory property of names is emphasised, while in others the individualising property is stressed. According to Goodenough, 'naming customs and modes of address appear to counter-balance the effect that the workings of the social system tend otherwise to give to people images of themselves and others' (1965, p. 275). Other researchers showed that where the naming practice is to give several different names to the same individual, one name may be used mainly as an individualiser (for instance, a nickname) and another as a social classifier. But this is not a rule and names may serve both functions in some communities (e.g. Dorian, 1970).

Alford (1988) provided supporting evidence for the notion that a naming system must fulfil both classification and differentiation functions. Correlations show that in societies where given names are unique, people tend to be addressed and referred to by kin term, which clearly categorises a person. Furthermore, high name uniqueness is correlated with low occurrence of nicknames, the differentiation function already being fulfilled. High name uniqueness tends to be found in technologically simple societies, and is also associated with strong religious beliefs. One reason for the attribution of unique names appears to be the existence of various name taboos. In some cultures, for example the Ona from South America and the Aranda from central Australia, the dead are never mentioned for fear of upsetting either ghosts or living people. With such beliefs, unique names would provide a way of keeping such problems to a minimum. A somewhat less interpretable result is that name uniqueness correlates positively (and significantly) with the occurrence of cannibalism, but one should not make a meal of this finding.

Social categorisation from the name seems to be more straightforward in less industrialised areas than in more industrialised ones. However, classifying people according to their *ethnic* origin often remains possible from their names. Some families of immigrants, being aware of this classifying power of names (and of the possible consequences of this classifying act), may change their original name into a patronym which is more typical of the country in which they live. This kind of procedure is allowed in several European countries in order to facilitate the integration of immigrants. But this is not always without problems. A few years ago, a family of North African immigrants who had lived in Belgium for many years decided to adopt a Belgian-sounding name. Unfortunately, one Belgian family bearing the same name reacted very strongly against the fact that 'their' name could be attributed to the North African family, and this made the procedure much more complicated.

Anthropology has thus stressed the categorisation and differentiation functions of people's names. We return to these two requirements in Chapter 2, in which we explore the functions and meaning of proper names from a cognitive viewpoint.

PROPER NAMES AND COGNITIVE PSYCHOLOGY

The cognitive approach to proper names is concerned with the mental representations and mental processes required to recognise and recall proper names. Cognitive models should be able to account for the patterns of errors and difficulties that people experience with proper names in their everyday lives, in laboratory experiments and following neurological damage.

Cognitive psychologists therefore seek the answers to some questions of practical significance such as: Why is retrieval of proper names so vulnerable to cognitive ageing? Why do some brain-damaged patients show a strong impairment of proper name production while the production of other kinds of words is well preserved? In fact, data from sources as diverse as laboratory experiments, diary studies of name processing difficulties in everyday life and neuropsychological single case studies suggest that the retrieval of proper names is particularly difficult. On one hand, access to semantic properties of a specific entity (an individual, a country, a river, a piece of music, etc.) is easier than access to the name of that item. On the other hand, the retrieval of proper names (and more particularly the retrieval of people's names) is more difficult than common name retrieval. What is it either about proper names themselves or about the way in which they are processed which makes retrieval of proper names so vulnerable? These issues might also be investigated by turning the question around and asking, 'What properties of a name make it easier to recall?' Therefore, cognitive psychology holds the prospect of eventually being able to offer some practical advice which could help normals, the elderly or the brain-injured with their everyday difficulties in recalling people's names. In addition, principles could be developed which would aid the generation of memorable names. This work might have applications in the commercial world for development of product names.

The study of the cognitive aspects of proper name processing could equally well provide a powerful tool which would enable us to increase our understanding of human cognitive processes generally. For example, the following issues of broad theoretical significance are all addressed using proper names in studies reviewed in this book: the effect of frequency of occurrence on cognitive processing; the suggestion that names learned early in life are more robustly represented, and the issues of meaning and uniqueness on cognitive processes. Thus, proper names can provide a domain in which cognitive psychologists can study issues of wider significance than proper name processing.

Current cognitive psychologists' interest in proper names is closely linked to the development of research on familiar face processing during the 1980s. Indeed the study of face naming logically followed the study of face recognition itself and the study of person identification from faces. Thus the class of proper names on which cognitive psychologists have concentrated is that of people's names.

The major part of the present book deals with the recognition and the production of proper names (Chapters 3–8). However, we begin our review of the cognitive psychology of proper names in Chapter 2 by considering the properties required by proper names and the functions that they serve from a cognitive point of view. The processes of differentiation and categorisation (already discussed in relation to anthropology) and the meaning of proper names (discussed in relation to philosophy of language) are two issues which have important implications for cognitive models of proper name processing. Analysis of these aspects of proper names from a cognitive point of view forms the basis of Chapter 2.

Chapter 2

Cognitive properties of proper names

The central contemporary question in the cognitive psychology of proper names is 'Why are they particularly difficult to recall?' Before considering the evidence that they are indeed more difficult to recall (see Chapters 3 and 5), and the theoretical explanations for the phenomenon (see Chapters 5, 6 and 7), we shall consider the cognitive aspects of the functions that proper names serve.

NEW PROPER NAMES

Proper names are continually being created. New streets and buildings are assigned proper names. New products with novel names are frequently introduced to the market. Therefore, the interpretation of newly encountered proper names and memory for them are significant cognitive aspects of our everyday lives. This observation raises a number of questions with both theoretical and practical implications. Do new proper names categorise and differentiate their referents? How are proper names created, and what constraints are there on their creation or selection? Do new proper names carry any meaning? If so, what meaning can be obtained from a new proper name?

New names are required whenever a new object or entity comes into being. For objects, a new name is required for a new *type* of object, not for every object produced, i.e. for a new chocolate bar, not every chocolate bar. For unique objects, names denote *tokens*, i.e. every new public building, bridge or person requires a name. The object may be entirely new (e.g. a piece of new technology, a computer file or a new chocolate bar), or simply the result of new discriminations being made, as when empires are carved up into smaller countries.

Some names are genuinely new, having recently been invented, and some have been around for a long time but are new to a particular person or culture. Names such as 'Lillehammer' or 'Yeltsin', while new to many people in recent years, have been known for a long while to millions of other people, and so have not just been invented. The emphasis here will be on new names and the processes by which they are created. So, words such as Yeltsin and Lillehammer are not of concern to us, their origin being lost in the mists of time; whereas recently created names, like the Commonwealth of Independent States, Apple Macintosh and Snickers, are of interest.

One type of new name is provided by names that consist of novel phoneme strings, which we will call *novel* names. Two well-known examples from the business world are Kodak and Exxon, which were explicitly chosen because of their novelty value, and in the latter case because of the absence of the double 'x' in most languages. Other than brand names, possibly the only other type of name that receives a completely new phoneme string is that of characters in films and books, e.g. Brubaker.

A second type of new name is what we will call *derivational* names, where the root of the word carries meaningful associations to the referent, but where the name as a whole is new. For instance, the new administrative capital of Brazil was called Brasilia in the 1960s. Other examples of this type of name are the new names of the countries that constituted the Union of Soviet Socialist Republics which are extremely similar to their former names, in most cases with Soviet and Socialist removed. So, in English, what was formerly the Kazakh Soviet Socialist Republic is now the Republic of Kazakhstan (Tarkhov, 1992). This type of name is also frequently used for new products, e.g. Healthilife vitamin products.

For some derivational names the information carried by the root is not quite so 'transparent'. As we shall see in more detail later, Rubin *et al.* (1991) have shown that certain semantic categories have characteristic surface forms associated with them. For instance, radioactive elements typically have four syllables and end in '-ium'. Roots such as '-ium' do not carry meaning in the same way that roots like 'Brasil-' or 'Kazakh-' do, perhaps because it is quite possible to conceive of names ending in '-ium' that are not radioactive elements, whereas objects whose names begin 'Kazakh-' are rather tied to a particular part of the former Soviet Union. Rubin *et al.* (1991), however, argued that this difference is a matter of degree rather than a difference in the kind of meaning carried.

Both the novel and derivational types of new words are phoneme (or grapheme) strings that are new to the language, whereas names of a third type are those that are old words or new combinations of old words. For British people at least, the words 'apple' and 'Macintosh' were familiar before they were put together to make the name of a computer, and 'boost' was a word before a chocolate bar was given the name. Plays and books and other artistic creations often fall into this category, as well as the names of new products, and we shall refer to these as *novel combination* names.

The requirements of categorisation and differentiation do not appear to apply uniformly to the proposed taxonomy of new proper names. For derivational names, the first function is necessarily fulfilled, although the name does not always identify or give uniquely specific information about the referent. Novel combination names may also be opaque; e.g. Apple Macintosh, which does not categorise itself as a computer company, but does differentiate itself from other computer companies.

Any novel names, such as Kodak, are by definition differentiated from all other entities and so face the converse problem of being inadequately categorised by their name. Thus, the principle regarding a classification system cannot apply to novel names since, by definition, they have no discernible meaning-based link with other words and so cannot be situated in a hierarchy where entities with similar meanings have similar names.

Since the clue to Kodak's sphere of competence cannot be derived from semantic associates to the name, the only way that such names can become meaningful is through familiarity with it. Kodak is intimately associated with photographic equipment, and so gets around the essential meaninglessness of its name. Generally, then, novel names must achieve high familiarity in order to be easily categorised.

THE FUNCTIONS OF PROPER NAMES

Baggett and Ehrenfeucht (1982) studied the attribution of names to unfamiliar objects and analysed the requirements that names should fulfil. They suggested principles that should be followed in order to derive 'good' names for new objects. First, names should form a classification system, so that a name consists of a generic term and one or more modifiers, e.g. smooth red wheel. This requirement appears to correspond to the two functions proposed by Alford, namely categorisation and differentiation. Second, names should be short and unique to the referent, termed informationally efficient by Baggett and Ehrenfeucht (1982). In addition, they suggest that names should be 'within the users' linguistic capacities', which presumably means that the new names should be novel combination names only. These principles led to objective criteria for the assessment of a name's utility. An iterative method was used, where a group of subjects initially made up names for pieces from a toy construction set. The experimenter selected the most appropriate name from all those generated on a combined basis of brevity and frequency of generation. Another group of subjects then attempted to match the experimenter designated name to the construction pieces. Their errors were corrected, and a surprise recall test followed. When systematic errors occurred, the proposed name was replaced by another generated by the initial group of subjects, and this procedure iterated until a set of names was obtained that was sufficiently transparent to be matched to their referent by naive subjects, and also easy to retain.

This purely pragmatic approach seems appropriate for new objects where, in addition to the categorisation and differentiation requirements, the memorisation of the names is particularly important. However, Carroll (1985) gives an example of another class of names where novel combinations are often to be found, and yet where the requirement that a name be short and easy to retain does not apply: the names of dishes served in restaurants do not need to be particularly easy to memorise, because the customer orders with the aid of a menu. The criteria for their creation are completely different, with attractiveness and other such variables becoming relevant.

Consider also the new names of cities in the former Soviet Union, which are not attributed according to ease of recall: there are overriding political considerations in many cases to declare oneself as part of a particular region, or to associate oneself with a particular person. Baggett and Ehrenfeucht's (1982) informational efficiency principle is not generalisable to all domains of words. The names of computer files are proper names according to most definitions because they refer to unique entities. Since this category is radically different from the other categories of proper names considered so far, it affords a look at the relationship between functions of names that are demanded by the category of proper name and the type of new name. In the course of work, computer users need to open files with specific contents. If the correct filename can be recalled, the task is easy; however, free recall is not necessary because a list of filenames is readily available on modern computers. The task thus becomes one of being able to recall the contents of a file from the name in order to choose the required file, and the names attributed might reflect this. Note that these demands are different from the other proper name categories already considered.

Carroll (1985) studied the attribution of names to computer files by asking twenty-two regular computer users to annotate a list of filenames that they themselves had created. They were asked to describe the contents of as many files as possible. The average number of files was 114 per person, and yet on average over 90 per cent of filenames elicited a satisfactory description of the contents, which shows that the naming process was successful using the criterion of ease of recall. Carroll demonstrates that the filenames are actually very structured, with a rich variety of coding schemes. In fact, Carroll managed to discern a coding scheme for 97 per cent of the files, which means that very few files are novel names because these could not fit into a coding structure. About fifty per cent of the filenames were based on a single word, though only a proportion of these were unabbreviated. Interestingly, the balance of single word- versus multiple word-based filenames differed between categories of filename. Over 60 per cent of text files took a single name that was unabbreviated, whereas only about one-quarter of programmes and procedures had such names. The files in the latter groups would generally be created in order to perform an operation on something, and many of the names were verb–noun mixes, e.g. makeasmu. This again emphasises that the characteristics of names vary according to the precise demands of the category.

Having demonstrated that proper names' functions and characteristics depend upon the category from which they are drawn and the type of new name, the next section considers whether certain characteristics of names may be general to *all* categories.

PHONETIC SYMBOLISM

Phonetic symbolism is a recurring theme in psycholinguistic research. The idea is that the sound–meaning relationships in a spoken language are not arbitrary, so that individual phonemes may have consistent meanings associated with them. This is interesting in relation to the creation of new words, which occurs particularly for proper names, as the name can be manipulated to suit the image that is to be conveyed.

Words encountered for the first time can seem funny or stern or Germanic, and many other qualities besides. Users of a language with genderised nouns know that one can have an impression that some newly encountered word is masculine (or neuter or feminine) without being able to say explicitly why that should be so. This too is an example of phonetic symbolism.

Various examples of phonetic symbolism have been reported over the years. In English, for instance, Bloomfield (1933) has pointed out that words associated with a stationary light tend to begin with the consonant cluster 'gl-', e.g. glare, glow, glint, gloom, whereas words beginning with 'fl-' tend to be associated with moving light, e.g. flash, flare, flicker. Jespersen (1922) noted that the /ʌ/ sound is found in many words with negative connotations, e.g. humdrum, dull. A further English example is the occurrence of the word ending '-umble' in words with connotations of vagueness (e.g. fumble, jumble, bumble, mumble), with the possible inclusion of humble, tumble and crumble.

The term 'phonetic symbolism' in a general way means any association between sound and meaning. The types of meaning that have been most explored empirically are 'low-level' associations of vowels with size. For instance, Tarte (1974) demonstrated that monolingual Czech speakers also assign /a/ to large figures, and /i/ to small figures, which is remarkable considering that Czech is Slavic and English is Germanic. Further evidence of cross-linguistic phonetic symbolism is found in some earlier studies showing that, when given pairs of English antonyms and their counterparts in some language that they do not know at all, subjects could pick out the correct correspondences above chance levels (Brown *et al.*, 1955; Brown and Nuttall, 1959). Sapir (1929) asked subjects to match monosyllables (differing only in their vowel) to objects. There was a large consensus among his subjects that monosyllables with /a/ match large objects and those with /i/ match small objects, with other vowel sounds associated with sizes in between.

The range of meaning that can be associated with phonemes is rather wider than associations with size, however. In fact, some of the first empirical studies of phonetic symbolism were carried out to determine the connotations of people's names. English (1916) presented subjects with non-words, and asked them to describe the person that 'must belong to the name'. For only five out of the fifty stimuli was there even a degree of consensus among the eight subjects regarding connotations of the name. For instance, Boppum was said to be a large fat man by six subjects and Zethe was deemed to be a girl by five subjects, whereas all agreed that Rupzoiyat was a young man. In a second experiment the task was reversed: subjects had to think of appropriate names for people upon seeing drawings of their faces, but English reports that there was little discernible agreement among subjects' responses.

Alspach (1917) studied the connotations of English's fifty nonsense words for one of the original subjects fifteen months after the first experiment and found considerable consistency in the replies. The subject was apparently a professor 'whose long experience in experiments of a similar nature contributed not a little to the success of our investigation' (p.437). Despite the small scale of the study, the responses are often pleasing:

> Snemth -- Feeling came at once for a character in Dickens . . . the shortness of the word seems to signify that you have not much respect for him . . . Thasp is a miner; a worker in metals. . . . Whin is a frail man with a high-pitched nasal voice.
>
> (pp.438–439)

These studies suggest that phonetic symbolism does exist for people's names, but that the mappings between phonemes and meanings might not be one-to-one. That is, more than one name might be appropriate for any given face or personality, and any given phoneme string might have a range of different connotations. It seems likely from the above examples that such connotations can be shared by more than one person, but on the other hand it would be surprising if they were universal.

Another type of 'higher' phonetic symbolism has also been reported. It was found that an angular shape was judged brighter, more aggressive, noisier and faster than a rounded shape, which was more peaceful, blunter and 'nearer' -- not so much phonetic symbolism as geometric symbolism (Köhler, 1947; Lindauer, 1990a, 1990b). The link with names is that these nonsense shapes are referred to by nonsense syllables. One irony of this work is that Fox (1935) cites Köhler's two shapes as 'takete' and 'baluma', Lindauer (1990) as 'taketa' and 'maluma', whereas Marks (1978) calls them the same as Köhler originally did, 'takete' and 'maluma'. Apparently, neither the final 'a' and 'e' nor the initial 'b' and 'm' were crucial for this instance of phonetic symbolism! Incidentally, without even seeing these two shapes, guess which is the angular one and which the rounded smooth one. Informal observations suggest that the effect is a very robust one.

There is not yet much empirical research on these higher level forms of phonetic symbolism. Yet it would be these higher level connotations that would be most relevant in name creation, particularly for the commercial branch of name creation. As an aside, the research described above has found cross-cultural constancies in phonetic symbolism, but only at a rather shallow level, where sounds are associated with dimensions like bigness. The richer forms of phonetic symbolism may, of course, be much more specific to individual languages and linguistic communities, but they are closer to what a word's sound actually connotes to a person.

As suggested above, the regularities in phonetic symbolism can be exploited by those wishing to create a specific image for their product. The only instance of research on this that we came across was by Schloss (1981). He noted that English words containing a /p/ or a /k/ are often rude. Indeed, although we would not like to claim any particular expertise in this, an informal perusal of English swear-words indeed shows that many have a /k/ phoneme in them, and the same can also be said of French. The implications for product names are unclear but Schloss noted that thirty-eight of the top 200 USA brand names in 1979 began with either K or C, and furthermore, that a total of ninety-three out of 200 contained a /k/ sound somewhere in the name.

Presumably the image being sought after is not one of vulgarity, and the /k/ phoneme perhaps conveys other qualities too, e.g. reliability, up-to-dateness; the very proliferation of the /k/ phoneme suggests that not all its qualities are bad ones! Indeed, it may be simply that /k/ is in some sense a 'strong' phoneme, one that is easy to identify. Dawkins (1989) gives the example of a line in the traditional Scottish New Year's Eve song, Auld Lang Syne. If one knows one line of the song, it is the refrain, 'For the sake of auld lang syne'; Dawkins points out that, in fact, the original was 'For auld lang syne', and he speculates that the distinctiveness of the dissident /s/ and /k/ sounds means that even if they are sung by a minority, they are much easier to hear than those who are singing the correct version, which has no distinctive sounds. Thus those in the process of learning the song will tend to sing the incorrect version, and the /s/ and /k/ 'intruders' will spread.

Work on the affective connotations of phonemes and phoneme clusters will allow principled choice of product names, and similarly, Lindauer's line of work could be developed to give appropriate names for new products, particularly those from domains where the shape is a salient aspect, e.g. cars, chocolates.

Another approach to this area is that taken by Rubin *et al.* (1991), who investigated subjects' notions of the surface forms of words from different categories. One group of subjects were asked to list all radioactive elements, all the types of pasta, all the names of brand name painkillers and all the names of laundry detergents that they could remember. Certain structural regularities emerged for each category. In each, the modal number of syllables grouped over 50 per cent of exemplars. There were consistent endings for three of the four categories and the roots also had regularities. For instance, the root of most exemplars of the radioactive elements was a proper name, whereas for detergents it was an already existing English word. In a second experiment, a different set of subjects generated one new exemplar for each of the four categories. This creative exercise allowed some subjects to excel, producing items such as 'oops' or a radioactive element and 'mussolini' for a type of pasta. Overall, the distribution of exemplars according to their structural characteristics (e.g. number of syllables, type of ending, type of root) was very similar for the exemplars *generated* in the first experiment and the exemplars *created* in the second, showing that subjects possess and can use category-specific structural information in name creation.

In a related vein, Carroll (1985) analysed the entries to a competition to choose the name of a building in New York and recorded a diversity of endings, e.g. -adome, -arama, -arium, -orium, and many had associations with apples, deriving from New York's nickname 'The Big Apple', e.g. The Applesider, The Core of the Apple. Thus, the phonological structure of the names of the building was much more variable than Rubin *et al.* found for the categories they studied. The winning entry was, in fact, the New York Conference and Exposition Center.

It should be pointed out that the information that subjects used in Rubin *et al.*'s (1991) neat demonstration is only stereotypical; that is, although in many countries most detergent names are words that already exist in English, the rule is not 100 per cent reliable and there are exceptions. Brennen (1993) has claimed that all phonology is plausible for people's names and yet it is possible that in a task such as Rubin *et al.*'s, some regularities would be found. We would argue that, rather than showing structural regularities in the category of people's names, these would be due to the stereotypical type of information that we may possess. For instance, we may be aware that a significant proportion of Norwegian names finish with the syllable '-dahl', or that many Bulgarian names finish with '-ov'.

There is a category of proper names that appears to have particularly rigid structural invariance in the English-speaking world, at least. Whenever a governmental scandal is uncovered, it is immediately referred to by a word ending in '-gate', with the first part of the word referring to the scandal itself. It stems from the Watergate scandal, which was so serious that it forced President Nixon to resign. The impact of the scandal is such that less serious intrigues involving governments (even on other continents) are still labelled ——gate; perhaps the name is created in order to associate the new scandal with the blockbusting one from the 1970s.

In sum, there appears to be some sort of universal phonetic symbolism, where phonemes or combinations of phonemes convey the same geometric, affective and tonal qualities to speakers of very different languages. This would apply to proper names as well as to common names, but we should beware of interpretations of this as evidence that human speech emerged as pure phonetic symbolism, because, as Brown *et al.* pointed out, sounds and meanings may have originally been arbitrarily related and phonetic symbolism has been selected for ever since (Brown *et al.*, 1955; Brown and Nuttall, 1959). The more reliable forms of structural invariance for proper names appear to be specific to categories of proper names, and possibly to cultures too.

PROPER NAMES AND MEANING IN COGNITIVE PSYCHOLOGY

Our aim in this section is to show, by means of an analogy with telephone numbers, that, psychologically speaking, proper names have a range of possible meanings.

In attempting to account for the elusiveness of people's names when recalling them, Brennen (1993) pointed out that, in contrast to other categories of words, almost unlimited combinations of phonemes are permitted. This has consequences for the process of recall because, as outlined in Chapter 5, completion on the basis of partial phonology is less likely to produce the correct response. Imagine hearing a person's surname under poor perceptual conditions. One might have difficulty being sure that one had heard the name correctly -- was it Milligan or Millicent, Waverley or Wegerle?

A similar problem would arise if one was hearing a telephone number read out -- was that two-six or two-three, five-nine or nine-nine? This is because, as for people's names, completion is not very useful for telephone numbers. Though it is not true that all digits in a telephone number are legal in all positions, because, for example, subscribers' numbers rarely have '0' in the initial position, a large number of possible combinations is permitted. As with people's names, given a small number of elementary building blocks (phonemes or digits), the set of possible exemplars is enormous. The idea is that recalling a person's name and recalling their telephone number are difficult because of the need to specify every component individually, and an analogy can be drawn between a phoneme in a proper name and a digit in a telephone number (Brennen, 1993).

In fact, this analogy can be extended beyond the *recall* of people's names and telephone numbers. Recently, philosophers have tended to insist on the lack of meaning for proper names (e.g. Kripke, 1980), and this idea has been proposed by cognitive psychologists and neuro-psychologists as a reason for the problems that proper names pose for recall (Cohen, 1990; Semenza and Zettin, 1988), as described in detail in Chapter 5. The reasoning is that if you know that someone's name is Mr Baker, it does not tell you anything else about him. However, this is not a view that we support. It is obvious upon reflection that if we know that someone is called Mr Baker, it is likely that the name refers to an adult male, it is rather likely that he speaks English, and we may be prepared to guess that he likes apple pie, and may expect him to have heard of Oscar Wilde. On hearing the names Michio Yamato, Natalia Todorova and Björn Bergström, you are likely to be right in assuming that the ethnic origin of these people is Japanese, Slavic and Swedish respectively. The point is that a surname gives some information as to the person's culture of origin.

The information is of variable precision. It will sometimes allow one to classify a person as from a particular culture with certainty, and at other times to narrow it down to a certain part of the world, and still others to be completely misleading. For instance, in some cases names appear normal to more than one culture. There are people called Anne Sinclair in both France and Britain, so that in some cases a person's name does not specify the culture of origin, although the person is unlikely to be either a cannibal or Italian or a man. Even knowing that a person belongs to a particular culture does not allow strong, definite conclusions to be drawn about him or her, but educated guesses can be entertained about certain properties the person may have, and thus the claim that names are arbitrary is not wholly true.

On the other hand, information carried by surnames is, by and large, not useful *intra*-culturally, with names from industrialised societies, at least. That is, knowing that he is Mr Baker does not tell us whether the person is married, what his job is, or indeed whether he has a job. In this sense, people's names might be arbitrary and the information given by the name redundant, because we would already know that the person with whom we were communicating was English-speaking.

One way of resolving the problem of whether proper names have meaning is to realise that there are many possible types of meaning that a name can have. In the philosophical literature, the key question with regard to proper names is, do they refer? That is, do they, in and of themselves, convey meaning? This type of meaning is somewhat different to that explored by psychologists. As discussed in Chapter 1, to some philosophers 'meaning' is independent of what is mentally represented. When a psychologist discusses the meaning of proper names however, the mental representation of the name in a subject's head is intended. Thus proper names have different meanings to different subjects, according to levels of expertise with different categories.

It is in this sense that telephone numbers too can carry meaning. In order to phone Belgium from abroad, you have to dial the international dialling code of the country you are in (00 in most countries) followed by 32, the code number for Belgium. Then you have to dial the number corresponding to the area to which you are dialling, followed by the number of the subscriber to whom you wish to speak. The international dialling code, the dialling code of the country and the area code are thus non-arbitrary, because, with sufficient exposure to them, one would subsequently be able to tell the geographical location of a particular telephone subscriber just by seeing the number. The subscriber's number, on the other hand, typically provides no further information as to location or anything else. Thus, subscribers' numbers in countries with this system of number organisation (e.g. Belgium, the United Kingdom) can be regarded as random digit strings. In other countries (e.g. France, Norway) the area code is the first two digits of a subscriber's telephone number, so knowing where a person lives specifies the first two digits. The next six digits can be any combination not beginning with '0'. Thus this type of telephone number is not a random digit string but a composite of a meaningful string (the first two digits) and a random string (the last six).

In the same way, proper names are sometimes composites of random and meaningful phoneme strings, and sometimes simply random phoneme strings (phonotactic constraints permitting). Flemish and Dutch names often begin with 'van', Scottish names with 'Mac' and Norwegian names often end with '-dahl'. These regularities can be considered to be the meaningful part, and, to most people, the root represents the meaningless part. However, for other people's names, no such meaningful part can be discerned.

This is a link with other types of proper name, because they too often have both meaning-carrying and random components in them. Many proper names include one part that specifies the referent's category and another that is unique to the referent. For instance, many cities around the world have 'City' as an integral part of their name, e.g. Guatemala City, New York City. The 'City' ending defines the category of the referent, whereas the first part (the name stem, in Carroll's (1985) terms) specifies which particular referent this is. In this case the ending can be considered to be the meaningful bit and the name stem the meaningless bit.

Filenames too, as explored by Carroll (1985), often represent such combinations, as do the titles of books, names of cities, countries, islands, lakes, mountains, rivers, etc. These categories demonstrate that the idea that proper names are meaningless does not hold water, at least not from a psychological point of view. In fact, Mill (1843), a proponent of the idea that proper names are meaningless, noted that they were not *necessarily* meaningless but that, for instance, if a town called Dartmouth was not to be found at the mouth of the Dart River then this was not a contradiction – it might be there and it might not; whereas it is a contradiction to say that 'the mouth of the Dart River is not at the mouth of the Dart River'. Carroll (1985) points out that philosophers have not always confronted their analyses of proper names with the whole range of proper names, and that some accounts can be falsified simply by considering a wider sample of proper names. For instance, Ziff (1960) appeared to assume that proper names have to be singular, but as we have seen, this is not the case, e.g. the Alps. And while it may be unclear what it means to ask what 'Katmandu' means, the meaning of other proper names, e.g. Buckingham Palace, Sydney Opera House, is much clearer.

Theories of proper name meaning often do not capture the full variety of types of meaning that they can have. Consider the analysis of some city names given above. While it is true that many cities end in 'City', it is not true that all referents whose names end in 'City' are in fact cities. Manchester City and Norwich City are well-known English football clubs, and the second word in their name tells us nothing more than that the place where the team is based is a city. This may be information, but it is not relevant to the referent. It is difficult to characterise the meanings that proper names carry in a summarised form: the variety is so great. Another example of the sometimes tenuous link between a name and its referent is provided by Lord Owen's observation during the Cold War that each word of the Union of Soviet Socialist Republics' name was, in fact, incorrect.

The classification of new names proposed above makes it clear why some proper names do not carry meaning. The novel names (that consist of phoneme strings new to the language and are unrelated to existing words) appear to possess only the random component. By definition they can have no meaning, and yet novel names can be found in a variety of categories of proper names, e.g. filenames, commercial products, personal names.

Derivational names, also by definition, have both meaningful and random components. They are previously unfamiliar words and perforce have a random component, but they are based upon an existing word, hence the meaningful component.

It may seem that novel combination names only have the meaningful component, because they are composed of previously familiar words.

Most titles of books and plays fall into this category, e.g. *The Day of the Jackal*, *An Inspector Calls*; but for some novel combination names it is much less clear that the name is meaningful, e.g. Apple Macintosh is the name of a computer.

In any case, from a psychological point of view, there are no grounds for distinguishing between types of referent that take proper names on the basis of whether they carry meaning or not. Some people's names carry meaning, others do not. Some names of cars do and some do not, and so on.

SUMMARY

When created, proper names might be genuinely novel lexical items, or they might be derived from existing words or existing combinations of words. The functions of different classes of proper names impose various constraints on proper names (for example, the degree to which names need to be recalled, sound attractive, differentiate or categorise). A number of different aspects of meaning can be derived from proper names. Phonetic symbolism suggests that the choice of phonology may not be entirely arbitrary. The structure of names within a category may mean that some characteristics of names become associated with a meaning. People's names can carry meaning in that it may be possible to make educated guesses about a limited range of a person's characteristics from knowledge of their name alone, although such information is not always reliable.

Chapter 3

Cognitive models of familiar face recognition and naming

INTRODUCTION

As we have already seen, one of the major reasons for cognitive psychologists' interest in the study of proper names derives from the particular difficulty which people appear to have in recalling proper names. The category of proper names which seems to pose the biggest problem is that of people's names: the feeling that a name is on the tip of the tongue is more frequently provoked when trying to recall a person's name than when recalling other types of proper name, e.g. names of cities, product names, etc. The studies of the so-called 'tip-of-the-tongue' states and the relationship between different types of proper names will be discussed in more detail in Chapter 5. In this chapter the cognitive approach to the study of recall of proper names will be reviewed. The focus is almost exclusively on recall of people's names, as this is the category of proper names with which the vast majority of research in this tradition has been concerned. Before addressing theoretical accounts of why people's names are so difficult to recall, it is necessary to introduce an information-processing model of face recognition and some methods, most notably repetition priming and semantic priming, which are commonly employed to test such models empirically. Finally, more recent work in which face processing is modelled by computer simulation of an interactive activation network will be discussed.

The first systematic study of the recall of people's names was reported by Yarmey (1973). However, it was only recently that this initial work was followed up in any detail. The new interest derives from theoretical and methodological advances in the domain of face recognition. The methodological developments derive mainly from the analogy that was drawn between the recognition of words and the recognition of faces; thus tasks employed to explore word recognition came to be used for face recognition studies. Bruce (1983) developed the 'face familiarity decision task' as an analogue of the lexical decision task which had previously been widely employed in studies of word recognition. In a lexical decision task a subject has to decide whether or not a letter string forms a word. A word will usually be presented in one half of the trials and a pronounceable non-word presented in the other half of the trials. In a face familiarity decision task, the subject has to decide whether or not a face is familiar. As a rule, half of the faces presented will be famous and half will be unfamiliar. Therefore, a lexical decision involves deciding whether a stimulus is represented in the subject's mental lexicon, and a face familiarity decision involves deciding whether a face is represented in the mental store of faces of familiar individuals. The point is that pronounceable non-words or unfamiliar faces could be meaningful if they had been encountered previously. The adoption of the face familiarity decision task enabled a host of experiments on familiar faces to be carried out which were analogous to earlier experiments in word recognition. These experiments provided empirical tests for the development of information-processing models of familiar face processing which were analogous to Morton's (1969, 1979) logogen model of word recognition.

THE BRUCE AND YOUNG FRAMEWORK OF FACE PROCESSING

A number of information-processing models of face recognition were published during the 1980s. Although there were some important differences between the models, they had much in common with each other. One aspect upon which they were all agreed was that access to a familiar person's name could only be achieved *after* accessing at least some other information specific to the individual (e.g. their occupation).

The Bruce and Young (1986) model specifies the relationship between different aspects and stages of face processing. It deals with many of the possible types of processing that one can undertake upon seeing a face (e.g. judging the facial expression, lip-reading, etc.). Some processes are assumed to operate in parallel, for example, processing facial expression and recognition of the identity of a face. Such parallel routes imply that these different types of processing task are undertaken by functionally separate pathways. (See Bruce and Young, 1986; Bruce, 1988, for detailed reviews of the evidence on which these claims are based.)

The route of interest here is the one that allows access to the identity of a person which culminates in access to the name of the person. This route consists of four serial stages. The first stage, which is common to all face processing tasks, involves formation of a structural code of the visual properties of the face. Structural codes of familiar faces are stored in face recognition units (FRUs). Each FRU represents the face of one familiar person. The function of a FRU is to signal the overlap between the perceptual input and the structural code of the face it represents. Bruce and Young proposed that a familiarity decision is based on the degree to

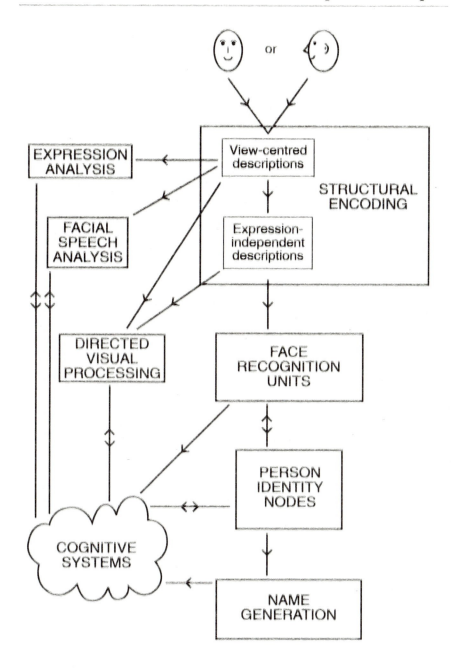

Figure 3.1 A functional model of face recognition
Source: Bruce and Young, 1986

Reprinted with permission

which a FRU is activated. An active FRU will pass activation to the person identity node (PIN) associated with the FRU. Activation of the PIN allows access to what Bruce and Young termed 'identity-specific semantic codes' (ISSC). Identity-specific semantic codes represent any information known about an individual except their name. For example, it would include their occupation, where they live, to whom they are married, personality traits, etc.

The only piece of information relating to the identity of the person which is not stored at the PIN is the person's name. As shown in Figure 3.1, the model claims that the name is stored separately, and can only be accessed *after* access to the person's PIN (i.e. access to a person's name from their face is dependent upon access to some other identity-specific semantic information related to them). In the next section we will consider in detail the empirical evidence relating to this postulated distinction between a person's name and the rest of the information associated with them.

NAMES ARE STORED SEPARATELY FROM IDENTITY-SPECIFIC SEMANTIC INFORMATION

A prime example of cognitive psychology's embrace of naturalistic methodology is the study by Young *et al.* (1985). They asked subjects to record any incidents that occurred in the course of their everyday lives concerned with the identification of persons. During an eight-week period all such incidents were described in each subject's diary. An indication was given to subjects of the type of 'error' that might occur, for instance, telling them that they might see a face and find it familiar but not be able to 'place' it, or that someone might come up to them and tell them that they had failed to recognise them on a previous occasion. In other words, the subjects were asked to note all instances where person identification did not occur faultlessly. The subjects reported a total of 922 incidents, which were categorised by the researchers according to incident type. Three error types predicted by the identity processing route of the Bruce and Young model were recorded. First, the occasions where subjects failed to recognise someone, and where it was subsequently brought to their attention. This involves a failure of the matching process at the recognition unit level. Second, subjects reported the 'familiarity only' error type, where the person's face was familiar but they had no further information about the person. This corresponds to a blockage between the FRU and the PIN level in the Bruce and Young model. Finally, there were, of course, instances where a face was recognised and identified but where the person's name was temporarily irretrievable. Whether the retrieval of the name was felt to be imminent or not, the existence of this error type argues in favour of an access of the name only after access to the semantics of the person involved. This conclusion is even stronger given that no subject ever reported recalling the name of a person without knowing who it was; that is, the case where a face is seen and the subject says, 'Ah, that's Boris Becker ... but how do I know him?' The Bruce and Young model predicts that such an error should be impossible. There was one type of incident that was unexpected: the 'resemblance-only' records, where subjects claimed that, for instance, a passer-by resembled someone else they knew, without however misleading them into thinking that it really was the other person. This class of error is accommodated by Bruce and Young (1986) by suggesting that the degree to which a FRU is activated can signal resemblance. In Hay and Young's (1982) earlier model, FRUs were envisaged as threshold devices that either signalled the presence of a stimulus or not. This binary operation follows Morton's (1969) original conception of the role of logogens in word recognition.

Young et al.'s (1985) diary study was replicated by Schweich et al. (1992); again the same sort of error types were found, and no errors of naming without recall of some identity-specific semantic information were reported. This study also looked at individual differences between young and old subjects, and a group of young subjects who, according to self-report, were particularly prone to face recognition errors. This so-called 'young impaired' group suffered a disproportionate number of face recognition errors but were not particularly impaired in naming, whereas previous reports of a particular problem in recalling people's names for elderly subjects was replicated.

These two diary studies have been backed up by a laboratory study of face identification, which used a face naming task to provoke the different knowledge states in their subjects (Hay et al., 1991). They never found a case of naming without recall of identity-specific semantics, whereas in one-fifth of trials in which subjects correctly recalled identity-specific semantic information about a face, they failed to recall the name. The majority of these failures were omissions, where the subject did not produce a name: there were very few instances of correct semantic information being produced along with an incorrect name.

The sequential access of the Bruce and Young model predicts that cues should be differentially useful according to the point of difficulty in processing. Hanley and Cowell (1988) tested the hierarchy of representation proposed by Bruce and Young (1986) by using a laboratory task similar to that employed by Hay et al. (1991). They presented their subjects with photographs of faces, half of which were famous and half unfamiliar. The subjects had to try to name the famous faces, and were often able to do so. However, three types of errors also occurred: one where subjects failed to recognise a familiar face; another where they recognised a face as familiar but were unable to say why they knew it; and the third type where a face was found to be familiar and correct identity-specific semantic information was provided, but the name was still unavailable. Each time one of these errors was produced, subjects were presented with one of three cues: a different view of the same person's face; detailed semantic information about the person; or information on the initial letters of the person's first name and surname. From the Bruce and Young model Hanley and Cowell predicted that: another photograph should provoke more naming than the other two cues for the 'failure to recognise' type of error; semantic information should allow access to the name more for the 'familiarity only' errors, and initial information should be most useful for the tip-of-the-tongue (TOT) state errors. The model's predictions were verified in all but one case. This exception involved the 'familiarity only' error, where the presentation of a second face did in fact facilitate name recall. This is a puzzling result, but for the TOT errors, only information about the initial letters of the name aided recall. A rich semantic description of the person did not help resolve TOTs.

In the neuropsychological literature there are case studies where the patient has a particular problem with recalling people's names while knowing very well who they are. Semenza and Zettin (1988, 1989) reported two aphasic patients corresponding to this description. The patients had no problem recognising people nor in saying from which category they came, but both had great difficulty in recalling the names of the same people. As both of these patients were Italian, one was able to say that a picture of Dante belonged to 'the father of our literature', a precise specification at the semantic level, but was unable to recall the person's name. This sounds very much like a tip-of-the-tongue state that normal subjects report, but the patients' performances were clearly pathological if one considers that one of them was unable to name *any* faces at all. A similar deficit was also observed on verbal fluency tasks, where the task was to produce as many exemplars from a particular category as possible within a short period of time. The number of people's names produced was vastly reduced compared to the number of exemplars from other categories. Lucchelli and de Renzi (1992) have reported a similar case, albeit a less severe deficit, but with the same pattern – recall of people's names is impaired even though the identity-specific semantic information can be recalled in a relatively trouble-free manner. As Flude et al. (1989) remarked, a demonstration of a patient with the opposite pattern of performance, preserved recall of names, in the presence of impaired recall of identity-specific semantics, would falsify Bruce and Young's proposal that names are stored separately from other semantic information about people (see Chapter 5). There are well-documented cases of patients who have difficulty recalling indentity-specific semantic information about people (Hanley et al., 1989; Ellis et al., 1989; de Haan et al., 1991). All of these patients also have problems recalling people's names. It therefore appears that their impairment in recall of identity-specific semantic information about familiar people also prevents them from recalling the relevant names.

Further support for the functional separation of a person's name from identity-specific semantic information comes from learning experiments in which information is associated with previously unfamiliar faces during the course of the experiment. Cohen and Faulkner (1986) presented subjects with unfamiliar faces and taught them various facts about the people in the photographs; for instance, their profession, their hobby and their name. Cohen and Faulkner found that names were indeed more difficult to recall than other pieces of information, but the main aim of this study was to reveal age differences in name recall. As they predicted, names were more difficult to recall for older subjects.

This paradigm of association of information to unfamiliar faces was developed by McWeeny et al. (1987). They asked their subjects to learn to associate just a name and a profession with each of sixteen unfamiliar faces, and the errors produced during learning were recorded. After being told each face's name and profession twice, faces were presented one by one and the subject had to recall the two elements of the information. Care was taken to ensure that the profession and the name were equally emphasised by reading the name and then the profession for half of the faces, and the profession and then the name for the other half. In many trials, subjects knew both elements or could not remember either. The trials of interest, however, were those where the subject recalled just one of the pieces of information associated with a face. They showed that when only one label could be recalled there was a much greater probability that it was the profession rather than the name. That is, subjects rarely recalled the name of a face without recalling the person's profession, but they quite often recalled the profession without the name. The feature of this experiment's design that makes the result so impressive was that some of the labels could be either a name or a profession, e.g. Baker, Porter. For half of the subjects a particular ambiguous label was learned as a name, whereas for the other half it was learned as a profession. The main result held even for these ambiguous labels, so that names were recalled less frequently than professions, even when the same items were involved. This result has been termed 'the Baker-baker paradox' by Cohen (1990b). The data show clearly that the difficulty in recalling people's names cannot be attributed to any features of the names per se (e.g. imageability, frequency or distinctiveness of names), because there is a recall disadvantage for proper names even when the same phonology is involved.

Mental chronometry studies have also been carried out in order to explore the functional relationship between a person's name and their professional category. Young et al. (1988a) asked subjects to perform binary decisions to famous faces. These decisions were either based on the category membership (politicians or pop stars) or on the first name of the person (David or Michael). The set of eight faces shown in the experiment was chosen so that half of the people were politicians and half were pop stars; furthermore, half of each occupational category were called Michael and half were called David. Two faces were presented in each trial. In one block of trials subjects had to make same/different judgements according to whether or not the two faces had the same *profession*, and in another block of trials the decision was according to whether the two faces had the same *first name*. Thus, all subjects performed both the semantic decision and the name decision to the same faces over the course of the experiment. This design meant that it was possible to compare a semantic decision to a name decision, using the same items and using decisions where the response set was binary in each case (same/different). It was found that the semantic decision was made more rapidly than the name decision, supporting the claim that names are accessed after identity-specific semantic information. This result is all the more important because of the small number of faces shown in the experiment which were all repeated to each subject many times.

Johnston and Bruce (1990) reasoned that although Young *et al.*'s (1988a) results were consistent with Bruce and Young's framework, there was a potential problem in their choice of name and semantic decisions. The name, they argued, is the property of a person, whereas the occupation of a person is a category to which they belong. If a category can be considered as a cluster of properties, then this extra semantic richness might have been the reason for the occupational decision being taken more rapidly than the name decision. In order to get around this problem, Johnston and Bruce identified semantic properties instead of semantic categories. They selected the properties of being dead or alive and American or British, and compared these to the property of being called John or James. Here the selection of stimuli was even more constrained; there was one exemplar from each of the eight possibilities obtained by crossing these three properties. Thus, there was one dead American called John (Wayne), one living American called John (McEnroe), one living Briton called James (Callaghan). Again subjects performed same/different matching tasks. It was found that the name decision was slower than decisions concerning either semantic property, despite the fact that they too were mere properties of the famous people.

There is then an array of evidence in favour of the box and arrow model separation of names from other identity information. It is impressive not only for the range of different paradigms providing converging evidence for the functional dependence of name retrieval on access to identity-specific semantic information, but also due to the relative lack of evidence *against* it. Names are associated with faces less quickly than are professions; the names of famous people are accessed less quickly than their professions, even when decisions are binary and the items have been seen many times in the experiment; brain-injured patients are reported with deficits for the recall of people's names with recall of facts about the same people intact, but patients who have difficulty recalling biographical information about a person also have difficulty recalling their name; diary and laboratory studies of normal subjects show that whenever a face elicits the correct name, it also elicits some correct identity-specific semantic information.

There are nevertheless some difficulties for the claim of serial dependence. As noted by Bruce and Young (1986), Williams and Smith (1954) report the case of a patient who was apparently able to name all his ex-army colleagues when presented with a group photograph, but did not seem to know how he recognised them. The key question for the model is whether or not he knew that they were all from the army. This is impossible to ascertain from the brief description given.

In the McWeeny *et al.* (1987) experiment reported above, trials in which subjects recalled professions without the names were very frequent, and significantly more common than the reverse. However, there were some trials where the name alone was recalled. Such trials might be thought to be illegal for the Bruce and Young framework. However, such a conclusion would require a strong and probably misguided claim as to what actually constitutes the identity-specific semantic information of the unfamiliar faces used in learning experiments. For famous faces, the occupational category may be considered an essential part of the information about that person. However, for an unfamiliar face encountered once in an experiment, the supposed occupational category is perhaps not so important: the identity-specific semantics of such a face might be merely that it was a face that was seen in a particular experiment. In order to demonstrate naming without understanding of the meaning for a face encountered only in an experiment, it is necessary to show that the naming occurred and that the subject was unable to say that the face had been encountered in the experiment. This seems to be a much less likely prospect.

Recently, Brennen *et al.* (in press) reported a French patient with Alzheimer's disease who, on some occasions named famous faces upon seeing them, but was unable to provide any semantic information about the people. This happened on a handful of occasions, mostly with two faces, Serge Gainsbourg and Catherine Deneuve, both extremely famous French entertainers. The patient failed to pick out the correct profession from a short-list, thus apparently violating the Bruce and Young model's hierarchical processing assumptions. The phenomenon of naming without semantics was elicited even more readily in object identification tasks, thus also posing a problem for sequential models of object processing. It should be noted however that overall, the patient's recall of proper names was not superior to her recall of common names: it was on individual trials that a proper name was recalled without appropriate common names. The pattern poses difficulties for Bruce and Young's models, but is not a case of selective preservation of proper names. Recent cases of selective preservation of proper name recall are described in Chapter 5.

The conclusion from this survey of evidence regarding the separation of names from identity-specific semantics is that there is much data in favour of it, and no clearly interpretable data against it. Ironically, such a situation is unsatisfactory because while there is a functional model that *describes* the relationship between identity-specific semantics and people's names, it in no way *explains* it. Indeed McWeeny *et al.*'s data appear to eliminate hypotheses based on the items themselves, or at least to show that they cannot explain all the difficulty that proper name recall presents. More recently, new explanations of the difficulty of the recall of proper names have been proposed that perhaps allow a way out of this impasse. These accounts are discussed in chapters 5 and 6.

At this point, we shall briefly summarise some of the evidence which supports the theoretical analogy between recognising familiar faces and recognition of words and objects on which the Bruce and Young framework is based, before introducing a more recent implementation of the Bruce and Young framework. The work reviewed in the rest of this chapter does not explicitly address any issues concerning recall of people's names, but some studies of recognition of people's names are discussed. The methods and models discussed below are central to theories of proper name processing which are discussed in subsequent chapters.

REPETITION AND SEMANTIC PRIMING OF FACES AND NAMES

The Bruce and Young (1986) framework and the concept of face recognition units was inspired by the logogen model of word recognition (Morton, 1969, 1979) and similar work on object recognition (e.g. Warren and Morton, 1982). A number of studies have shown that an analogy between recognition of familiar faces, names, objects and words is remarkably consistent over a range of tasks. Generally, faces are processed in a similar manner to objects, and names show similar effects to those observed in word recognition.

Repetition priming refers to the advantage in processing a stimulus that arises from recent exposure to the same stimulus. For example, if in a lexical decision task a subject has recently decided that 'clown' is a word and the same word is presented again, the subject will make the same decision more quickly than without the prior lexical decision to the stimulus (e.g. Scarborough *et al.*, 1977). The effect of repetition priming has been found to be modality specific. For example, reading the word 'clown' does not prime naming a picture of a clown, but prior exposure to the same or a different picture of a clown does (Warren and Morton, 1982). The effect is also relatively long-lasting; typically, it is observed after delays in the range of 15–30 minutes and after many intervening stimuli have been presented. The time taken to make a familiarity decision to a famous face has been shown to be sensitive to repetition priming from previous exposure to the face over a similar delay, and to be modality specific; face recognition is not primed by prior exposure to the celebrity's name (Bruce and Valentine, 1985; Ellis *et al.*, 1987).

Semantic priming refers to the advantage in processing a stimulus that arises from prior exposure to a related stimulus. For example, a lexical decision to the word 'butter' can be made more quickly if it is preceded by the word 'bread' (e.g. Neely, 1976). Similar effects of semantic priming are observed in familiarity decisions to faces of celebrities who are closely associated. For example, a familiarity decision to Stan Laurel's face will reduce the reaction time to make a familiarity decision to Oliver Hardy's face (Bruce and Valentine, 1986). Bruce and Valentine also found semantic priming between familiarity decisions to printed names of closely associated celebrities (i.e. deciding that 'Stan Laurel' is a familiar name speeds subsequent recognition of the name 'Oliver Hardy').

Semantic priming, unlike repetition priming, has not been demonstrated over intervals longer than 5 seconds, nor has it been shown to survive the presentation of an intervening stimulus between prime and target. This difference in the time-course of repetition priming and semantic priming has been observed for both words (Dannenbring and Briand, 1982) and familiar faces (Bruce, 1986). Semantic priming also differs from repetition priming in that it crosses stimulus domains. A familiarity decision to a celebrity's face will prime familiarity decision to a close associate's name (Young *et al.*, 1988b).

The striking similarities between word, object and face recognition also extend to studies of picture-word interference. In a series of experiments reported by Young *et al.* (1986b), subjects were presented simultaneously with a famous face and the name of a celebrity. They were instructed to make a decision about either the face or the name and to ignore the other stimulus. When the face and name were of different celebrities the presence of the irrelevant stimulus slowed the reaction time of the decision but the effect was dependent on the nature of the response required (naming or classification). The pattern of interference effects found between faces and names was very similar to that found between pictures and words in analogous experiments. Faces gave the same effects as pictures of objects and names gave the same effects as words.

The similarities between face and word recognition provide support for the idea of extending the concept of logogens or word recognition units to analogous face recognition units. The effects of semantic and repetition priming were assumed to be due to residual activity in a recognition unit resulting from either recent activation of the unit which had not yet dissipated (repetition priming) or activation originating in semantically related active recognition units (semantic priming). The effect of priming was assumed to occur because the threshold of the recognition unit was reached more quickly when the target face was presented as the rise in activation of the appropriate unit was starting from a point above the resting level.

The Bruce and Young framework used the same mechanism to explain both semantic and repetition priming. It was therefore difficult to explain why repetition priming lasts longer than semantic priming and why repetition priming is modality specific but semantic priming is not. A further difficulty for the Bruce and Young framework is posed by the demonstration of implicit recognition of familiar faces in some prosopagnosic patients. Prosopagnosia is a condition in which patients, following brain injury, are unable to recognise familiar faces. Once highly familiar faces evoke no feeling of familiarity at all, although many prosopagnosic patients can still comprehend the names of familiar people. However, some patients do show evidence of still recognising familiar faces in indirect tests of memory; that is, in tests which do not require any overt judgement that a face is familiar. For example, Young *et al.* (1988b) found that patient PH showed evidence of semantic priming from faces he did not recognise on the time required to judge that the name of a related person was familiar. The Bruce and Young framework has no means of explaining how such 'covert' recognition of familiar faces could occur in the absence of overt recognition. We shall discuss an implementation of the Bruce and Young framework in terms of an interactive activation and competition network which addresses these problems in the next section.

AN INTERACTIVE ACTIVATION IMPLEMENTATION OF THE BRUCE AND YOUNG FRAMEWORK

Burton *et al.* (1990) used an interactive activation and competition architecture (cf. McClelland, 1981) to implement the Bruce and Young (1986) framework. The great advantage of this approach is that the model can be simulated in computer software. It is therefore possible to examine the behaviour of the network under a variety of conditions to test whether the model does actually show the effects which have been observed in empirical studies (e.g. repetition priming and semantic priming). The ability of the network to model the empirical data can then be used to judge how successfully the model simulates the processes involved in human face recognition. The interactive activation and competition architecture (IAC) is one of a much wider class of connectionist models (see Quinlan,

1991 for a review). The IAC model uses localised representations. One processing unit in the IAC model represents one FRU or PIN in the Bruce and Young model. The processing units in the IAC model are clustered into pools of units of similar functions. For example, there is a pool of FRUs and a pool of PINs. This makes the architecture of the model similar to the structure of the Bruce and Young framework. All units within a pool are connected to every other unit in the pool by inhibitory links. For example, if one FRU becomes active it will inhibit all other FRUs. The strength of the inhibition is a function of the level of activation of the active unit. All links between units in different pools are excitatory and bi-directional. For example, there would be an excitatory link which would connect the FRU which represents a familiar individual's face to the PIN for the same person. Figure 3.2 shows the architecture of the model used by Burton *et al.* (1990). There are four pools of units: face recognition units (FRUs), person identity nodes (PINs), semantic information units (SIUs) and name input units (NIUs). Note that name input units represent the input of written names; there are no units to represent recall of names in this version of the model. Inputs to the network are simulated by setting the activity of an FRU (to simulate presentation of a face) or an NIU (to simulate presentation of a name) to a level of 1 (maximum activation). Reaction time can be simulated in the network by observing the number of processing cycles that are required for the relevant unit (e.g. a PIN) to exceed a threshold activation as the activation spreads throughout the network with each cycle.

There are two major differences between Burton *et al.*'s implementation and the original Bruce and Young (1986) model. First, PINs are no longer seen as the units at which identity-specific semantic information is stored. SIUs represent specific biographical information, PINs are merely entry nodes to access SIUs (i.e. SIUs can only be activated from FRUs or NIUs by passing activation via a PIN). Second, face familiarity decisions are now assumed to be based on the activity of a PIN reaching a threshold rather than based on the activity of an FRU. In fact, all routes that can be used to identify a person, e.g. face, name, voice, gait, pattern on sweater, would converge at the PIN gateway. It is supra-threshold activation at the PIN level that causes a person to be found familiar. Semantic information becomes available by activation of the corresponding units, which are linked to the PIN of a particular person.

The Burton *et al.* IAC model (1990) has a number of advantages over the original Bruce and Young framework. First, the model is able to account for the differences in the time-course and modality specificity of repetition priming and semantic priming. Burton *et al.* proposed that the mechanism for repetition priming of face recognition was an increase of the weight of the connection between the FRU and PIN of a stimulus face. Thus when a face is seen, the strength of the connection increases

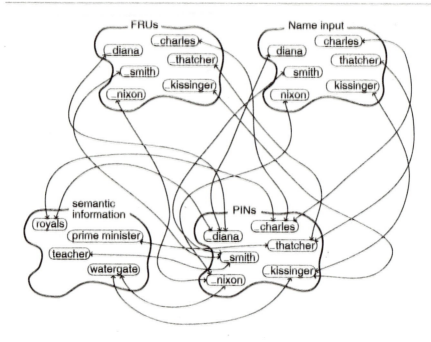

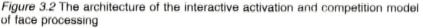

Figure 3.2 The architecture of the interactive activation and competition model of face processing

Source: Burton *et al.*, 1990. Reprinted with permission

and only very slowly decays. If the face of the same person is encountered again, the activation of the PIN reaches threshold more quickly (i.e. in fewer processing cycles) because more activation is passed to the PIN from the FRU via the increased weight on the connection (see Figure 3.3). The effect of repetition priming is modality specific because the increased weight is on the modality-specific input to the PIN (i.e. names access the PIN via NIU–PIN links but faces access the PIN via FRU–PIN links).

The effect of semantic priming is simulated by the spread of activation between PINs via common SIUs. For example, if Stan Laurel's face is presented the corresponding FRU and PIN become activated. The PIN would pass activation to the relevant SIUs, for example, a unit representing a comedy actor. The PIN representing Oliver Hardy would also be connected to the same SIU. As the links are bi-directional, activation from the active common SIU(s) will be passed back to partially activate Oliver Hardy's PIN. Although activation of Oliver Hardy's PIN would remain below threshold it would be raised above its resting level. Thus, if Oliver Hardy's PIN is now activated by presentation of either his face or his name, activity in his PIN will rapidly reach threshold as it is starting from a point above the resting level (see Figure 3.4). Thus residual activation in

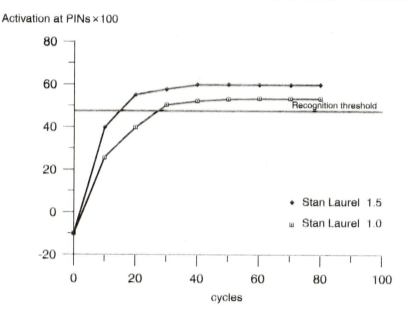

Figure 3.3 Repetition priming in an IAC model of face processing. The activation curves of Laurel's PIN following input to his FRU under two conditions: (1) when his FRU–PIN connection strength is set to 1.0, and (2) when his FRU–PIN connection strength is set to 1.5. The increase in connection strength between (1) and (2) simulates the effect of repetition priming

Adapted from Calder, 1993, after Burton *et al.*, 1990. Reprinted with permission

PINs spread via common SIUs provide the mechanism for semantic priming. As PINs are multi-modal gateways to the semantic system (i.e. they receive inputs from both faces and names) semantic priming crosses modalities. If the face or name of an unrelated person was presented after Stan Laurel's face in the above example, the PIN of the unrelated person would become highly activated. The inhibition spread from this strongly activated PIN would rapidly dissipate the activation of any partially activated PINs. Therefore, the effect of semantic priming would not survive any intervening stimulus. This simulation of semantic priming is consistent with the empirical data which show that the effect of semantic priming is short-lived.

A further advantage of the IAC model is that it is also able to account for covert recognition of faces in prosapagnosic patients without requiring any further processing mechanisms or pathways to be postulated.

Burton *et al.* (1991) modelled prosapagnosia with covert recognition as a reduction in the connection strengths of the links between FRUs and PINs rather than a complete disconnection. Burton *et al.* showed that if

Activation at PINs × 100

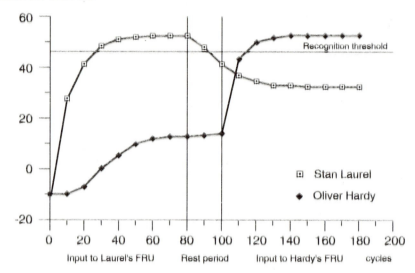

Figure 3.4. The activation curves for Laurel's FRU and PINs are shown following an input to Laurel's FRU, followed by a rest period of twenty cycles (corresponding to a prime target inter-stumulus interval) and finally an input to Hardy's FRU

Adapted from Calder, 1993. Reprinted with permission

the weights of all FRU–PIN links were reduced to 50 per cent of their original value, presentation of a face did not induce sufficient activity in the PIN to reach the recognition threshold. Therefore, the face would not be consciously recognised. However, presentation of an unrecognised face produced sufficient residual activation of the PIN to give the normal semantic priming effect on the unimpaired recognition of familiar names. Therefore, attenuation of FRU–PIN links with unimpaired NIU–PIN links enables prosopagnosia with covert recognition to be simulated.

In summary, the Burton *et al.* (1990) IAC model provides an impressive account of the available data on repetition and semantic priming by use of simple and plausible mechanisms. Simulations of 'lesioned' networks show that this approach can provide a parsimonious account of covert recognition in prosopagnosic patients. The simulations using an IAC model described so far have not attempted to simulate name retrieval. Burton and Bruce (1992) report a simulation of name retrieval. However, in order to simulate the available data they abandon Bruce and Young's claim that names are stored in a functionally separable component from identity-specific semantic information. As we have seen, there is a broad base of evidence to suggest that names are stored separately from biographical information. In this book, we shall take the stance of supporting the separation of names and identity-specific semantic information for both empirical and conceptual reasons. This issue and Burton and Bruce's (1992) simulations are discussed in detail in Chapter 6.

SUMMARY AND CONCLUSIONS

Bruce and Young (1986) proposed an information-processing model of face recognition, based on an analogy with the logogen model of word recognition. A serial hierarchy of representations for face processing was postulated in which a structural code of the face is formed and matched to face recognition units. Identity-specific semantic information about a familiar individual can then be accessed and finally their name can be retrieved. Name retrieval is dependent on retrieval of some identity-specific semantic information. Evidence for this serial dependence is found in diary studies, learning studies, mental chronometry and in neuro-psychological case studies. The analogy between familiar face recognition and word recognition is supported by comparisons of the effects of repetition and semantic priming. However, the Bruce and Young framework cannot account for the different time-course of repetition and semantic priming or covert recognition in prosopagnosic patients. An implementation of the framework using an interactive activation and competition model successfully addressed these issues.

Chapter 4

The recognition of proper names

The work reviewed in Chapter 3 showed that failure to recall proper names is a common error reported in diary studies of cognitive failures in everyday life. Difficulty in recall of proper names was commonly reported by elderly people in a questionnaire study of everyday memory ability (Cohen and Faulkner, 1984). Production of a proper name on seeing a familiar face or building is, of course, only one aspect of proper name processing. We are also able to recall the appropriate semantic information about a familiar person or building on seeing a printed or written proper name or on hearing the spoken name. Proper names can therefore form the input to cognitive processing as well as be the product of it. Of course, the same distinction between input and output applies to common as well as proper names. In short, we can speak about objects and events in the world as well as read and understand speech. In this chapter we will focus on the processing of proper names from print or sound, and thus concern ourselves principally with input rather than output. We have already discussed some aspects of the recognition of printed words and proper names in Chapter 3, in particular work on repetition and semantic priming. We begin by examining the development of proper name processing in infancy, before going on to discuss information-processing models of adult processing of people's names and the factors which affect recognition of heard and seen names.

PROPER NAME ACQUISITION BY INFANTS AND YOUNG CHILDREN

The task facing infants is to learn the difference between proper and common names. What sort of objects take which type of name? It is claimed that infants have acquired this information at a very early age. Natural languages are extremely complex entities, yet normal babies learn one (and often more than one) language in only a matter of years. This observation has led many to assume that humans have innate linguistic capacities, which facilitate and structure the process of language acquisition. Our concern here is not to give even a summary of language acquisition processes, but rather to pinpoint landmarks on the road to adult proper name processing. The first step towards learning *any* words at all would appear to be the ability to discriminate between phonemes, for this would appear necessary in order to provide a framework for categorising linguistic input. In fact, we will see later that it has been suggested that phoneme discrimination plays a particularly important role in the recall of proper names.

Ingenious work by Bertoncini *et al.* (1988) has shown that even very young babies can make distinctions between phonemes. The babies listened to sets of phonemes, and the rate of sucking on a 'blind nipple' was measured. Sucking rate is a common methodological tool used to study infants' capacity to discriminate between stimuli; it relies on the phenomenon of habituation, where babies will suck vigorously when presented with novel stimuli, and will gradually reduce in frequency if the same stimuli are presented again and again. By exposing babies to a fixed set of four syllables (e.g. bi, si, li, mi) in the first phase of a certain experimental session, and by then introducing another phoneme in the second phase (e.g. di), it was possible to conclude that, since the babies increased their sucking rate after the addition of the new syllable, they were able to discriminate between it and the others in the original set. The mean age of these subjects was less than five days old. The responses showed that infants in this age group did not make all discriminations, but infants tested at two months were able to detect a change in a consonant *or* in a vowel. Also using a sucking paradigm, Mehler *et al.* (1988) showed that newborns can distinguish between utterances in their own (or rather their culture's) language and utterances in a foreign language. Intriguingly, the infants were not capable of discriminating between two foreign languages, suggesting a rapidly learned capacity favouring discriminations in the 'ambient' language. One group of babies for whom these results held had an average age of five days.

A later part of the language acquisition process must then be the learning of words and more specifically the *names* of things. We shall see that there are developmental changes in word-finding difficulties that give an insight into the underlying functional organisation of the naming system. First, we need to consider that, in the same way as they need to learn about verbs, adjectives, tenses, adverbs and the like, infants also need to learn to distinguish between proper names and common names.

In a child's world, proper names are typically given to important animate objects, or toys modelled on animate objects. Common names suffice for other objects. Besides this semantic distinction, proper and common names are also distinguished syntactically: a common name takes an article before it (in English, 'a', 'an' or 'the'), whereas (animate) objects referred to by proper name typically do not.

Young children's sensitivity to semantic and syntactic constraints on proper name usage was first studied by Katz et al. (1974). They reported two experiments aimed at elucidating children's acquisition of names for objects. Children aged around 2 years old were encouraged to play with two objects. Furthermore, the objects were either blocks or dolls. The blocks were very similar to each other, being of the same size and texture and differing only in colour. Likewise for the dolls, the only difference between them being hair colour.

One of the objects was given a nonsense syllable as a name (e.g. 'zav') and the other was referred to merely as 'this one here', or 'the other one'. One critical manipulation was the presence or absence of an article before the name, as the object was being introduced; either it could be introduced as 'Zav' or as 'a zav', taken to imply Zav as a proper name and a common name, respectively.

In accordance with semantic constraints, it was assumed that it would not be appropriate for a block to take a proper name, whereas for a doll it would be. In accordance with syntactic constraints, only objects named without an article should receive a proper name interpretation.

In the course of play with the objects (either blocks or dolls for any one given child) reference was made at least five times to the named object before the data collection. This took place when the two objects were equidistant from the child, and consisted of the experimenter asking for a simple action to be performed with 'Zav' or 'the zav' (according to condition); for instance, to put it on a pencil. The measure was the proportion of trials on which the child picked the object designated in the first phase as 'Zav' or as 'a zav'. The results showed that the blocks were equally likely to be picked, whether or not one had been introduced as 'a zav' or as 'Zav'. This was also true for the dolls when one had been introduced as 'a zav' (inducing a common name interpretation). However, when one doll had been introduced as 'Zav' it was picked on three-quarters of trials. This pattern was exactly as expected if the children were sensitive to both the syntactic and semantic constraints, but unfortunately it was true only for girl subjects; boys chose the designated object and the other one with equal frequency in all conditions. The authors offer no explanation for this sex difference, instead focusing on the (indeed) remarkable performance of the girls, who were sensitive to both the semantic cues (block versus doll) and syntactic cues (article versus no article).

Gelman and Taylor (1984) cited the failure to find the effect with boys as one reason for replicating Katz et al.'s data, and also changed the design in two respects; they pointed out that since the children in the original study had only two blocks or dolls from which to choose, the interpretation of a 50 per cent choosing rate is ambiguous. It could mean, as Katz et al. in fact concluded, that children had imposed a common name interpretation, taking 'Zav' to refer to a category of items. However, it is also consistent with the children making no such interpretation and simply guessing. In Gelman and Taylor's experiments distractor items were included during the test phase in order to distinguish between these two possibilities.

The second change was that the objects to be named were unfamiliar to the subjects, pre-experimentally. The attribution of names to objects for which a name is already known poses problems for the interpretation of the results because it is unclear how children understand such new names. According to the contrast principle (e.g. Clark, 1988), no two words can have the same meaning. So, in cases where children are taught a new label for an object that already has a name, for example, a block or a doll, a proper name interpretation may be encouraged, as the common name interpretation is 'already taken'. Conversely, the interpretation of a new name for an unfamiliar object might be preferentially a common name interpretation. Thus Gelman and Taylor maintained the animate/inanimate distinction by using 'weird' blocks and stuffed animals, instead of the blocks and dolls as used by Katz *et al.* (1974).

Gelman and Taylor's subjects were on average about six months older than Katz *et al.*'s, the mean being 2½ years old. The results showed that the named toy was chosen significantly more often in the proper name/stuffed animal condition than in the other conditions. That is, a proper name interpretation was made more often; there were no differences between the other conditions. Thus, backing up Katz *et al.*'s conclusions, under appropriate syntactic conditions, labels given for animate objects were interpreted as proper names. Labels given for inanimate objects were not interpreted as proper names. Thus the knowledge that some objects may take proper names and some not is present at an early age.

Rates of choosing outside the category of object (i.e. a block when a monster was named, and vice versa) were low for all conditions except the proper name/block condition, where in one-third of the trials a stuffed animal was chosen. This was interpreted as a refusal to label an inanimate object with a proper name, but this conclusion must be tempered because this tendency was found only in boys. The main result, however, was found for both sexes.

In a subsequent study, Hall (1991) studied the effect of recognising an object and having a name for it upon proper name attribution in the same experiment. The findings reported by Katz *et al.* (1974) and Gelman and Taylor (1984) that infants use syntactic and semantic cues when interpreting labels is not called into question, but Hall (1991) points out that the lack of a difference between proper names attributed to unfamiliar and familiar objects is inconsistent with studies investigating acquisition of other types of name (e.g. Soja *et al.*, 1992). So despite the fact that Katz *et al.* (1974) showed that labels could be interpreted as proper names when attributed to familiar objects, and that Gelman and Taylor (1984) showed the same for unfamiliar objects, Hall (1991) argued that a replication was worthwhile, since the subjects in the two studies were of different ages and there were also procedural differences between them. He used two toy monsters and two toy cats as the unfamiliar and familiar animals respectively. He used the same method as Gelman and Taylor and the measure was the proportion of trials on which a child would choose the named toy after it had been syntactically labelled as a proper name. In two studies he found that only familiar objects received a proper name interpretation, whereas unfamiliar objects received a common name interpretation. This result was supported by comparing the proportion of children in different conditions who used a proper name interpretation in every trial. In both studies, only two out of ten children in the unfamiliar condition always chose the named toy, whereas seven out of ten did so in the familiar condition. Despite studying children of very similar age and background, these results are in direct contrast to Gelman and Taylor's (1984) results, but are consistent with the literature on the acquisition of other types of name.

Furthermore, Hall divided the familiar condition into two: for instance, one set of children were introduced to one cat as 'Zav', and the other cat as 'the other one' as in previous studies. In the familiar-explicit condition, one cat was referred to as 'Zav' and the other as 'this kitty here' or 'this cat here', in accordance with the child's spontaneously produced names for it. There were no differences between the two familiar conditions, suggesting that Hall's effect is due to the fact that the toy already has a name, and not to whether a name has been explicitly mentioned.

RECOGNITION OF PROPER NAMES BY ADULTS

We have reviewed the development of processing spoken proper names in children. In the remainder of this chapter we will consider information processing models of adults' processing of proper names (more specifically people's names). The majority of the work concerns recognition of visually presented (i.e. written) names. Therefore, before we go on to discuss the factors which affect adults processing of proper names, it is appropriate briefly to consider the relationship between recognition of written names, spoken names and production of names.

RECOGNITION AND PRODUCTION OF NAMES: SEPARATE PROCESSES?

The theoretical stance which we take in this book postulates that the representations accessed when processing seen or heard names are separate from the representations accessed in production of names. This distinction is widely held by researchers who develop information-processing models of face and name recognition (e.g. Bruce and Valentine, 1985, 1986; Young *et al.*, 1986a; Young and de Haan, 1988). The distinction has arisen because, almost invariably, the models were proposed to account for data from experiments which have involved visual presentation of names and faces. In the visual domain the case for separate input and output representations is robust, and is derived from Morton's (1979) model of word recognition. Recognising a printed name requires a mapping from orthography to identity-specific semantics, whereas production of a name requires a mapping from identity-specific semantics to phonology. The two processes seem to have little in common. However, in developing a model of proper name processing, we have to consider the processing of both auditory and visual input of names. In the auditory domain, recognising a spoken word or name requires a mapping from phonology to semantic information, whereas speech production requires the same mapping but in the opposite direction (i.e. from semantics to phonology). The issue is whether a single lexicon can handle mappings between phonology and semantics in either direction, or whether two separate lexicons exist, one of which handles the mapping required for speech perception and the other handles speech production. In contrast to models of visual word recognition, most models of speech production and perception make the assumption that both perception and production of language are mediated by a common lexicon (e.g. Levelt, 1989). Roelofs (1992) proposed a model in which a semantic lexicon but not the phonological lexicon is common to perception and production (see Chapter 8). Therefore, the separation of input and output representations is a controversial one. Currently, models of face and name processing differ from models of speech production. If recognising a heard name is to be considered as an act of speech perception, and if face naming is considered to be an act of speech production, models of name processing, face naming and speech production should be compatible. In order to achieve compatibility between the models developed in these areas of research, a consistent position on the relationship between auditory input and naming output needs to be developed. (See Chapter 6 for detailed discussion of speech production models and their role in the development of models of face naming.)

At present there is insufficient evidence to come down firmly in favour of either a common lexicon or separate lexicons for speech perception and production. The evidence relating to this issue will be discussed in Chapter 8. In the models we present in this book, we prefer to follow the dual lexicon route for two reasons. First and most importantly, we believe that on balance the evidence favours this view (see Chapter 8). Our second reason is really one of convenience. We present models which are intended to account for recognition of both visually and auditorily presented names. Processing of visually presented names requires separate representations for recognition and speech production. If we make the same assumption for auditorily presented items, for clarity we can include in our models only a single input route which could apply equally to processing of visual or auditory input. Therefore, we shall not specify whether the input route is intended for processing of auditory or written stimuli. However, we are not suggesting that the same input representation mediates recognition in both modalities. There would be a recognition unit which mediates recognition of the visual form of a word and a separate unit which mediates recognition of the auditory form of the word (Morton, 1979). Therefore, each modality requires its own set of recognition units and the required modality-specific pre-processing. In the interests of clarity, we shall show only one set of recognition units which could apply equally to either modality. Thus it should be borne in mind that in the case of lexical input, there is another set of input representations which provide access to a multi-modal semantic system for the alternative modality. Of course, this issue does not arise in the case of face recognition units, as faces can only be recognised by the visual modality.

FREQUENCY AND FAMILIARITY OF PEOPLES' NAMES

Much of the recent theoretical development in information-processing models of face recognition has been based on an analogy between recognition of familiar faces and words (Bruce, 1979; 1981; 1983). The framework proposed by Bruce and Young (1986) has been successful in accounting for similarities and differences between face, word and object recognition in a range of experimental paradigms, including repetition and semantic priming and interference studies (see Chapter 3 for a brief review of this work). Most of these experiments were inspired by an analogy between familiar faces and words, but have in fact involved a comparison between processing of people's faces and names. The hidden assumption underlying work of this nature is that words and names are equivalent and are processed in the same way. This assumption is based on the view that names are merely arbitrary verbal labels and begs the question whether a distinction between words and proper names should be made in the analogy with familiar face recognition.

Valentine *et al.* (1991) make the point that the effects of word frequency have been largely ignored in the analogy between face recognition and word recognition, despite ubiquitous effects of word frequency reported in the word recognition literature. For example, subjects decide more quickly that a high frequency word is a word (rather than a non-word) than when they make the same decision about a low frequency word (Scarborough, *et al.*, 1977). Valentine *et al.* suggested that there are two reasons for this oversight.

First, there is some theoretical debate about the locus of word frequency effects. Traditional models of word recognition have attributed the effects of word frequency to frequency-sensitivity of the identification process. For example, in a model based on the concept of recognition units (e.g. Morton's logogen model), the recognition units for high frequency words could either have a lower threshold or a higher resting level of activation than the recognition units for low frequency words. Recently, it has been argued that the identification of visually presented words is not frequency-sensitive but that the major effects of frequency arise from later task-specific processes (Balota and Chumley, 1984; 1985). Monsell *et al.* (1989) review the evidence for the loci of word frequency effects and present evidence that the primary locus of frequency effects is indeed the identification process.

A second problem in exploring the effects of frequency in the analogy between faces and words is that the appropriate analogy is not immediately clear. One possibility is to draw an analogy between the frequency of a word and the degree of familiarity of a face. Initially, this analogy appears to be entirely appropriate. Subjective ratings of familiarity with a face are negatively correlated with reaction time in a face familiarity decision task (Valentine and Bruce, 1986b). Bruce (1983) has argued that a face familiarity decision task (in which a subject decides as quickly as possible whether or not a face is familiar and indicates the decision by pressing one of two response buttons) is analogous to a lexical decision task (in which subjects decide whether a letter string is a word or a non-word). Usually, the non-words in a lexical decision task are pronounceable, so the task is equivalent to asking a subject whether a letter string is familiar. Therefore, the effect of familiarity of a face in a familiarity decision task is analogous to the advantage found for high frequency words in a lexical decision task.

There is, however, a sense in which the familiarity of a face differs from the frequency of a word. The word frequency of a common noun is an estimate of its frequency of occurrence. Such occurrences might refer to its use to denote a type or a token. For example, the word 'dog' would be used to refer to any dog (a type) or to the family pet (a token). In contrast the familiarity of a face is always associated with the same individual (a token). This distinction between type and token is more problematic when we consider proper names.

A full name or an initial and surname may be familiar because it is the name of a familiar individual in the same way that an individual's face might be familiar. Valentine *et al.* (1991) referred to this as the *familiarity* of a name. It is important to note that the familiarity of an individual's face and the familiarity of their name are not equivalent. For example, an actress's face may be more familiar than her name. It is possible to recognise an actress and to know which films she has appeared in without knowing her name. It is also possible for a name to be more familiar than a face. For example, a newspaper columnist's name might be familiar but her face might be entirely unfamiliar. Thus, familiarity of names and faces are properties specific to the individual.

A surname or a first name might also be familiar because it is shared by more than one known person. For example, the surname 'Moore' might refer to Roger Moore (actor), Patrick Moore (astronomer), Dudley Moore (actor) or many other individuals who share the same surname. Valentine *et al.* (1991) refer to a measure of the number of people who have the same name as the *frequency* of the name. The number of times a name is encountered will depend on the frequency of the name and the degree of familiarity of known people who have that name. Measures of word frequency are estimates of the number of times a word is encountered and therefore are analogous to the combined effects of the familiarity and frequency of a name. It should be noted that the familiarity of a name can only be assessed for a name that is unique to an individual (e.g. an initial and surname or full name), but name frequency can be estimated only for either a first or surname alone.

The visual or auditory recognition of proper names must have some processing in common with word recognition. Proper names and common names can only be distinguished subsequent to lexical identification. People's names have some properties in common with words and some properties in common with faces. Words and names can refer to any example of their referent. For example, the word 'Moore' can apply to all individuals who have the surname Moore. Like faces, names can be used to access identity-specific semantic information. For example, reading the name 'Roger Moore' accesses information about an actor who was well-known for playing the part of James Bond in a series of films.

A FUNCTIONAL MODEL OF RECOGNITION AND RECALL OF PEOPLE'S NAMES

Valentine *et al.* (1991) outlined a functional model of the processes involved in recognising and recalling people's names (see Figure 4.1). They suggested that recognition of people's names is mediated by a set of name recognition units (NRUs). Name recognition units are analogous to face recognition units (FRUs) and are functionally the same as the units referred to as name input units (NIU) by Burton *et al.* (1990) (see Chapter 3). Just as there is postulated to be one FRU which represents the description of each known face, there is one NRU which represents the name of each known individual. The input to name recognition units could be first or surnames alone, initial and surnames or full names. The NRUs mediate between the word recognition system and access to identity-specific semantic information about individuals. There are postulated to be word recognition units (WRUs) or logogens for all lexical items including words that are encountered in the context of proper names. The output of WRUs which represent lexical items that occur in familiar names form the input to the appropriate NRU(s). WRUs representing a first name and surname may be connected to the same NRU. A WRU representing a common first name or surname may be connected to many NRUs. Thus there would be one WRU for 'John' which would be activated by reading the name 'John Wayne' or 'John Major' and one WRU for 'Moore' which would be activated by reading the name 'Dudley Moore' or 'Roger Moore'; however, these names would each activate a different NRU.

Valentine *et al.* (1991) proposed that lexical output codes can be accessed directly from name recognition units. This route is analogous to the direct route from word recognition units to lexical output codes. Young *et al.* (1986a; 1988b) report some evidence that lexical output codes (name codes) can be accessed in parallel to identity-specific semantic information from written names but that lexical output codes can only be accessed from faces via access to identity-specific semantics. The evidence for direct access to lexical output codes from NRUs and WRUs will be discussed in more detail in Chapter 7.

Valentine *et al.* (1991) explored the effects of surname frequency and name familiarity in a number of name processing tasks in which students acted as subjects. It was predicted that if the task only required names to be processed to the level of words, the effects of name frequency and familiarity should be analogous to the effects of word frequency in word processing tasks. If, however, the tasks required individuals to be recognised from their names, the effect of surname frequency would be analogous to the effects of distinctiveness found in familiar face recognition tasks. Monsell *et al.* (1989) argued convincingly that the primary locus of the effect of word frequency is at the level of unique identification of a lexical item. Therefore, Valentine *et al.* (1991) argued that an effect of surname frequency on processing of familiar names will only be observed if the task requires the stimulus to be uniquely identified (i.e. if a specific item in the mental lexicon must be identified as having been presented). The implications of these general predictions for each task employed are described in more detail below.

Four sets of ten initial and surname combinations were selected for use in the experiments designed to test these predictions. One set of names contained celebrities who had high frequency surnames and were familiar to British students; for example, R. Burton (Richard Burton – actor) and P. Newman (Paul Newman – actor). Another set consisted of celebrities with low frequency surnames; for example, M. Jagger (Mick Jagger – pop star) and R. Redford (Robert Redford – actor). Corresponding sets of unfamiliar initial and surname combinations were compiled. Examples of high frequency, unfamiliar names were R. Morgan and K. Wright. The low frequency, unfamiliar names included G. Twigger and R. Waycot.

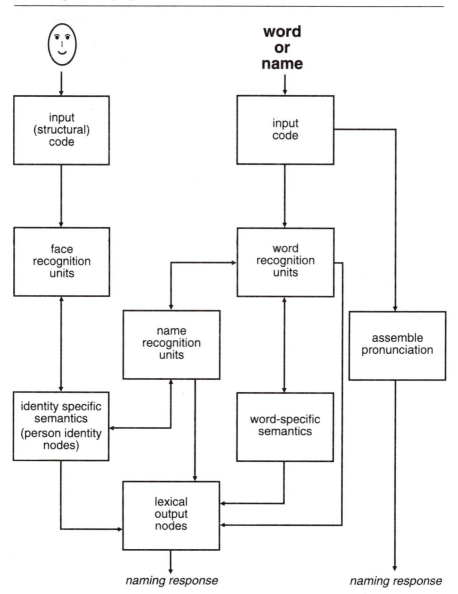

Figure 4.1 A functional model of face, name and word recognition proposed by Valentine *et al.* (1991). The routes for face and word recognition are standard models adapted from Bruce and Young (1986), except that a route for naming unfamiliar words is shown. Valentine *et al.* labelled the final stage 'phonological output codes'. Since then, Brédart and Valentine (1992) have argued that lexical access should be split into two stages (see Chapter 5). To be neutral on this issue the final stage has been relabelled 'lexical output codes'

Reprinted by permission of Lawrence Erlbaum Associates Ltd, Hove, UK

Surname frequency was estimated by counting entries in the local telephone directory. High frequency surnames were defined as surnames which had more than one occurrence for every 5,000 entries in the directory; low frequency surnames had at least one entry in the directory (i.e. they did occur as surnames) but did not have more than one occurrence for every 50,000 entries. Subjects who did not take part in any of the subsequent experiments rated each initial and surname combination for its familiarity on a seven-point scale. The two sets of 'familiar' names were matched for their subjective familiarity as were the two sets of 'unfamiliar' names. The mean number of letters in the surnames in each condition was also matched, and irregularly pronounced names were avoided as far as possible.

The first task that Valentine *et al.* (1991) investigated was designed to tap proper name processing at the level of recognising the stimuli as words. A nationality decision task was used in which subjects were required to classify names as 'British' or 'Belgian'. Such a decision could be based upon the degree to which the input code resembles an English orthography. However, if a word recognition unit for the name exists, the activation of the word recognition unit could also provide an input to the nationality decision process (cf. Bruce, 1986 for an analogous effect of familiarity on judging the sex of faces). A 'British' decision made on the basis of activation of a WRU would almost certainly be correct, as the Belgian names used in this experiment were unfamiliar to the British students who acted as subjects.

The nationality decision task was chosen because it provided the best analogy to a lexical decision task, although by no means a perfect one! In a lexical decision task subjects have to discriminate between words and pronounceable non-words. The decision is therefore one of whether a letter string is familiar. The equivalent task using surnames (is a letter string a surname?) is not a usable task because almost any pronounceable letter string could be a surname. The set of plausible items is far greater for proper names than for words (Brennen, 1993; and see Chapter 5, this volume). Subjects can, with some considerable degree of accuracy, assume that an unfamiliar letter string is not a word. However, it cannot be assumed that a letter string cannot be a surname simply because it does not seem familiar. Therefore, a decision about the national origin of a name was selected as a task which subjects would be able to perform with sufficient accuracy and which would only require processing to the level of an input code or word recognition unit.

In each trial, the subjects saw a single initial letter and surname in the centre of a computer screen. Their task was to decide as quickly as possible whether it was most likely to be the name of a British or Belgian person, and to indicate their response by pressing one of two keys. The stimuli consisted of the set of forty British names described above, mixed at random with an equivalent set of Belgian names. The reaction time of subjects' correct responses to the set of British names was analysed to explore the effect of surname frequency and familiarity of the initial and surname combination. The Belgian names were included to create the task demand (i.e. half of the names were British and half were Belgian). The Belgian names had been selected in terms of their familiarity and surname frequency to Belgian subjects. However, these criteria were not applicable to British students. Therefore, no predictions of effects on the reaction time (RT) to Belgian names were made.

The results, as iIllustrated in Figure 4.2, showed that names of famous people were correctly classified as British more quickly than the names of unfamiliar people. In addition, high frequency surnames were classified as British more quickly than low frequency surnames. The effects of name familiarity and surname frequency were not simply additive in this task. Comparisons between the mean RTs in each condition show that all of these effects are attributable to the mean RT to names of unfamiliar individuals with low frequency surnames being slower than the mean RTs to items in all of the other three conditions. The mean RTs to familiar names with high or low frequency surnames and to unfamiliar names with high frequency surnames did not differ from each other.

The results indicate that it does not make any difference whether the source of the perceived familiarity of a surname arises because it is the name of one highly familiar individual, or because it is a common surname and has been encountered in connection with many individuals. So long as it has been encountered frequently in the past, subjects are able to rapidly classify the name according to its national origin. Word recognition units are less likely to have been formed for low frequency surnames that are not the names of famous people than for any of the other stimuli. Therefore, decisions to these stimuli are less likely to be speeded by activation of a WRU representing the stimulus.

This pattern of results is consistent with an analogy between the nationality decision task and a lexical decision task. In a lexical decision task, high frequency words are accepted as words more quickly than are low frequency words. It has already been argued that the combined effects of name frequency and name familiarity would provide an estimate of the number of previous occurrences of a surname and therefore the combined effects of both factors are analogous to word frequency. Provided the item has been encountered many times before, either because it is the name of a famous person or because it is a common surname, a rapid RT was obtained.

At first sight, this line of reasoning might lead to the expectation that the effects of frequency and familiarity would be additive: i.e. that names that were both famous and high frequency would be responded to more quickly than other items. However, no effect of surname frequency on the

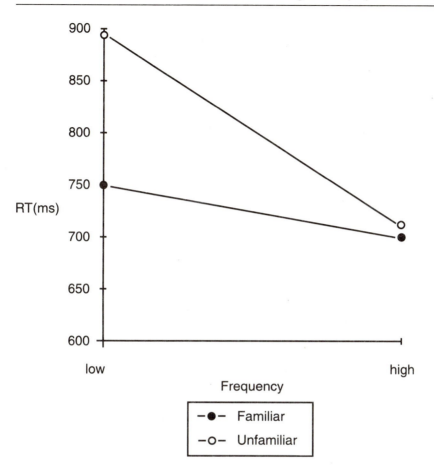

Figure 4.2. Mean reaction time to correctly classify names as 'British' as a function of familiarity and surname frequency (filled circles = names of celebrities, unfilled circles = unfamiliar names). The stimuli consisted of an initial and surname

Source: Valentine *et al.* (1991), Experiment 1. Reprinted by permission of Lawrence Erlbaum Associates Ltd, Hove, UK

RT of responses to familiar names was found. In fact, an analogy with the effects of word frequency would predict this lack of an effect. The nationality decision task does not require unique identification of the stimulus lexical item. Nationality decision could be based on the orthography of the stimulus and/or activation from an activated WRU. However, it is not necessary to identify *which* WRU has been activated in order to make a positive decision. If the combined effects of surname frequency and name familiarity are analogous to the effect of word frequency, and unique identification is the primary locus of the effect of word frequency, no effect of the frequency of a familiar surname would be predicted in a task which does not require unique identification. However, in the case of unfamiliar names an effect of surname frequency would be expected, as unfamiliar, high frequency names are much more likely than unfamiliar, low frequency names to be represented in the visual lexicon.

We do not mean to suggest that lexical decision or familiarity decision does not require unique identification. Logically, either decision could be based on a 'familiarity' signal based on any active recognition unit or units. However, the data suggest that lexical and familiarity decisions are indeed based on unique identification of a specific active recognition unit (Monsell *et al.*, 1989; Valentine and Ferrara, 1991).

In summary, RT of nationality decisions are slower to unfamiliar, low frequency surnames than to the other stimuli, because they are less likely to be represented by WRUs. Stimuli in the other cells of the design are either common or familiar surnames and so are highly likely to be represented by WRUs. The lack of an effect of surname frequency on RT of nationality decisions to familiar names is attributed to the lack of a task demand to uniquely identify the stimulus – which is a process believed to give rise to an effect of word frequency.

In the second experiment reported by Valentine *et al.* (1991), subjects saw the same British initials and surnames as were used in the previous experiment but this time they were instructed to read the surnames aloud as quickly as possible. The latency to start articulating the name was measured by use of a voice-activated switch.

There is evidence to suggest that high frequency words can be read aloud more quickly than low frequency words (Monsell *et al.*, 1989; Seidenberg *et al.*, 1984). Generally, surname frequency and name familiarity had a similar effect on naming latency as was found on nationality decision. The latency to read aloud unfamiliar, low frequency surnames was slower than the latency to read aloud surnames that were either those of celebrities or common surnames. According to the model shown in Figure 4.1 (p. 60) which is derived from the dual-route model of reading, known words (or names) which are represented by WRUs can be read aloud by directly accessing a stored lexical output code from an activated WRU. If the word is not represented in the visual lexicon, however, it can only be read by use of orthography-phonology conversion strategies. A similar interpretation of the results as offered for the nationality decision can be made. Surnames that are either high frequency or familiar will be represented in the visual lexicon and can be read via the direct whole word route, accessing stored lexical output codes. Surnames which are not associated with celebrities and are low frequency are less likely to be represented by a WRU and can only be read aloud by assembling pronunciation from sub-lexical processes. To the extent that assembly of pronunciation is slower than direct access of stored lexical output codes, the RT to read aloud unfamiliar, low frequency surnames will be slower than the RT to read aloud surnames that are either familiar or high frequency or both.[1]

One aspect in which the pattern of results obtained for naming latency differed from those obtained in the nationality decision task was the effect of surname frequency on RT to familiar names. The latency to read aloud familiar, high frequency surnames was shorter than that to read aloud familiar, low frequency surnames. In order to read aloud a surname (or word) via the lexical route, the WRU which represents the stimulus word must be correctly and uniquely identified. If this were not the case the correct lexical output code could not be selected. Therefore, the view that the primary locus of the effect of word frequency is unique identification was supported by these experiments using surnames. An effect of surname frequency was found in a task that requires unique identification of a familiar surname (reading a surname aloud) and no effect was found in a task which did not demand unique identification of a familiar surname (nationality decision).

Having demonstrated that the effects of surname frequency and name familiarity are analogous to the effects of word frequency in two tasks which only require names to be processed by the word recognition system, Valentine et al. (1991) went on to examine the effects of surname frequency in tasks which require familiar individuals to be recognised from their name. The British set of initials and surnames, which had been used in the previous two experiments, were presented in a name familiarity decision task. The subjects had to decide as quickly as possible whether or not the initial and surname presented was that of a familiar person. The subjects pressed either a 'yes' or 'no' button and the response latency was recorded. The mean RT to correctly accept as familiar the initial and surname of celebrities with high frequency surnames was *slower* than the mean RT to famous low frequency surnames. For example, subjects were faster to recognise that 'M. Jagger' (Mick Jagger – pop star) was familiar than they were to recognise that 'M. Jackson' (Michael Jackson – pop star) was familiar. A similar effect was observed for the RT to correctly reject unfamiliar names. Subjects were faster to correctly reject stimuli which included a low frequency surname than they were to reject stimuli which included a high frequency surname.

The effect of surname frequency was the reverse of that observed in the nationality decision and naming latency tasks. When a familiarity decision

---

[1] The status of the direct, non-semantic lexical route for reading words aloud is examined in detail in Chapter 7. We argue that Hillis and Caramazza's (1991) summation hypothesis should be preferred to the postulation of a non-semantic route for reading. The summation hypothesis provides an account of why the RT to read aloud a surname represented by a WRU would be faster than the RT to read aloud a surname that has not been encountered before. See Chapter 7 for a detailed discussion of the summation hypothesis.

was required, there was an advantage for *low* frequency surnames as opposed to an advantage for *high* frequency surnames in the nationality decision and naming task. Valentine *et al*. (1991) argue that the critical difference between the tasks is that a name familiarity decision requires access to memory for familiar individuals. The functional model of name processing proposed postulates that familiar name recognition is mediated by a set of name recognition units, each representing the name of a familiar individual. Presentation of an initial and a high frequency surname will activate the NRUs for several familiar people to some extent. For example, 'M. Jackson' will activate the NRU for Michael Jackson the pop star but will also activate to some extent the NRUs for Janet Jackson (his sister), Jesse Jackson (American politician), and any other Jacksons known to the subject. In contrast, the stimulus 'M. Jagger' probably activates no NRU other than that representing the name of the member of the Rolling Stones. Therefore, presentation of a low frequency surname will activate fewer NRUs and it will be easier to uniquely identify a match between the stimulus and a stored representation of a familiar name because there will be less 'noise' from competing NRUs representing individuals with the same surname.

The effect of surname frequency on name familiarity decision is analogous to the effect of facial distinctiveness on face familiarity decision. Valentine and Bruce (1986a, 1986b) found that familiar faces that have been rated as distinctive are recognised more quickly than familiar faces that have been rated as more typical in appearance. Young and Ellis (1989) propose an account of the effect of distinctiveness on face familiarity decisions which is based on competition from FRUs which represent faces similar to the stimulus face. There will, by definition, be more competition from faces similar to typical faces than from faces similar to distinctive faces. The account of the effect of surname frequency on name familiarity decision offered by Valentine *et al*. (1991) and the account of the effect of distinctiveness on face familiarity decision described by Young and Ellis (1989) are directly analogous. Both depend on the view that a familiarity decision requires unique identification; that is, a decision must be made as to which single recognition unit has been activated. In fact, unique identification is not a logical requirement of a familiarity decision. The decision could be based on the level of activation summed across all recognition units. This process could distinguish familiar from unfamiliar items but not uniquely identify which recognition unit has been activated. Valentine and Ferrara (1991) argued that the effect of distinctiveness in face recognition could only be squared with a large body of work on the representation of concepts if the assumption is made that familiarity decisions to meaningful stimuli are in fact based on a process involving unique identification.

In order to test the interpretation of the effect of surname frequency on name familiarity decision, Valentine *et al.* (1991) examined the effect of presenting full names rather than initials and surnames as the stimuli. They argued that a first name and surname should reduce the ambiguity of the stimulus. The presence of both names would activate the 'target' NRU more strongly and inhibit activation of 'competitor' NRUs representing other individuals with the same surname. Therefore, including first names should reduce or remove the competition from partially activated NRUs and reduce or remove the effect of surname frequency. This experiment was carried out in Liège, working in a different linguistic context and using a different set of stimuli (the set of Belgian names used in the nationality decision task).

The effect of surname frequency on name familiarity decisions to initials and surnames was replicated. Subjects were quicker to correctly accept stimuli with low frequency surnames as familiar than they were to accept stimuli with high frequency surnames. Subjects were also quicker to correctly reject unfamiliar low frequency surnames than they were to reject unfamiliar high frequency surnames. When a full name was presented the effect of surname frequency on RT to accept familiar names was completely removed as predicted (see Figure 4.3). In fact, there is a non-significant trend for names with high frequency surnames to be accepted faster than names with low frequency surnames. However, the effect of surname frequency on RT to reject unfamiliar names was unaltered by inclusion of a first name – subjects were still quicker to reject full names which included a low frequency surname (see Figure 4.4).

Valentine *et al.* (1991) argue that if the stimulus name is unfamiliar, no one NRU will be strongly activated by either an initial and surname or a full name, but in both cases there are likely to be more competing name recognition units for individuals who share the same surname as a high frequency stimulus surname than a low frequency surname. These NRUs will be activated to some extent and in the absence of one very strongly activated NRU, the greater degree of activation induced in other NRUs by a high frequency surname is sufficient to slow down the rejection of the name compared to the RT to reject a name with a low frequency surname, even in the presence of a first name.

In a final experiment Valentine *et al.* (1991) demonstrated an effect of surname frequency in another task that requires access to memory for individuals. The effect of surname frequency on classifying the initials and surnames of celebrities according to their occupation was similar to the effect found in a name familiarity decision. Subjects were quicker to classify low frequency surnames as politicians or pop stars than they were to classify high frequency surnames. This task requires not only identification of the familiar person from their name but also access to identity-specific semantic information. The finding that the effect of surname frequency is similar in a name familiarity decision task and a semantic

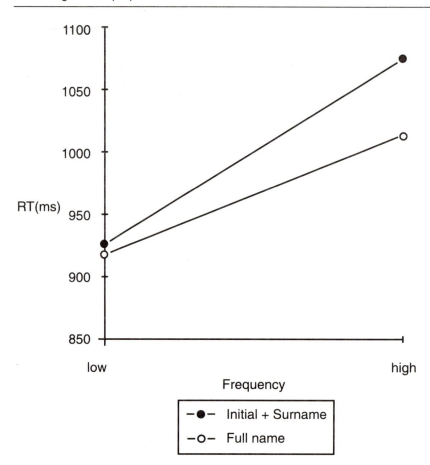

Figure 4.3 Mean reaction time of correct responses to familiar names in a familiarity decision task as a function of format of name and surname frequency (filled circles = initial and surname, unfilled circles = full name)

Source: Valentine *et al.* (1991), Experiment 4. Reprinted by permission of Lawrence Erlbaum Associates Ltd, Hove, UK

classification according to occupation is consistent with the view that it is the process of unique identification that is faster for low frequency surnames.

So far, the discussion of the effect of surname frequency has been restricted to the effect on processing of seen names. Would the same effects of surname frequency be observed for recognition of auditorily presented names? The approach we have adopted here would predict that the same effects would be observed regardless of the modality of the input. Following Morton (1979), we would argue that the WRUs and NRUs are modality-specific and that there are analogous pools of WRUs

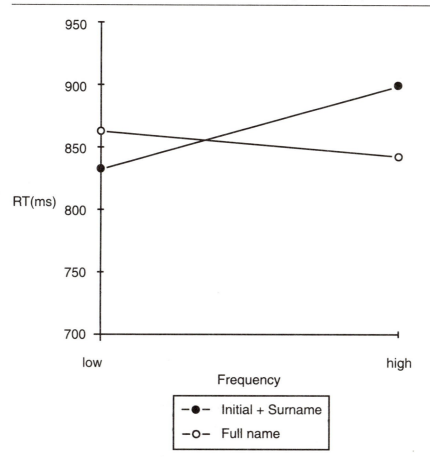

Figure 4.4 Mean reaction time of correct responses to unfamiliar names in a familiarity decision task as a function of format of name and surname frequency (filled circles = initial and surname, unfilled circles = full name)

Source: Valentine *et al.* (1991), Experiment 4. Reprinted by permission of Lawrence Erlbaum Associates Ltd, Hove, UK

and NRUs which act as word and name detectors for auditory input. Brédart and Valentine (1992) used the stimuli employed by Valentine *et al.* (1991, Experiment 3) in a name familiarity decision task in which the names were presented from a tape recorder using headphones. The results were similar to those obtained using visual presentation: name familiarity decisions were faster to initial and low frequency surname combinations.

To summarise, the central notion of the model proposed by Valentine *et al.* (1991) is of a set of name recognition units, analogous to face recognition units which receive input from word recognition units and enable access to identity-specific semantics via person identity nodes. This framework appears to account for the pattern of effects of surname frequency and name familiarity observed in a variety of name processing tasks.

REPETITION PRIMING BETWEEN PROPER NAMES AND COMMON NAMES

One feature of the proposed framework, which is critical in the account of the effects of surname frequency, is that proper names are initially processed by the word recognition system. Only after the constituent lexical items of proper names have been identified in the mental lexicon are they processed by the person recognition system. In the case of people's names, person recognition begins by activation of name recognition units.

It is not uncommon in western societies for words to occur as people's surnames. For example, in the UK the surnames of the last two prime ministers (Thatcher, Major) are both English words. If such surnames are initially processed by the word recognition system, it should be possible to demonstrate facilitation of processing between a lexical decision and a name familiarity decision made to the same lexical item, by use of a repetition priming technique. The phenomenon of repetition priming is well established in lexical processing. If, say, a lexical decision to a specific word is repeated during an experiment, the decision is generally made more quickly on the subsequent encounter in comparison to the RT of lexical decisions to words that have not been 'primed' by a recent presentation (see Chapter 3).

Valentine *et al.* (1993) used this strategy to look for repetition priming from lexical decisions to name familiarity decisions and vice versa. Two sets of names of celebrities whose surnames are English words were compiled. In one task subjects saw the celebrities' full names, mixed in a random order with invented names (comprised of familiar first names and surnames) and other celebrities' names. The subjects made a name familiarity decision to each stimulus. In the second task the celebrities' surnames alone (which were words) were mixed at random with other words and non-words and subjects made lexical decisions to each stimulus. Each subject took part in both tasks. One set of celebrities' names which were also words appeared in both tasks. The set of names which was 'primed' was counterbalanced so that, across subjects, responses to the same items made up the 'primed' and 'unprimed' trials.

It was found that correctly deciding that a celebrity's full name is familiar facilitated a subsequent lexical decision to the word which occurred as the surname. RT of correct lexical decisions were faster to 'primed' than to 'unprimed' items. Repetition priming was also found to occur when the tasks were carried out in the opposite order: a lexical decision facilitated a subsequent name familiarity decision. In a further experiment, Valentine *et al.* (1993) found there was as much repetition priming between a name familiarity decision task and a lexical decision task as there was when the same decision to the same items was repeated. The latter result suggests that the effect of repetition was not being mediated by subjects recalling the response that they made to the stimulus in an earlier trial (i.e. retrieval from episodic memory). If this was the case, repeating the stimulus and its processing should lead to a greater effect of repetition than that found when a different decision is made to the stimulus on the second encounter.

The pattern of repetition priming that would be predicted from the theoretical framework of name recognition depends on the exact locus of the effect of repetition. Recent experimental evidence and connectionist modelling suggests that the mechanism of repetition priming involves an increase in the weight of links between pools of units or levels of representations (e.g. Burton et al., 1990; Vitkovitch and Humphreys, 1991; Monsell et al., 1992).

Valentine et al. (1993) point out that their results do not unambiguously locate the specific locus or loci of repetition priming. By analogy to the simulation of repetition priming effects using an interactive activation model reported by Burton et al. (1990), the effects of repetition priming would be located at the links between word recognition units and the semantics of words for lexical decisions; and between word recognition units and name recognition units for name familiarity decisions. In the case of name processing an additional possible locus is at the links between name recognition units and person identity nodes.

These links can only account for repetition priming between name familiarity decisions and lexical decisions, if it is assumed that the links – at least as far as name recognition units are concerned – are automatically activated whenever a word that is also a proper name is encountered; and conversely, that the links up to the semantics of words are activated whenever a proper name that is also a word is encountered. Although this assumption sounds a little bizarre it is consistent with work on the resolution of lexical ambiguity of homographs. It is well established that both meanings of a homograph can be available simultaneously, although the activation of meanings can have a different time-course and are subject to effects of frequency and context (e.g. Tanehaus et al., 1979; Onifer and Swinney, 1981; Seidenberg et al., 1982; Simpson and Krueger, 1991).

A further possible locus of repetition priming which could account for the results reported by Valentine et al. (1993) would be an increase in the weight on the links from the input code to the word recognition units. However, there is not likely to be a single locus of repetition priming; an increase in the weight of links between *all* levels are potential loci of repetition priming. Furthermore, there is not likely to be even a single mechanism. Undoubtedly, repetition priming can be mediated by episodic retrieval under some circumstances (Monsell, 1991; Wheeldon and Monsell, 1992).

The suggestion that the semantics of words which are encountered in the context of surnames are automatically activated can be directly tested. If this is so, seeing the name of a celebrity with the surname 'Baker' should produce a semantic priming effect on to a lexical decision to a related word (e.g. bread). Thus, if a lexical decision to a word that is semantically related to the meaning of a celebrity's surname is made up to about five seconds after seeing the full name it should be made more quickly than a lexical decision to an unrelated word. Experiments to test this prediction are currently being carried out in Durham.

Further predictions arise from our interpretation of repetition priming effects in terms of an increase in the weights on links between representational units rather than in terms of mediation by recall from semantic memory. Would deciding that an unfamiliar name is unfamiliar give rise to repetition priming of a subsequent lexical decision to the word which served as the surname? (e.g. would deciding that 'John Bush' is not a familiar name prime a lexical decision to 'bush'?). If repetition priming results from an increase in weights of links following activation, it should be predicted that priming would be obtained. The word recognition unit for the surname would have had to have been activated in order to decide that the name was unfamiliar (i.e. not represented by an NRU). If this activation led to automatic activation of word semantics and a subsequent increase in the weight on links, a repetition priming effect would be expected.

If the order of the tasks were reversed (i.e. name familiarity decision to an unfamiliar name is preceded by a decision that the surname is a word), an account of repetition priming based on increased weights on links could predict a negative priming effect (i.e. RTs to primed items would be *slower* than RTs to unprimed items). If the subject makes a lexical decision to a word that occurs as a surname (e.g. bush), the presentation of the word would activate name recognition units for individuals who have that surname and the weights on the appropriate links would be increased. If the subject is subsequently required to make a name familiarity decision to a full name which is unfamiliar but includes the primed surname (e.g. John Bush), the competition from the primed name recognition unit(s) representing the known individual(s) with the same surname would slow down the decision that the stimulus is not a familiar name.

If a negative priming effect was obtained in the experiment described above, the explanation is in terms of competing activation from name recognition units of known people with the same surname. Unfamiliar names for use in the experiment could be created by exchanging the first names of celebrities' names. If so, it will always be the case that there is likely to be a familiar competitor. The framework predicts that if there is no other known person with the same surname, the negative priming effect should not be obtained. It might be difficult to choose surnames which are clearly used as surnames, but for which one can be sure a person with the surname is not known to the subject. Drawing on Brennen's (1993) work on the set size of plausible phonology (see Chapter 5), one strategy would be to use as surnames English words which do not normally occur as surnames (e.g. Michael House, John Wheel, etc.). An alternative approach would be to examine the effect of surname frequency. The effect of negative priming should be frequency sensitive. More competition (and therefore more negative priming) should be found for name familiarity decisions to unfamiliar full names with common surnames than for unfamiliar names with rare surnames. These predictions are all derived from the theoretical framework of name processing proposed by Valentine *et al.* (1991), coupled with an account of repetition priming resulting from a change in the weights of links. The results of such experiments would provide further tests of the theoretical stance that we are proposing in this book.

AN INTERACTIVE ACTIVATION IMPLEMENTATION OF THE FRAMEWORK FOR PROCESSING PEOPLE'S NAMES AND WORDS

In this chapter, we have reviewed studies of the effects of surname frequency and familiarity on the recognition of people's names. The relationship between proper name and common noun processing has been examined by use of a repetition priming technique. We have argued that all of the available experimental evidence is consistent with the proposed framework for recognition and production of people's names. The approach taken has been to derive predictions by reasoning from the way in which we believe such an information-processing system would behave if implemented. These predictions have been tested experimentally. We have then considered how the results obtained could be accounted for by the theoretical framework. If our conclusions based on this approach are correct, it should be possible to implement the framework in computer software, to simulate the various experimental effects found in the normal population and to 'lesion' the software to produce simulations of the patterns of dissociations reported in the neuropsychological studies described later in this chapter.

Burton and Bruce (1993) have reported on an implementation of the Valentine *et al.* (1991) framework using a simulation of an interactive activation and competition (IAC) network. This work follows the approach of their earlier IAC simulations of normal and impaired face processing and naming (Burton *et al.*, 1990; 1992; see also Chapter 3, this volume). Their model is illustrated in Figure 4.5. The architecture differs from that proposed by Valentine *et al.* (1991) in a number of respects. First, Valentine *et al.* did not explicitly show semantic information units (SIUs). They followed the Bruce and Young framework by including only person identity nodes (PINs) as the stage of access to identity-semantic information. Burton and Bruce (1993) adopted the strategy used in their earlier simulations (Burton *et al.*, 1990) of assuming that identity-specific semantic information is stored at SIUs which can only be accessed via PINs.

Burton and Bruce (1993) also follow a strategy adopted in an earlier paper on naming faces (Burton and Bruce, 1992) of assuming that nodes representing full names are included in the pool of SIUs (see Chapter 6). This strategy involves abandoning the assumption that names are stored separately from identity-specific semantics. For the present discussion, we merely note that this departs from the Bruce and Young framework. It is not a move with which we agree. The issue is discussed at length in Chapter 6. Furthermore, Burton and Bruce include nodes representing both identity-specific semantic information and the semantic represen-tations of words within the pool of SIUs. This amendment is entirely in keeping with the spirit of the Valentine *et al.* framework (1991). As dis-cussed, Valentine *et al.* did not show any representation of identity-specific semantics other than PINs. Burton and Bruce (1993) point out that, as we can access general semantic information via PINs, the representation of identity-specific semantics and other semantic information must be highly interconnected. For example, on seeing a face of a famous American, it is possible to access the semantics shared by Americans and to access the word 'American' if asked what the person's nationality is. Burton and Bruce (1993) achieve this interconnectivity by including all 'semantic' units in a single pool. A final difference between the architecture of Burton and Bruce's (1993) IAC model and the framework proposed by Valentine *et al.* (1991) is that Burton and Bruce did not include a direct link from name recognition units (NRUs) to lexical output units (LOUs).

Burton and Bruce (1993) simulated presentation of a name by activating a unit representing a first name and a unit representing a surname in the WRU pool. The first names were all equally common; the surnames ranged from being unique to an individual to being shared by five people. Naming latency was simulated by examining the asymptotic levels of activation of lexical output units. (It is always the case that units which reach a higher asymptotic level of activation also reach a threshold faster.) The lexical output units representing common surnames reached a higher asymptote than unique surnames, for both first and surname combinations represented in the NRU and PIN pools and for unknown combinations. Thus, the simulation is consistent with the finding that common surnames could be named faster than rare surnames.

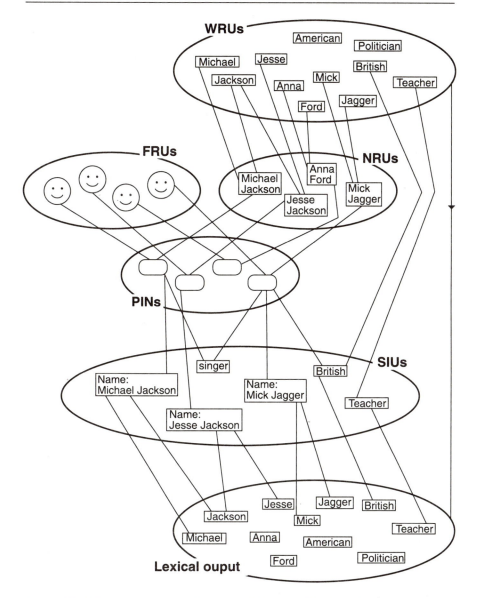

Figure 4.5 The architecture of Burton and Bruce's (1993) implementation of the Valentine *et al.* framework using an interactive activation and competition model

Reprinted by permission of Lawrence Erlbaum Associates Ltd, Hove, UK

In order to examine the effect of surname frequency on familiarity decision, Burton and Bruce studied the activation of PINs, the level at which it is believed familiarity can be determined. They found that the activation of a PIN in response to a known first name and rare surname combination was greater than that observed when a known first name and common surname combination was presented. It is not possible to simulate the effect of surname frequency on rejection of unfamiliar first and surname combinations, as there is no mechanism to model rejection latencies. Burton and Bruce point out that the effect of surname frequency on activation of PINs is rather weak, but claim that the simulation is consistent with the data reported by Valentine *et al.* (1991).

Valentine *et al.* (1991) found that familiarity decisions were made more quickly to familiar low frequency (rare) surnames than to common surnames *only when an initial and surname was presented*. In a condition in which full names were presented, *no effect of surname frequency was observed* (Experiment 4). In their simulations Burton and Bruce activate units representing a first name and a surname. Therefore, they have inadvertently simulated a condition in which no effect was observed in the behavioural data. The same criticism applies to their simulation of the effect of surname frequency on naming latency, although in this case we do not know whether an effect would be observed if full names were presented. A more plausible simulation of presentation of an initial and surname would have been to activate the WRU representing the surname fully (set the activation to 1) and to only partially activate WRUs representing first names which share the initial letter presented (e.g. set the activation of these units to 0.1). We do not know whether the IAC model proposed by Burton and Bruce (1993) could simulate the behavioural data reported by Valentine *et al.* (1991) in this manner. This example serves to show that the analogy between experiment and simulation can be problematic and that careful consideration must be given to this issue if the simulations are to address the issue intended in a satisfactory manner.

Burton and Bruce (1993) did not carry out a simulation of the experiments in which repetition priming between proper names and common names was observed (e.g. from familiarity decision to 'George Bush' on to lexical decision to 'bush' (Valentine *et al.*, 1993)). However, they point out that their assumption that repetition priming reflects an increased weight on links would give rise to this effect if the increase in weights were applied indiscriminately across the network whenever both of the linked units were simultaneously active.

THE NEUROPSYCHOLOGY OF COMPREHENSION OF PROPER NAMES

The considerable theoretical development in our understanding of face recognition in recent years has been largely due to some compelling neuro-psychological evidence. Therefore, the pattern of deficits of recognition and production of common and proper nouns is potentially an important source of evidence of the organisation of proper name processing. In this section, we will discuss some evidence that suggests that proper names may be processed differently from other word categories. Evidence of dissociations between proper and common name processing in comprehension of names will be reviewed. The issue of how our theoretical framework of proper name processing can account for the neuropsychological evidence will also be addressed and potential dissociations which can be predicted or excluded by the framework will be identified. Dissociations between production of proper names and common names are discussed in Chapter 5.

Saffran *et al.* (1976) found that two deep dyslexic patients, who tended to make paralexic errors in reading (misread words), could read aloud lexical items which were part of a proper name more accurately than they could read the same item presented as a single word. For example, 'olive' was read as 'black' and 'robin' was read as 'bird', but 'Robin Kelly' and 'Olive Cooper' were read correctly. A similar although less powerful effect was found when the words were embedded in a phrase which restricted its meaning (e.g. a *heart* attack). Saffran *et al.* argue that proper names and words in restrictive phrases are read more accurately because there are fewer semantic associates activated by the stimulus. They suggest that the semantic substitution errors made by deep dyslexics may be because the normal process of spreading activation in the semantic system leads to selection for articulation of non-target items which are activated due to their semantic relationship to the stimulus. The semantics of a word may be suppressed by presenting the item in the context of a proper name. As an unfamiliar proper name will have fewer semantic associations than the word counterpart, deep dyslexics are less likely to make paralexic errors when reading proper names. They also point out that the fact that proper names did elicit some word-type semantic errors (e.g. 'Jill Frost' read as 'Jill Snow' and 'Ed Prince' read as 'Ed King') suggests that both words and proper names might access the same lexical entry (cf. Valentine *et al.*, 1991).

There is some evidence of a different degree of lateralisation between word recognition and proper name processing. Saffran *et al.* (1980) found that normal subjects' accuracy of written report of first names was equivalent in both visual fields, but performance was superior for right visual field presentation of all other word categories tested.

Dissociations between comprehension of proper names and common names

Van Lancker and Klein (1990) report case studies of four patients who acquired global aphasia following left hemisphere brain damage. Their ability to recognise proper names was assessed by requiring the patients to select the photograph from an array of four famous faces which matched a spoken or written name. Although all the patients were severely impaired in their ability to recognise common nouns, as assessed by standardised tests, they performed within the normal range when matching famous faces to spoken names and to names which were presented both verbally and visually. The same pattern of preserved proper name matching in the presence of impaired common noun matching was found when subjects were asked to select the appropriate name or word from an array of four written responses to match either a spoken or pictured object or celebrity.

In terms of Valentine *et al.*'s (1991) framework, the dissociation reported by Van Lancker and Klein (1990) could arise from impaired access to semantic information from word recognition units in the context of unimpaired access to identity-specific semantic information via name recognition units. The impairment could either be to the links from word recognition units to units representing semantic information, or to the semantic units themselves. Impairment to the links would give rise to modality-specific impairment as there are assumed to be separate sets of WRUs for auditorily presented and visually presented words. However, Van Lancker and Klein's patients were impaired in their comprehension of both seen and heard words. This pattern of impairment is more consistent with damage to the semantic information units themselves, rather than to impaired access to intact units. As we assume that there is a single multi-modal semantic system, damage to the units representing semantic information would result in an impairment to comprehension of both written and spoken words.

The opposite dissociation of impaired recognition of proper names in the context of unimpaired processing of common nouns and other word categories could occur if the access to identity-specific semantics via name recognition units and word recognition units is impaired while access to word semantics remains unimpaired. If Van Lancker and Klein's patients are interpreted as suffering from an impairment to the representation of semantic information, a case forming a double-dissociation has been reported in the literature. Hanley *et al.* (1989), Ellis *et al.* (1989) and de Haan *et al.* (1991) report patients who suffer impaired access to identity-specific semantic information which is not modality-specific in the context of unimpaired word recognition skills. These patients are unable to recognise the names or faces of familiar people.

The Valentine *et al.* (1991) framework suggests that it should be possible to find patients who are impaired in their recognition of either people's names or common names in only one modality. Such impairments would arise from damage to the links connecting word recognition units to units representing the semantics of words or the links connecting name recognition units to PINs and identity-specific semantics. Modality-specific impairments to access to semantics from written or spoken words do occur, in cases of semantic access dyslexia (e.g. Warrington and Shallice,

1979) and post-access word meaning deafness (e.g. Kohn and Freidman, 1986) respectively. (See Ellis and Young, 1988 for a review.) We know of no reports that such impairments are specific to either people's names or common names.

A footnote in Van Lancker and Klein's (1990) paper reports data collected from a patient with right hemisphere brain damage, who showed unimpaired comprehension of words but recognised only 47 per cent of famous names. (The mean for normal controls on the tests are approximately 85 per cent or better.) It is not clear from the brief description provided whether this patient is impaired in her or his comprehension of both visually and auditorily presented names, and whether (s)he is also prosopagnosic. If the patient is impaired in recognition of names presented in both modalities and is prosopagnosic, the deficit could be caused by damage to representation of identity-specific semantic information as in the cases reported by Hanley *et al.* (1989), Ellis *et al.* (1989) and de Haan *et al.* (1991). Otherwise the case could be indicative of a double dissociation between recognition of people's names and common nouns. It remains to be seen whether a detailed account of this dissociation will be published.

Goodglass and Butters (1988) and Goodglass and Wingfield (1993) report a double dissociation in the comprehension of a class of common names (body parts) and a class of proper names (place names) in group studies of aphasic patients. In both studies Wernicke's aphasics and global aphasic patients show relative preservation of comprehension of geographical place names (e.g. Europe, Hawaii) compared to body part names (e.g. ear, nose), but anomic aphasics showed better comprehension of body parts than geographical place names. Comprehension was tested by pointing (at their own body or at a map as appropriate) in response to spoken requests ('Show me . . . ?'). No tests of written stimuli are reported. These data suggest a double dissociation between comprehension of place names and body parts; however, due to the limited range of stimuli tested it is not clear whether the impairment should be considered a double dissociation between comprehension of proper names and common names. In fact, inspection of Goodglass and Wingfield's data shows that the groups of Wernicke's aphasics, global aphasics and anomic aphasics all performed at a very similar level in their comprehension of place names (56.7 per cent, 52.4 per cent and 59.2 per cent respectively). However, a word discrimination task was included in this study in which patients had to point to one of six objects, letters, forms or actions depicted on a card which matched a spoken name. Both Wernicke's aphasics and global aphasics performed better in locating places on a map than in the word discrimination task but worst in the identification of body parts. Conversely, anomic aphasics performed better on body part identification than in word discrimination and worst on locating places on a map. Thus when performance in word discrimination is taken as a baseline for auditory comprehension, evidence of a double dissociation for place names does emerge. As no written stimuli were tested, we do not know whether the impairments would affect the visual modality. Taken together with the group design, it is impossible to ascertain whether a *modality-specific* double-dissociation exists between any pair of individual subjects for geographical place names.

Wapner and Gardiner (1979) report data of a relatively spared capacity to recognise proper names in aphasic patients, broadly similar to the cases reported by Van Lancker and Klein (1990). One task was designed to test comprehension of common object names. Patients were given a picture of a living-room. They were then read a list of words which included objects depicted in the drawing of the living-room and were asked to point to the object if it was included in the drawing. Some names of objects not shown in the picture and other inappropriate word categories were included in the list. Patients were asked to reject these items, for example, by shaking their head. A similar task was constructed to explore patients' comprehension of proper names using the same procedure. However, in this case names of American cities were included in the list of spoken words and patients were asked to point to their location on a map of the USA.

A group of fourteen aphasic patients were better able to respond appropriately in the task which involved names of cities than they did in the object location task. However, no control group was included in the study and the overall level of performance is somewhat ambiguous from the description of the design. Therefore, it is not possible to ascertain the relative difficulty of the two tasks for normal subjects or whether performance was impaired on both tasks relative to normals (although it seems likely that this is the case). However, the data is suggestive of the possibility of preservation of comprehension of proper names, in the context of impaired comprehension on common nouns as reported by Van Lancker and Klein (1990), except that in this case the impairment of proper name comprehension was tested using names of cities instead of people's names.

Warrington and McCarthy (1987) report on a patient (YOT) who showed preserved comprehension of proper names associated with impairment to comprehension of common nouns, but in this case the impairment for common nouns was category-specific. In general, YOT's comprehension of objects was significantly more impaired than her comprehension of foods and living things. More specifically, her comprehension of small manipulable objects was more impaired then her comprehension of large man-made objects. Exploration of her comprehension of proper nouns is of particular interest to the present discussion. YOT showed a preserved ability to point to a written word in an array which matched a spoken proper name. She showed preserved ability to match famous people's names, countries and cities. However, she was severely impaired in matching common surnames, boys' names and girls' names. YOT also showed preserved ability to match a spoken word to the appropriate picture in an array for the categories of famous people, famous buildings and countries.

Warrington and McCarthy interpret the dissociation found between preserved verbal-to-visual word matching of famous names, but impaired matching of common first names and common surnames as a preserved ability to match proper names with a unique referent. The famous names used were single word names of historical figures which had a clear single referent (e.g. Napoleon, Churchill). Common first names and surnames do not have a unique referent in this sense in the absence of a specific context. This distinction is supported by the preserved comprehension of countries, cities and famous buildings; all are classes of proper names with unique referents.

YOT's pattern of preserved comprehension of proper names can be interpreted within the theoretical framework proposed by Valentine *et al.* (1991) by the same impairment as the patient described by Van Lancker and Klein (1990); namely, impaired access to, or damage to, the representation of semantics required to comprehend common names. Famous names which specify a unique referent can be processed by an intact output from word recognition units to name recognition units and subsequent access to identity-specific semantics. However, common surnames or first names alone will be insufficient to uniquely specify a familiar individual's name. Although several NRUs might be partially activated by a name (e.g. David), no one unit will be able to become more strongly activated than its competitors and therefore identity-specific information cannot be accessed. This interpretation relies on the assumption that in the absence of a uniquely identified name recognition unit becoming strongly activated, first name or surname matching would be based solely on the word recognition system. This interpretation also requires that there are units which are functionally equivalent to name recognition units which mediate recognition of names of famous buildings, countries and cities in order to account for YOT's preserved matching of these categories of proper names.

McCarthy and Warrington (1985) describe a patient who shows selectively preserved comprehension of proper names. In this case, the patient was severely impaired in his naming and comprehension of action verbs, but his ability to name common nouns and proper nouns was well preserved. Therefore this patient does not show a dissociation between processing of common and proper nouns.

In summary, neuropsychological studies show evidence of relative sparing of proper name comprehension in the context of impaired comprehension of common names. The Valentine *et al.* framework can account for this dissociation but would predict that cases should be reported in which comprehension of people's names in either the visual or auditory modality is impaired, but comprehension of common names and recognition of familiar faces is unimpaired. No such cases have been reported to our knowledge. The neuropsychology of proper name *production* is discussed in Chapter 5.

A final note of caution in the interpretation of the data obtained from aphasic patients needs to be considered. The interpretation of the patients' deficits are based on the assumption that word–object matching, face–name matching or auditory–visual word or name matching demonstrates 'comprehension'. However, this need not necessarily be so. In the case of face and name recognition, the interactive activation model proposed by Burton *et al.* (1990) specifically postulates that face–name matching could be achieved at the level of the person identity nodes without any access to identity-specific semantics. The interpretation we have described would predict that patients reported by Warrington and McCarthy (1987) and Van Lancker and Klein (1990) are able to access person identity nodes. We do not know, however, whether they 'comprehend' the people's names in the sense of being able to retrieve identity-specific semantics. In order to address this issue it would be necessary to test whether such patients can classify people's names according to their occupational category or, for example, whether they are dead or alive. It is only really justifiable to use the term 'comprehension' if the patients are able to perform such semantic classification tasks.

SUMMARY AND CONCLUSIONS

In this chapter we have evaluated the framework for face, name and word recognition proposed by Valentine *et al.* (1991). This framework incorporates relatively 'standard' models of face and word processing (cf. Bruce and Young, 1986). The main thrust of the framework is to make explicit the relationship between recognition and production of people's names and other words. It was proposed that recognition of people's names is mediated by name recognition units (analogous to face recognition units) which receive their input from the output of word recognition units.

Experiments on the effect of surname frequency support the framework for processing of visually presented names. If the task does not require access to memory of an individual, high frequency surnames are processed more quickly than low frequency surnames, an effect which is analogous to the effects of word frequency. If access to memory for a known individual is required, the effects of surname frequency are analogous to the effects of distinctiveness in face recognition. Low frequency or 'distinctive' surnames are processed more quickly.

Repetition priming studies support the hypothesis that recognition of surnames and common names share some common pathways or representations. It was found that deciding that 'George Bush' is a familiar name primes the lexical decision to 'bush' and vice versa.

An implementation of the proposed framework using an interactive activation model could probably be consistent with the observed effects of surname frequency and repetition priming. However, there are some problems with the simulations reported as tests of the empirical data on the effect of surname frequency.

Neuropsychological evidence is broadly consistent with the framework. Patients with impaired word recognition but intact recognition of people's names could have an impairment affecting the representation of semantic information accessed from word recognition units in the presence of preserved representation of identity-specific semantics. The framework suggests that double-dissociations between general lexical processing abilities and proper name processing could exist for modality-specific impairments to recognition of lexical input. Such dissociations could arise from impairments to the links from recognition units which access semantic information or identity-specific semantics. However, cases forming a clear double-dissociation have yet to be reported.

The neuropsychological evidence suggests that a dichotomy between all classes of proper names on the one hand, and all other classes of words on the other, will be inadequate as a psychological model of the relationship between proper name processing and word recognition. Some patients show impairments to processing of all classes of proper names, while others show preservation or deficits in processing only some categories of proper names. One distinction that emerges from the literature is that people's names can dissociate from other classes of proper names. The theoretical framework discussed in this chapter applies only to one category of proper names – people's names. Further research and theoretical development is needed to explore the relationship between other classes of proper names with processing of people's names and words.

Chapter 5 examines the relationship between retrieval of proper names and common names, including neuropsychological case studies of name production. The ability of the Valentine *et al.* (1991) framework to account for the empirical evidence relating to production of names is evaluated in Chapter 7.

The use and structure of proper names differs between cultures (see Chapter 1). The data we have reported here have been concerned almost entirely with names of people which consist of a first and family name within a western society. Even within such a culture some names do not conform to this pattern (for example, royalty, e.g. Queen Elizabeth; and some pop stars, e.g. Sting). Working within a cognitive framework, it is easy to be less mindful of the cultural and societal influences on the processes studied than perhaps we should be. Working with proper names, however, it is difficult to ignore these limitations. In order to develop a complete cognitive psychology of proper name processing, use of proper names in others cultures must be studied.

Chapter 5

The retrieval of proper names and common names

INTRODUCTION

In this chapter we shall review the phenomena that arise in everyday life as things are named. We shall be concerned with naturally arising phenomena related to retrieval of proper names in adults and elderly people, and with the performance of brain-injured patients. It will be suggested that the category of words for which there is most recall difficulty is that of proper names. Indeed, the idea that access to proper names is harder than access to common names is shared by most researchers in the field. However, the corpus of data supporting this idea is not yet very abundant. This corpus comprises four sources of data: studies of self-evaluation of memory in elderly people; diary studies of naming difficulties in everyday life; laboratory studies of retrieval blocks; and neuropsychological single case studies of brain-damaged patients. Explanations of these empirical observations will be considered in detail.

'Naming' means recalling the correct verbal label that is associated with a particular concept. Typically, of course, *le mot juste* is *spoken,* but this is not the only way to show that one has recalled a name. One could also spell it out with writing blocks, type it, or write it. These different output systems have errors associated with them, but first we shall consider the potential pitfalls that are common to all output modalities.

In the course of everyday conversation or casual introspection, words (or even streams of words) spring rapidly to mind. We are unconscious of the processes by which a particular word becomes conscious, or even of how it is spoken: word finding just happens to be a skill at which human adults are extraordinarily proficient (MacKay, 1987). In order to investigate this process that works so smoothly and effortlessly, cognitive psychologists have borrowed a strategy from other disciplines, such as engineering and neuropsychology, where light is shed on the workings of a system by studying its patterns of breakdown. What happens when the system does not work? It is evident that attempts to name do occasionally fail to produce the target word. Let us now consider the various ways in which such failures manifest themselves.

THE TIP-OF-THE-TONGUE STATE

In English, the notion of 'having a word on the tip of your tongue' has passed into common usage, and indeed, the tip-of-the-tongue state (henceforth TOT) is possibly the type of naming error that is most integrated into 'folk psychology'. Everyone has suffered instances of being unable to recall a person's name, which can prove rather embarrassing when they are in front of you, waiting for you to introduce them to someone. In fact, psychologists are not unanimous on how to describe having a word on the tip of your tongue. A classic data-gathering exercise on this sort of name recall failure was carried out by Brown and McNeill (1966), and they claimed to be studying the tip-of-the-tongue *phenomenon*. A recent review of work in this area was about the tip-of-the-tongue *experience*, (A.S. Brown, 1991). Other studies however, have referred to the tip-of-the-tongue *state*. There seems to be little difference between the first two descriptors, but calling something a 'state' suggests that it is a unitary entity. When, for experimental purposes, one needs to know what having something on the tip of the tongue means in practice, it is as well to think of the phenomenon as being a single state, and we shall talk of TOT states, though we shall see later that this is not necessarily appropriate. Turning to such experimental definitions of TOT states, let us consider Brown and McNeill's pioneering study. Their definition of a tip-of-the-tongue state was that it 'involves a failure to recall a word of which one has knowledge' (Brown and McNeill, 1966, p.325).

Furthermore, they deemed that in order to be considered a TOT the state requires more than just this conjunction: recall of the word must also be felt to be imminent. Subsequent studies have not all used this terminology or this definition, and there is confusion in the literature regarding TOTs. For instance, failures to name are not all called the same thing: Cohen and Faulkner (1986) talk about 'name blocks', Read and Bruce (1982) talk about 'difficult name retrievals'. Also, Brown and McNeill's definition clashes with the use of TOT in at least two other studies. S.M. Smith *et al.* (1991) explored a new technique of teaching subjects facts about imaginary animals with made-up names. Using these TOTimals they showed that subjects were often able to recall a fact about an animal but not its name, and they suggested that this technique is a useful laboratory tool for generating TOTs. A reservation about this technique however is that it is uncertain whether subjects who were unable to recall a name of a TOTimal would *ever* be able to recall it. That is, did subjects really 'know' the names of the TOTimals? S.M. Smith *et al.* (1991) argue that the subjects did know because they were able to recognise the name when it was presented among three close alternatives. However, we would argue that recognition and recall must not be confused, and that subjects learning TOTimals would occasionally find themselves unable to recall a name, in spite of having some partial phonological information about the target, and that they would remain unable to name it, however long one gave them in which to recall the name. A further study bears this point out (B.L. Smith *et al.*, 1991). Adults were taught the names of rare (but real) objects, and the recall attempts during learning were recorded. Even when names were incorrectly recalled, there was a high structural overlap between the errors and the targets. We would predict that normally after producing an error, subjects in the B.L. Smith *et al.* (1991) study would be unable to correct it, perhaps even knowing it to be incorrect: the words were simply underlearned. Furthermore, we would predict that the amount of partial knowledge that subjects possessed would have allowed them to perform a four-choice recognition test which S.M. Smith *et al.* (1991) gave their subjects. This suggests that name recall failures in S.M. Smith *et al.*'s (1991) study were also instances of underlearning of the names, which means that the name recall failures are not TOTs according to Brown and McNeill's definition; rather, they are cases of where the memory trace is insufficient for ever generating the name. For a word recall failure to be considered a TOT the failure must be temporary, meaning that on prior and future occasions the word could be produced.

Ryan *et al.* (1982) asked subjects to learn a list of paired associate words, and in the test phase one of the pair was presented with the subject having to recall its associate. Some of the failures to name were accompanied by a feeling that the word was known, which the authors classed as TOTs. This does not seem to be the same thing as a normal TOT, where the meaning of the word is known to the subject and just the phonology is missing. It seems to fall victim to a criticism of much research on the feeling-of-knowing (FOK) phenomenon, when subjects report that they feel recall is imminent because they feel that it *should* be imminent. In this case they would have just been taught these pairs by the experimenter, which might lead to the self-presentational strategy of saying that recall was imminent. Furthermore, as we shall see more clearly later, when subjects are in a TOT they invariably know the meaning of the item for which they are looking. It is not at all certain that the blocks that Ryan *et al.*'s subjects experienced involved access to the meaning of the missing word, despite their claim that the phenomenology of a name block in the experiment was the same as a normal everyday TOT.

In order to clarify this conceptual and terminological fog, let us agree with Brown and McNeill (1966) that a TOT implies a failure to recall a word of which one has knowledge and where recall is felt to be imminent. In many cases of word recall failure however, recall may not feel imminent, even though we believe that we *do* know the word in question. These cases would correspond to word recall failures with a feeling of knowing, but are not TOTs because recall may be distant.

One of the most bizarre uses of the terminology however comes from some work on olfaction, where subjects were asked to name different odours that were presented to them (Lawless and Engen, 1977). When the subject found the smell familiar but could not name it, these authors classified the response as a tip-of-the-*nose* state. This is a misnomer because all name recall failures are by definition linguistic failures, regardless of the input modality: a concept can be activated by reading from definition, by seeing a face of a familiar person, by hearing a piece of music and, of course, certainly by smelling things, but in each case a failure to name the concept is a lexical failure. One of the few things that can be on the tip of the nose, it seems to us, is a sneeze, which brings us full circle, since Brown and McNeill (1966) likened being in a TOT to being on the brink of a sneeze!

Brown and McNeill's classic study involved reading definitions of rare words to their subjects, who then had to try to provide the target words. In a forerunner of ecological cognitive psychology, they asked subjects when in a TOT state to guess the number of syllables in the target word, the initial letter, and furthermore to record any words that came to mind while searching for the target. They reported that subjects had accurate knowledge of both length and the initial letters of TOT-inducing words, and that spontaneously offered target-related words were often similar to the target words in sound or in meaning. The results are often cited as vindication of our intuition that we are in fact able to give structural information about words that we are temporarily unable to recall. However, we should note the caution advised by Koriat and Lieblich (1974), who asked 'What does a person in a TOT know that a person not in a TOT doesn't know?' They point out that there are structural and statistical regularities in languages that give information about words. That is, even without knowing a word at all, one is more likely to guess that its name consists of one, two or three syllables than to guess it has four, five or six syllables. Furthermore, of course, the twenty-six letters of the English alphabet are not equally likely to be the initial letter, and one would be more likely to guess that the word would begin with a 'T' than with a 'K'. So, in experiments like Brown and McNeill's, where definitions are read to subjects, there will be trials on which the definition does not provoke the feeling that it is on the tip of the tongue; the warning provided by Koriat and Lieblich (1974) is that when in this state subjects may be able to guess or deduce some of the structural and phonological information that has been taken as evidence for a TOT state. This does not mean however that all partial information provided in TOT states is a spurious by-product of the statistical knowledge that we have of our language.

A further criticism was outlined by A.S. Brown (1991), who pointed out that the study by Brown and McNeill (1966) and subsequent studies have often encouraged one particular type of partial knowledge, typically structural knowledge, e.g. initial letter, number of syllables, etc. For a more complete idea of subjects' partial knowledge, the instructions should be to report *any* knowledge that is evoked when searching for a word, as in Lovelace (1987). This criticism alerts us to the fact that partial knowledge other than structural information about the target word might exist.

A further study of the partial knowledge of word structure to which we may have access, without being able to recall the word, was carried out by Rubin (1975). He presented subjects with four definitions that had previously provoked TOT states, and whenever a TOT was provoked subjects were asked to write down any letters that they thought were in the word. In this way, it was possible to deduce the structure of partial knowledge *for individual words*, by recording the number of times each letter within the word was recalled by a subject experiencing a TOT, given that the recall of the letter immediately to its left or right was also correct. So from the left of each word he recorded the number of times the initial letter was recalled, the number of times the second letter was recalled, and so on. Similarly, the same procedure was used from the right end of the word. Thus for the cue, 'The first name of the character Scrooge in Dickens' Christmas Carol', the following structure was obtained:

	E	B	E	N	E	Z	E	R
Left	10	4	1	1	0	0	0	0
Right	0	0	0	0	0	0	4	4

Subjects appeared to retrieve clusters of letters rather than letters at random, and these clusters seem to be found at the beginning or the end of the words. Rubin's conclusion was that 'word-name memory does not consist solely of inseparable strings of letters' (1975, p.396); in fact, the point can be reversed to saying that word name memory is not a collection of single equally memorable letters. The linguistic unit appearing to govern the letter clusters of partial knowledge was the morpheme rather than the syllable. Rubin's results hardly seem explicable by subjects guessing letters in the words, and so they provide excellent evidence of partial knowledge.

Yarmey (1973) was the first to investigate TOT states for proper names, by presenting subjects with photographs of the faces of famous people which they had to try to name. Often, of course, subjects could either name the face straight away or they didn't even find the face familiar, but occasionally they found that they were sure they knew the person but that they could not remember his name. In these cases subjects were encouraged to recall all they could about the person. Yarmey reported that there were high success rates when guessing initial letters of words on the tip of the tongue – 68 per cent correct for first names, and 59 per cent for surnames. The number of syllables was correctly guessed on over 70 per cent of TOTs, but it is hard to interpret this particular result since it is likely that the chance levels of guessing would also be high (Koriat and Lieblich, 1974).

Brennen *et al.* (1990) induced TOTs by reading out definitions of famous people and famous landmarks to subjects. The study compared the ability of different cues to resolve TOTs, and found that the initial letter(s) of the name(s) of the target reliably resolved the TOTs, whereas a picture of the target did not resolve more TOTs than mere repetition of the original TOT-inducing information. This is in spite of the fact that a picture of the referent uniquely specifies it, whereas the initial letters do not. This pattern was found for the names of both famous landmarks and famous people, providing some evidence of like organisation of representations of these two types of proper name. These experiments do not in any way lead one to conclude that the semantic system and the output lexicon are organised differently for proper names than for common names; rather, the fact that proper names are often difficult to recall was exploited in order to explore the meaning–naming relationship.

PARAPHASIAS

A paraphasia is the term for an incorrect verbal production. When someone says, for instance, 'I rushed home as soon as I had got my exams', the word 'exams' has slipped into the person's sentence instead of the word 'results'. The speaker (or writer or typist) may or may not be aware of the inappropriate production, and there is a variety of possible relationships between the target and the actual production. Uttering 'lion' instead of 'tiger' is an example of a semantic paraphasia. 'Plum' in place of·'plug' would be a phonemic paraphasia, and 'window' instead of 'windscreen' is an example of a mixed semantic *and* phonemic paraphasia. Of course, it is not logically necessary that an incorrect production should result in another word, but there is an oft-observed lexical bias, such that rogue utterances often consist of other words. For semantic paraphasias this is of course necessary, because non-words have no meaning; but what about phonemic paraphasias? A phonemic paraphasia can be considered to be an approximation to the 'meant' word, with one or more erroneous phonemes.

These categories are self-evident when a common name is a target, but are they so for proper names? If a semantic paraphasia is considered to be the substitution of one word for another that has a similar meaning then it is not clear what could be meant by a semantic paraphasia of a proper name. As we saw in Chapter 1, it has been forcefully claimed that proper names do not have a meaning: 'Reagan' in and of itself does not mean anything. Knowing that Ronald Reagan is a Republican, is American and was a B-movie actor does not give you any information about someone else whose surname happens to be Reagan. On the other hand, if a semantic paraphasia is the substitution of one word by another from the same category, then a semantic paraphasia for a proper name is the replacement of a person's name; for instance, with another person's name from that same category, e.g. saying 'Prince' instead of 'Michael Jackson' (substituting the name of one pop star with the name of another).

For common names, a word from the same category that replaces the 'intended' word will sometimes not change the meaning of the 'intended' sentence. For instance, in most families, 'Where are the kids?' or 'Where are the children?' would be understood in the same way, whereas for proper names, any change of target word alters the meaning of the utterance: 'Steven Spielberg's new film is a comedy' or 'Oliver Stone's new film is a comedy'. This fact means that we should expect to detect a higher proportion of proper name semantic paraphasias than common name semantic paraphasias, because the former type will distort the speaker's original meaning, which may be detected either by the speaker, or even by the interlocutor if the new meaning is sufficiently unexpected. For common names, a word replacement will sometimes not change the meaning of the utterance, and in these cases it therefore cannot be detected by the interlocutor, and may even go undetected by the speaker. This possibility of circumlocution for common names which is impossible for proper names is an idea to which we shall return later when considering different possible explanations of the difficulty we have in recalling proper names.

PROPER NAME RETRIEVAL BY OLDER ADULTS

The TOT study by Brown and McNeill (1966) has inspired much research on adults' difficulties with naming, and as we have seen, there is a growing research area into adults' difficulties in recalling proper names in particular. In this section we shall consider the problems faced by older adults in naming things. This topic is experiencing a growth in interest at the moment with both experimental studies and naturalistic 'diary' studies.

An important phenomenological point is that older adults' TOTs often appear to be unaccompanied by partial information such as the initial letter, similar sounding words, etc. Persistent alternates also seem to be less frequent for the elderly.

Diary studies

So-called diary studies have, in recent years, become an important part of the tool-kit of the cognitive psychologist. In the spirit of corroborating experimental results from the lab with 'real-world' behaviour, diary studies consist of asking subjects to monitor their everyday life for a particular set of phenomenological experiences. In the studies reported here, subjects were invited to record their own naming difficulties experienced in everyday life. There have been several diary studies in which subjects were invited to record, among other things, their retrieval blocks in the production of proper names (Reason and Lucas, 1984; Cohen and Faulkner, 1986; Burke *et al.*, 1988, 1991). The objective of the three later studies was generally to search for age-related differences. They all showed that the occurrence of TOTs involving proper names is higher for older subjects than for younger subjects. Unfortunately, not all of these studies reported, or allowed, statistical comparison of the occurrence of blocks for proper names and blocks for common names.

Burke *et al.* (1991) compared the occurrence of TOTs from three categories of words involved in reported retrieval incidents: proper names, object names and abstract words (non-object words, adjectives, verbs and adverbs). Three samples of subjects participated: a young group of undergraduates (mean age 19 years), a mid-age group (mean age 39 years) and an older group (mean age 71 years). Over the four-week period of data collection the subjects recorded 686 TOT states. Subjects from the three samples reported more TOTs for proper names than for the other two kinds of words. No TOTs involving closed class or function words were reported. Sixty-five per cent of reported TOTs involved proper names. TOTs on object names and abstract words represented 12 per cent and 23 per cent of TOTs, respectively .

The number of TOTs reported was significantly lower for the young group relative to both of the other groups. Furthermore, there were differences in the proportions of TOTs in the three word classes between subject groups. Proper name TOTs were more frequent for mid-age and older subjects than for the younger subjects, TOTs for objects' names were more common for older adults compared to the two other groups, and TOTs for the abstract words were more frequent for the younger group. The finding that older subjects experience more TOTs for proper names has already been reported.

Burke *et al.* (1991) also divided the proper name TOTs into subcategories of names of personal acquaintances, famous people, famous places and names of books, films and television programmes. Older adults reported more TOTs for acquaintances and for place names than the other two groups, place names caused more problems for mid-age than younger adults, and young adults experienced more TOTs for titles than the older adults.

As pointed out by these authors, it is necessary to be cautious in interpreting such differences found in diary studies such as these, since they covary with factors like the number of times that subjects *attempted* to recall words from a particular class. The interpretation of age differences is also difficult because the varying life styles of the different age groups may lead to different demands on their word retrieval systems. For instance, youngsters at university may meet new people more regularly than older people, thus making TOTs for this category more likely. The effect of this may be to exaggerate any real underlying differences between the word retrieval system of an older person and that of a young person; or it may have the opposite effect, cancelling out or changing the direction of any difference: studying the data of a diary study does not allow us to know. Laboratory studies on the other hand allow control of many of these factors.

Laboratory studies

Burke *et al.* (1991) carried out a complementary laboratory study with a subset of the younger and older subjects from the diary study. In fact this is the only experimental study comparing the incidence of retrieval blocks to proper names and to common names that has been reported in the literature. They attempted to provoke TOTs by reading general knowledge questions to subjects and included five types of target words: abstract nouns (e.g. 'What do you call a feeling of resentment, often at some fancied slight or insult? [usually follows the verb "take"]'; target: umbrage); object names (e.g. 'What do you call the vessel, usually an ornamental vase on a pedestal, which is used to preserve the ashes of the dead?'; target: urn); adjectives and verbs (e.g. 'What is the word that means to cause to explode or to set off, for example, a bomb?'; target: detonate); place names (e.g. 'What was the name of the capital of the Aztec empire, which was located where Mexico City is today?'; target: Tenochtitlan), and names of famous people (e.g. 'What is the last name of the cosmonaut who was the first person to orbit the earth?'; target: Gagarin). The young subjects were around 20 years old and the older subjects around 70 years old.

The results showed that older subjects experienced more blocking states than young subjects only for names of famous people but not for the other four kinds of words. In older subjects, blocks to people's names were more frequent than blocks to the other kinds of words including place names, i.e. another kind of proper name (see p. 114). Here again however, there are problems of interpretation. For instance, older subjects have more TOTs in some categories but they also have more 'Know' responses and fewer 'Don't know' responses for the same categories, and therefore, as Burke *et al.* (1991) recognise, it is probable that the class was simply more familiar for the older subjects. As Burke *et al.* also explain, if there are more 'Know' responses then there are fewer questions that could potentially result in TOTs. So, in order to calculate unbiased TOT incidence rates, the authors used A.S. Brown's (1991) prescription for controlling item difficulty across categories. The idea is to calculate TOT rates as a fraction of un-successful retrievals, i.e. (number of TOTs)/(number of TOTs + number of 'Don't knows'), instead of (number of TOTs)/(number of trials). Computing TOT rates in this way, Burke *et al.* showed that older people were more likely to experience a TOT for object names, adjectives and verbs and names of famous people, even when the successfully recalled items are not considered.

A potential problem with these data is that it is likely that some 'Don't know' responses could not result in TOT states either, because they had never been encountered and would thus have been permanently irretrievable; if they were anything like the authors of this book, some subjects may never have heard of the old Aztec capital Tenochtitlan! The ratio of real interest is (number of TOTs)/(number of names for which a lexical representation exists), and so it would be more convincing to show higher TOT rates in older adults after following Brown's prescription and then conditionalising upon correct recognition of the target item.

Thus, this study demonstrated what was suggested by data from subjective evaluation of memory difficulties and by diary studies: Ageing affects the retrieval of proper names, and in particular the retrieval of people's names, in a much more dramatic way than it affects the retrieval of common names.

Another piece of evidence for a differential effect of ageing on proper name retrieval and common name retrieval comes from Maylor's work. Maylor (1990a) and Maylor and Valentine (1992) reported a deleterious effect of age on retrieving people's names, while in a further study she reported no age effect on retrieving infrequent common names (Maylor, 1990b). Of course, this is not a perfect test of the differential effect of ageing on the retrieval of different kinds of words because different subjects participated in each of the studies. However, the participants were recruited from the same pool of subjects, and the characteristics of the samples (vocabulary and intelligence scores) were very similar.

Self-evaluation of memory difficulties

Several questionnaire studies on everyday memory abilities showed that older people evaluate the increased occurrence of retrieval blocks as their most frequently experienced memory difficulty (Cohen and Faulkner, 1984; Martin, 1986) and also as the most noticeable age-related cognitive change (Sunderland *et al.*, 1986). Elderly subjects' ratings of their ability to retrieve both proper names and object names are poorer than those of younger people, but the age difference is greater for proper names than for common names (Cohen and Faulkner, 1984). In fact Lovelace and Twohig (1990) found that the inability to retrieve proper names was cited as the main retrospective memory difficulty by 60 per cent of older people interviewed. However, the fact that older people report particular difficulty in retrieving proper names is only weak evidence of the relative vulnerability of proper name retrieval. Indeed, subjective evaluation of memory difficulties has proved to be a very weak indicator of memory abilities as measured by standardised tests (Rabbitt, 1982; Sunderland et al., 1986; Abson and Rabbitt, 1988; Devolder and Pressley, 1991), and older people's self-evaluation scores are better correlated with evaluations of depressive mood than with their tested memory performance (Perlmutter, 1978; Popkin et al., 1982; Williams et al., 1987; Bolla et al., 1991; Larrabee et al., 1991).

NEUROPSYCHOLOGY OF NAMING

A common consequence of brain injury is the loss of the ability to name things. Linguistic problems following a focal brain lesion are grouped under the heading of *aphasic* symptoms, and naming difficulties have been referred to as the 'master symptom' of aphasia due to the fact that there are few, if any, cases of language problems that are not associated with naming difficulties. There is a variety of different aphasic 'syndromes' which are anatomo-clinical groups into which aphasic patients have been categorised by clinicians and neurologists in the nineteenth and twentieth centuries. The most common is Broca's aphasia where the lesion is typically to the motor region of the left frontal lobe. As a result, Broca's aphasia is often associated with a right-sided hemiplegia. The verbal output of Broca's aphasics is slurred, as the problem is in the motor control of the vocal apparatus. Broca's aphasia is often free from comprehension disorder. Less common is Wernicke's aphasia, which *is* associated with a comprehension disorder and typically the lesion is in the left temporal lobe. The patient may also be prone to talking in neologisms that do not make any sense to interlocutors. Commonly too, patients with Wernicke's aphasia are unaware of their deficits. Pronunciation of words however, unlike in Broca's aphasia, is intact and fluent.

There are many other described syndromes, but unfortunately they are by no means mutually exclusive because different authors have different ground rules. This heterogeneity derives from the fact that different taxonomies come from different hospital neurology departments where they play a purely pragmatic role, enabling speech therapists and neuropsychologists working in the same institution to class patients similarly. This means that Broca's and Wernicke's are two of the few syndromes for which there is widespread agreement. In itself this makes it difficult to know without a detailed study of the performance whether a 'sensory' aphasic from one institution is very similar to a 'sensory' aphasic from another, or to determine that one researcher's 'semantic' aphasic is another's 'anomic' aphasic. Furthermore, it is now widely recognised that the syndrome approach has a tendency to group very different patients under the same heading. In order to be classified as a conduction aphasic, for instance, there is necessarily some leeway in the degree of fluency required and the extent to which long sentences are understood, and sometimes the main symptom that two conduction aphasics will have in common is a naming difficulty, which is not at all specific to conduction aphasia. A final major problem is that up to 50 per cent of aphasic patients cannot be accurately placed within any one syndrome (Benson, 1988).

Notwithstanding these problems, studies of the naming performance of aphasic patients has been carried out by grouping together all the Brocas, all the Wernickes, all the conduction aphasics, and so on, in order to compare the mean performances of each group of patients on various tasks (Goodglass et al., 1976). One solution to this taxonomic problem has come from the burgeoning field of cognitive neuropsychology. The approach has been to carry out single case studies on patients' deficits, describing them with reference to functional models of normal performance of the tasks, and not with reference to syndromes of behavioural symptoms. This approach has in fact facilitated the construction of functional models, which has allowed researchers to pose more intricate questions about naming performance.

A most intriguing set of patients has been reported, where the subject has difficulty naming things from certain categories but not from others (Goodglass et al., 1966). In recent years there has been an energetic search for such cases, leading to a lengthy list of so-called category-specific deficits. Affected categories include body parts (Dennis, 1976), colours (e.g. Beauvois and Saillant, 1985), letters (Goodglass et al., 1986) and animals (Temple, 1986). Hart et al. (1985) reported another case where there were only two categories affected. The patient had a satisfactory level of comprehension and naming for all stimuli except fruits and vegetables.

Sometimes there are cases of *preservation* of single categories; for instance, the domain of colours was the only domain nameable by Yamadori and Albert's (1973) patient. Also, McKenna and Warrington (1978) and Warrington and Clegg (1993) reported patients whose linguistic abilities appeared to be restricted to naming countries.

Brennen (1993) carried out a review of these cases, finding regularities in the data patterns. It is the case, for instance, that stimuli which patients were able to name were also understood (e.g. as shown by semantic classification tasks). Thus, the patient reported by McKenna and Warrington (1978) who could *name* only countries could also *match* countries to appropriate objects, demonstrating access to semantic information about this domain. In all other tested domains he could neither name stimuli, nor was he able to demonstrate evidence of semantic access. He scored zero on the token test, implying severe comprehension difficulties. This suggests a dramatic functional lesion of the semantic system, with sparing of the category of countries, and no phonological deficit. Hart *et al*.'s (1985) patient, who was able satisfactorily to name stimuli from all tested categories except fruits and vegetables, was unable to categorise pictures of fruit and vegetables, implying a semantic deficit affecting only the representation of fruits and vegetables.

This last case has been much cited; however, there is a misunderstanding in the literature (e.g. Baddeley, 1990; Shallice and Kartsounis, 1993) that this paper showed that the output lexicon is organised along semantic lines. It is worth repeating that the patient in question made numerous errors when categorising fruits and vegetables, and thus did not show evidence of preserved semantic access to these categories. The most parsimonious explanation is that this patient had a semantic deficit for the categories of fruits and vegetables which underpinned his naming deficit for these categories.

In summary, it has not been demonstrated that the output lexicon is categorically organised for any 'mainstream' semantic categories. As we shall now see, the only category of names for which there have been reports of a category-specific deficit in the *absence* of an underpinning semantic deficit is the category of proper names.

Proper name anomia

The neuropsychology of the comprehension of proper names was reviewed in Chapter 4. There have also been several cases of impaired proper name production in the literature. These patients show an impairment of proper name retrieval, or more specifically an impairment of the retrieval of people's names, contrasting with an absence of word-finding problems for common names. The opposite dissociation has been described only recently, and twice in the same issue of the journal *Memory* (Semenza and Sgaramella, 1993; Cipolotti *et al*., 1993). In this section, we will first describe the cases of proper name anomia, and then the recent cases of proper name preservation, in order to find the best way of accounting for this pattern of data.

Several cases of proper name anomia have been described in neuropsychological literature. Occasionally impaired production for several types of proper names is observed, while other patients are selectively impaired in producing *people's* names only.

P.C., a patient described by Semenza and Zettin (1988) was a 62 year-old businessman with a university education. He suffered a left parieto-occipital vascular accident that resulted in a right hemianopia and a jargonaphasia which rapidly improved. When the reported investigation started, P.C.'s spontaneous speech showed no pathological signs. P.C.'s complaint was of his dramatic inability to retrieve proper names other than his own.

P.C.'s scores for object naming in visual presentation tasks were perfect. He made no error and no omission in naming either objects or pictures from different categories (vegetables, fruits, body parts, colours, letters, means of transportation, types of pasta or pieces of furniture). His performance when naming people was quite different. He was unable to name any of the twenty pictures of famous people that were presented to him, but he was able to provide correct details about these people (for instance, 'Prime Minister, he is the first socialist holding this position in our country'). In all the cases, P.C. had no difficulty in matching names and pictures of famous people in a multiple choice test. His performance on geographical names was no better. He was unable to name well-known cities either from a blank atlas or from pictures, but he was able to match pictures and points on a map (e.g. placing a picture of the Eiffel Tower in the correct location). P.C. was also unable to name rivers, countries and mountains, but again he was able to produce a fair amount of information on most of these items. He never failed to correctly locate these geographical items on a map.

P.C.'s performance in naming from definition was similar. His scores were excellent when producing common names, while his performance was very poor when producing proper names. Finally, P.C.'s performance in giving names from a category in one minute was within normal limits for common names (vegetables, fruits, birds, clothes, body parts, sports, and so on), but far below the performance of a control group when the task required the production of people's names or geographical names.

Semenza and Zettin (1989) describe another case of proper name anomia. L.S. was a 41-year-old man who was employed in a hardware shop, and who suffered a fronto-temporal lesion after a riding accident. A few months after the accident, no pathological signs were detectable in L.S.'s spontaneous speech apart from a dramatic inability to produce proper names. This deficit affected both oral and written production but L.S.'s auditory and written comprehension of proper names was preserved.

In visual confrontation tasks, L.S. was 100 per cent correct with real objects and 98 per cent correct with pictures as far as production of common names was concerned. However, his performance with proper names was clearly lower. He was able to name most members of his family but he could name only two out of the twenty-five presented pictures of famous people while being able to provide correct biographical information about the people he could not name. Furthermore he had no problems in matching people's names with pictures in a multiple-choice test. L.S. could name six cities from fifteen presented pictures and four cities from fifteen map sites, but he was able to match all the items in 'name/picture' pairs and to give correct information about these cities. He was able to name three out of eight rivers, two out of eight countries and two out of eight mountains indicated on a blank atlas. Again, he was able to provide a fair amount of correct information for all the items.

L.S.'s performance in naming from definition show a parallel pattern: high performance in naming animate beings, inanimate objects, abstract nouns, adjectives, verbs and numbers but poor performance in naming people, cities, mountains and countries.

In summary, L.S.'s pattern of dissociation was rather similar to that shown by P.C.: an impaired ability to produce different kinds of proper names together with a preserved ability to retrieve common names. We turn now to the description of two other patients who showed a more specific deficit: their retrieval difficulties were limited to people's names.

McKenna and Warrington (1980) briefly described the case of G.B.L., a 55-year-old secondary school teacher. She was admitted to hospital for investigation of intermittent visual and memory disturbances. In fact, she had suffered a small left posterior temporal lesion. Her spontaneous language appeared normal. Her reading, spelling, verbal comprehension and verbal fluency were entirely normal. Her score on the Oldfield naming test was perfect (100 per cent correct). In contrast, her performance was very poor in naming well-known personalities: she was able to name only three out of twenty pictures while she could give relevant descriptions of the presented people for all but two items (for instance, she provided the following description of Mr Heath: 'Conservative, was Prime Minister, organist, comes from the South Coast'). She was able to name famous politicians or national leaders from definitions for nine out of twenty items. But she did not show the same difficulty in naming towns on a map. She was able to name sixteen of twenty Europeans towns and all the British towns pointed to on a blank map.

Although G.B.L.'s verbal fluency was normal, her ability to generate proper names from categories paralleled her naming difficulties. She was able to provide twenty-two town names in one minute but only two political leaders and three English Prime Ministers in the same amount of time.

McKenna and Warrington concluded that G.B.L. showed a nominal deficit affecting one particular kind of proper names (people's names), while another class of proper names (names of towns) and common names were spared.

More recently, Lucchelli and de Renzi (1992) described another patient showing a selective inability to produce people's names. T.L. was a 67-year-old typographer showing a left thalamic lesion following a vascular accident. Language and memory problems recovered a few days after the accident apart from a serious difficulty in retrieving people's names and telephone numbers. At the time of the investigation, T.L.'s spontaneous language showed no pathological signs.

T.L.'s scores on naming from pictures and from definitions, in the common name domain, reached 96 per cent and 95 per cent correct responses respectively. By contrast, T.L. could name relatives and acquaintances on verbal description in only 77 per cent of cases. This score in a task which presumably poses no problems to a normal person was judged as low. Moreover, T.L. was able to name famous people from pictures or definitions for about half of the items, while he could provide unequivocal biographical details in 90 per cent of naming failures. Several tests indicated that T.L. had no problem with recognition of people's names.

T.L.'s ability to name people was impaired but the retrieval of names of cities, states, rivers and mountains (from definitions or from a blank map) was preserved. There was one exception: names of streets. However, as Lucchelli and de Renzi noted, this exception is more apparent than real since almost all of the names of streets included people's names.

The investigation of verbal fluency showed a marked reduction in the generation of names of people in comparison to various categories of common names but also to other kinds of proper names like names of geographical sites, football teams or cars. For instance, T.L. was able to generate two names of football players and two names of politicians in one minute while he could provide sixteen names of Italian cities, fourteen states, ten football teams and ten brand names of cars in the same interval. A recent case with a pattern of performance very similar to that of T.L. has been reported by Fery *et al.* (1995).

A recent paper by Carney and Temple (1993) reported the case of a patient, M.H., with a profile similar to the above patients. Naming people was the only remaining linguistic deficit. This appears to fit the established pattern with category-specific aphasias: that in the absence of comprehension deficits, the only category that is impaired is that of proper names. However, these authors make the claim that the patient shows a naming deficit specific to *faces*, which would be a sort of optic aphasia restricted to faces – a rare beast indeed. This account, intriguing as it is, is unwarranted by the data, because recall of people's names was tested only by presentation of faces. The strong prediction based on previous data is that Carney and Temple's patient would have similar problems naming people from description, from voice or from any other modality. If this is so, then it is a new case of personal name anomia, and not, as tentatively suggested by Carney and Temple (1993), a category-specific disorder of the output lexicon.

Shallice and Kartsounis (1993) reported on a patient, W.K., whose main complaint was an inability to recall people's names. It was demonstrated that the problem was more marked for the names of people first encountered during the previous twenty years, and also for the names of concepts acquired over the same period, e.g. AIDS, video, etc. Rather than implying a category-specific deficit for proper names, it was proposed that

W.K. suffered from a combination of two separate impairments: verbal memory loss and retrograde amnesia. As Shallice and Kartsounis acknowledge however, it is not clear how far this scenario is true of the other proper name anomics.

One interesting feature of these cases of proper name anomia is the lack of uniformity of lesion site. P.C had a left parieto-occipital lesion (Semenza and Zettin, 1988), L.S. had a fronto-temporal lesion (Semenza and Zettin, 1989) and T.L. had a left thalamic lesion (Lucchelli and de Renzi, 1992). M.H. had suffered multiple cerebro-vascular accidents, leaving no dominant lesion but a number of small ones (Carney and Temple, 1993). Since the only symptom common to these patients was a difficulty recalling proper names, this heterogeneity of lesion site makes it unlikely that there is a neuroanatomical site dedicated to proper name phonology. Instead, it seems to argue in favour of an explanation of these neurological deficits in terms of a reduction of efficiency of name retrieval, where proper names pose particularly high demands on the system.

A FIRST CONCLUSION

To summarise, the idea that access to proper names (or to people's names) is more difficult than access to common names is essentially motivated by data from research on ageing and neuropsychology. First, access to proper names is more vulnerable to cognitive ageing than is access to common names. Second, several patients showing an impairment of proper name retrieval in the context of preserved access to common names have been described. The idea that proper name retrieval is more difficult than common name retrieval is supported also by the absence of the reverse dissociation. However, there is now reason to doubt this simple conclusion.

RECENT NEUROPSYCHOLOGICAL CASE STUDIES

The recent cases of preservation of proper name access show that the notion that proper names must always be more difficult to recall than common names is incorrect. Semenza and Sgaramella (1993) and Cipolotti et al. (1993) both report case studies where proper name recall was better preserved than common name recall. In order to explain our interpretation of these new case reports it is necessary to discuss the relationship between different types of dissociation involving proper name processing.

First, we note that Semenza and Zettin's (1989) claim that Warrington and McCarthy (1987) observed selective sparing of proper names which, taken with their patient, forms a double dissociation, is misleading because the case did not involve the preservation of the *recall* of proper names. The patient, Y.O.T., was a severe global aphasic, with an almost complete inability to understand or to produce speech, who showed a preserved ability to match proper names and pictures of famous people, buildings and cities. Better comprehension of famous people's names, in comparison to common names, was also reported by Van Lancker and Klein (1990). These authors described four global aphasics who performed better with proper names than with common names in tasks that required matching a photograph or a spoken name to one of four written names, or to match a spoken or a written name to one of four photographs (see Chapter 3). But neither Y.O.T. nor the four cases described by Van Lancker and Klein show a pattern of disturbances opposite to proper name anomia, which would require impaired production of common names with spared production of proper names. In fact, neither of the patients reported by Semenza and Zettin (1988, 1989), nor the ones reported by Warrington and McCarthy (1987) and by Van Lancker and Klein (1990) could name faces, and *all* of these patients could match names to faces, so clearly there are no grounds for claiming any sort of double dissociation at all between proper and common name production.

On the other hand, imagine a patient who is able to name neither objects nor familiar people in a confrontation naming task, and yet in spontaneous speech produces proper names and very few common names. This is in fact a description of Semenza and Sgaramella's (1993) jargonaphasic patient, who temporarily demonstrated readier access to proper names than to common names. Note that the patient did not name objects or people while not being able to describe them; proper names were produced in spontaneous speech, and because the patient's comprehension was affected at the time of testing, it is difficult to know whether the patient *could* have produced common names. Nevertheless, the case does suggest that proper name production can be preserved relative to common name production.

Another aspect of the patient's performance that requires explanation is the finding that cueing with the initial phoneme of a name he was trying to recall when confronted with a picture led to successful naming only for names of relatives, and not for objects. Again, people's names appear to be preserved, in some sense, relative to common names.

How can the patterns of impairment observed in Semenza and Sgaramella's patient be explained? Contrary to the preliminary conclusion above, proper name production appears to be less impaired than common name production. As the authors point out, the data is compatible with Valentine *et al.*'s (1991) model of face and name processing, because access to the phonological output system from common name and proper name referents are separate. On the other hand, we note that Semenza and Sgaramella's phonemic cueing data certainly appear to be difficult to account for in terms of Brennen's (1993) plausible phonology hypothesis (see p. 111). The initial phoneme should tend to specify a lexical item more when it is a common name than when it is a proper name, and so be a better cue.

In the same issue of *Memory*, there is another article on the neuropsychology of proper name output. Cipolotti *et al.* (1993) present a patient who is very different from Semenza and Sgaramella's, but who allows the same general conclusion to be drawn: proper name retrieval can be spared relative to common name retrieval. They report a severely aphasic patient, M.E.D., whose performance declined over the course of investigation and who died in the month following neuropsychological investigation. The neuropsychological investigation took place over a period of eleven days. Spoken word to picture matching was intact at first but deteriorated over the period of testing. Her naming (oral and written) was impaired at first, and by the end of testing was reduced to almost nil. The observation of interest was that during the course of the decline of written naming, common names appeared to be affected before proper names. Early on in testing, M.E.D. showed better written naming of country outlines than of objects, and Cipolotti *et al.* claim that word length and word frequency could not account for this result. It is impressive, for instance, that the patient could not name a picture of a key or a clock, but could name the outline of Spain and India.

In sum, proper names appeared, for a short while, to be preserved relative to common names, as could be accounted for in terms of Valentine *et al.*'s (1991) model (see Chapter 8). There are potential problems with Cipolotti *et al.*'s demonstration however. There are two reasons for doubting that the proper names and common names used in the naming tasks were equated for frequency for this patient. First, the frequency norms used were North American and the patient lived in Britain. So, the low frequency scores for Scotland, Ireland and Wales, and for that matter other European countries, would probably be a sizeable underestimate of their real frequency for the patient. Similar reservations hold for the requency of items from the Graded Naming Test (McKenna and Warrington, 1978) where past English monarchs and European leaders would presumably be of much higher frequency in Britain than in the USA. Second, the description of M.E.D. includes the biographical detail that she had lived abroad in at least three countries other than Britain, which will have heightened her geographical awareness, and so for her the true frequencies of the names of countries may have been much higher than average.

The evidence from normal adults in a range of experimental and naturalistic paradigms is that proper names are harder to recall than common names. The neuropsychological literature was until recently in accord with this, but now there are neuropsychological demonstrations that proper names are not always more difficult to recall than common names. These demonstrations do not alter the conclusion from experimental studies that for normal adults the retrieval of proper names is relatively vulnerable. The rest of the chapter will cover attempts to account for this experimental evidence from normal adults. In considering them, it will be useful to bear in mind the recent neuropsychological data. Explanations that, at least potentially, could account for the recent neuropsychological data on the preservation of proper name recall, should be considered more viable.

The classical Bruce and Young (1986) model provided an explanation for the fact that accessing people's names is more difficult than accessing biographical information known about these people. However, this model as well as its more recent revisions either in the form of a serial framework (Brédart and Valentine, 1992) or in the form of an interactive activation network (Burton and Bruce, 1992) do not *explain* why retrieving proper names is more difficult than retrieving common names. In fact these models did not deal with the specificity of lexical access to proper names at all. Explanations in terms of the extra difficulty of recalling proper names are needed.

LACK OF MEANING, ARBITRARINESS AND THE TYPE/TOKEN DISTINCTION

For Cohen (1990b), the difficulty in retrieving proper names is due to the fact that proper names are not meaningful. Proper names are detached from the semantic network representing conceptual knowledge. Cohen argued that if her hypothesis was correct, then proper name retrieval should resemble retrieval of other meaningless information about a person: associating a name to a person would be as difficult as associating a non-word to that person. She obtained data that fitted quite well with this prediction. In her experiments subjects were shown photographs of unfamiliar faces and had to learn information about each person. Three types of information were supplied: names, occupations and possessions. The possessions were either non-words or real words, and the results showed that recall of names was no better than recall of meaningless non-word possessions. For instance, learning that a person is called Mr Collins was as difficult as learning that this person has a 'wesp'. In a second experiment, Cohen showed that recall of a meaningless occupation (Mr Collins is a 'ryman') was also as difficult as name recall and was of course more difficult than recall of a meaningful occupation.

Recently, however, Brennen (1993) has pointed out the importance of taking the acquisition phase into account when explaining name recall. Learning a name like 'Ragnhild Dybdahl' requires two processes: (1) learning the phonology of the name, and (2) associating the phonology to the person. Thus two steps are in fact necessary to learn names whose phonology was previously unfamiliar. To learn names which were known prior to the learning episode (i.e. names composed of first names and surnames already encountered in other names), only the second step is necessary. This analysis provides an explanation of Cohen's (1990b) data, without invoking link-up with the conceptual system. Labels that are pre-experimentally unfamiliar will always be at a disadvantage in these paired associate tasks. This does not invalidate the idea that proper names are difficult to recall because of their 'meaninglessness', but leaves the database in need of reinforcement. Brennen (1993) acknowledges that his analysis predicts that a non-word occupation (e.g. wesp) should be harder to learn than a familiar but 'meaningless' name (e.g. Collins). However, Cohen found that recall of such items was equivalent. Brennen suggests that a paradigm which is more powerful than a face–name learning experiment may be required to detect better recall of people's names than non-words.

Burke *et al.* (1991) have proposed a model of proper name production in which this idea of names being detached from conceptual representations is also important. Burke *et al.*'s model is based on MacKay's (1987) 'Node Structure Theory', which was developed originally to provide a general account of speech production and speech comprehension. All links in the network are bi-directional, i.e. they exert both feedforward and feedback influences.

Burke *et al.*'s model of object naming includes visual concept nodes (see Figure 5.1a). Each of these nodes represents the appearance of an object. The role of these nodes appears to be similar to that of Warren and Morton's (1982) pictogens. Each visual concept node is connected to several propositional nodes and to a lexical node. Propositional nodes represent semantic information about the category of which the object is a member. Each propositional node represents a property of the category. Propositional nodes are also connected to the lexical node. Lexical nodes store neither phonological nor semantic information. They are connected to the phonological system in which nodes representing syllables, phonological compounds and features are hierarchically organised.

Burke *et al.* designed a slightly different network for the case of proper names production (see Figure 5.1b). This network also includes a visual concept node level. Each visual concept node represents the appearance of a person (for instance, Mr Bush). These units seem to be similar to face recognition units as far as faces are concerned. The relevant visual concept node is connected to propositional nodes which represent information known about Mr Bush. But neither the visual concept node nor propositional nodes are directly connected to the lexical node 'Bush': a node representing a proper noun phrase such as 'George Bush' mediates between the visual concept node or the propositional nodes and the lexical node 'Bush'. Therefore, the difference between lexical access to proper

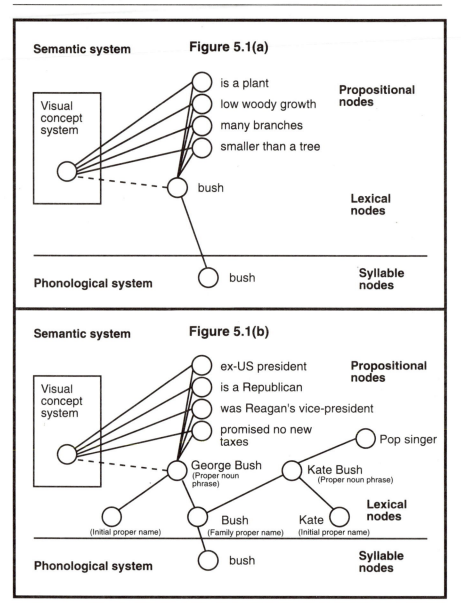

Figure 5.1 An account of lexical access for the common name 'bush' (a) and the proper name 'Bush' (b) in terms of node structure theory

Adapted from Burke *et al.*, 1991. Reprinted with permission

names and common names lies in the fact that for proper names a lexical node 'Bush' is connected to semantic information only via nodes for 'George Bush', 'Kate Bush' and other known people who bear the surname 'Bush'. The lexical node for the common name 'bush', on the other hand, is directly connected to propositional nodes representing properties defining the 'bush' semantic category. So, in the case of lexical access to the common noun 'bush', a large number of connections linking the propositional nodes to the lexical node 'bush' provide summation of priming that will make activation of the lexical node and its connected phonological nodes likely. This summation of priming from propositional to lexical nodes makes common nouns relatively invulnerable to problems of lexical access like TOTs. But if the proper name 'George Bush' is to be produced, no such summation of priming occurs at the lexical node for 'Bush'. The proper noun phrase 'George Bush' receives convergent connections but the lexical node itself (which is the gateway to the phonological system) is only indirectly linked to the propositional nodes through a single link. This makes proper names more vulnerable to difficulties of lexical access.

Other authors have adopted a view based on Katz's distinction between type reference and token reference. Semenza and Zettin draw on it and claim that the function of proper names is simply to refer to the objects so named and not to describe them by any property: 'Names have no sense, that is, they do not describe any property or imply any attribute' (Semenza and Zettin, 1989, p.679). Lucchelli and de Renzi (1992) expressed a similar idea: they saw proper names as tags that permit to identify their bearers but that on their own tell nothing of the properties of these bearers.

However, the notion of arbitrariness to which many authors refer should be made more explicit. On some definitions, arbitrariness does not distinguish between proper names and common names. The relationship between the meaning of a word and the word form itself is, except for onomatopoeias, arbitrary. This relationship is arbitrary in the sense that there is no necessary reason why the label 'baker' is used to denote those people who bake bread (de Saussure, 1916). French speakers use the word 'boulanger', Italians call them 'panettieri', Spaniards call them 'panaderos' and so on. But this relationship is conventional, i.e. all the members of a given linguistic community share the same label to denote a particular category.

In what supplementary sense then, are proper names supposed to be arbitrary? Cohen (1990) and McWeeny et al. (1987) argued that names are arbitrary because the label 'Baker' says nothing about the identity of Mr Baker, which is exactly the same reason Semenza and Zettin (1988, 1989) gave in order to attribute the feature of meaninglessness to proper names. Indeed, this seems plausible. Imagine that you meet somebody for the first time and that you are told that this person is a baker. In this case, you can automatically infer a number of properties about that person (inferences that may or may not be correct). Being a member of the 'baker' category, this person presumably bakes bread, gets up early, sells cakes, kneads dough and so on. By contrast, if you meet somebody under the same conditions and you are told that this person is called 'Baker', the information that is derivable may not be as useful. One may deduce, for instance, that the person is English-speaking. This is the intercultural information referred to in Chapter 1. The *intra*-cultural information, however, is much more limited. One might think that the name is an upper-class name, or that it comes from the North of England, or the South of France.

The fact that a proper name conveys so little information about the entity it names (and even that may be misleading) seems to be a consequence of the fact that proper names typically denote individuals and not categories in which exemplars inherit properties defining the category. Denoting a category to refer to one exemplar ('This man is a baker') allows inheritance of properties from the denoted category to the referred exemplar. Such inheritance of properties is not possible if a proper name is used. The name 'Baker' is not a label for a category within which exemplars (James Baker, Norma Jean Baker, Ginger Baker, Ben Baker or Samuel Baker) share a number of properties specific to people called 'Baker'. Apart from some very general properties like 'human beings' or 'belonging to an Anglo-Saxon culture', James (politician), Norma Jean (actress), Ginger (rock musician), Ben (football player in a famous cartoon) and Samuel (explorer) do not share many properties. Furthermore, these general properties are shared by others with different surnames.

In short, explanations of the vulnerability of proper names retrieval in terms of meaninglessness, arbitrariness, pure reference or token reference are very similar. They all rely on the same claim about proper names: a proper name conveys almost no information about the entity it names.

NAMING A PERSON REQUIRES THE RETRIEVAL OF ONE SPECIFIC LABEL

Another factor that might contribute to making person naming difficult lies in the fact that person naming requires the retrieval of one specific label: the name of the individual. Such a constraint holds to a lesser degree for object naming. First, many common names have synonyms. This is not the case for people's names or proper names in general. People (or other unique entities) generally only have one name. Cohen and Faulkner (1986) put this point well: 'It is probable that retrieval failures for object names are less noticeable since synonyms . . . can be substituted and effectively mask the lapse' (p. 187).

There are however some interesting exceptions to the rule that people have only one name. In particular, artists often bear a pseudonym. For instance, the two names 'Norma Jean Baker' and 'Marilyn Monroe' can be used to refer to the same person. However, artists represent only a small proportion of the individuals we know. Moreover, artists' real names are often not known to us. Many people know that Marilyn Monroe's real name was 'Norma Jean Baker', and some know that Bob Dylan's real name is 'Robert Zimmerman', but how many know that Kirk Douglas's name is 'Yssur Danielovitch Demsky'?

Another important difference between naming objects and naming people lies in the fact that in different conversational contexts, labels from different levels of categorisation of an object may be relevant to refer to that object. In order to name the last piece of clothing you bought, you may use words such as 'trousers', 'jeans' or 'Levis' or the even more precise '501'. Such a degree of freedom does not exist in naming people. Naming a person requires the retrieval of a label bound to one particular level of categorisation: the level of individuals. You can use the expression 'the author of relativity theory' to refer to Albert Einstein but this is obviously not an act of *naming* Albert Einstein. 'The author of relativity theory' is not the name of Albert Einstein. In contrast, 'trousers', 'jeans' or 'Levis' are three different names for the same object.

The fact that naming a person requires the retrieval of one particular label is likely to contribute to making person naming difficult. This hypothesis has been tested by studying faces that have the exceptional property of bearing two names (Brédart, 1993). The faces were those of actors playing well-known, nameable characters. For instance the names 'Harrison Ford' and 'Indiana Jones' may be used to name the actor who portrayed this character in films. If this hypothesis is correct, then retrieval blocks should occur less frequently when naming faces that may be referred to by giving the actor's name or by giving the character's name than in naming faces of actors playing characters whose names are not known to subjects, or than in naming characters played by actors whose names are not commonly known. This is due to the fact that when naming faces that bear two names, difficulty in accessing one name may be bypassed by producing the other name. Examples of faces with two names used in Brédart's study are Sean Connery alias James Bond, Tom Selleck alias Magnum and Peter Falk alias Columbo. Naming such faces was first compared to naming faces for which only the actors' names were known. These are, for instance, Julia Roberts as Vivian Ward in *Pretty Woman*, Richard Gere as Zack Mayo in *Officer and a Gentleman*, Woody Allen as Kleinman in *Shadows and Fog*.

As predicted, blocks were less frequent for faces with two names (mean rate = 3.1 per cent) than for faces with one name (mean rate = 15.9 per cent) in a naming context that allowed production of either names of actors or names of characters. In a second experiment, naming faces with two names was compared to naming faces for which characters' names only were known (e.g. Rick Hunter played by Fred Dryer, Zorro played by Duncan Regehr or Spock played by Leonard Nimoy). Results showed that the occurrence of retrieval blocks was less frequent for the former category of faces (mean rate = 2.8 per cent) than for the latter (mean rate = 12.5 per cent).

These results clearly showed that when bypassing a block is possible by producing another name, the rate of 'visible' blocks dramatically drops and consequently supports the hypothesis that the habitual requirement in person naming of retrieving one specific label is a factor that contributes to making person naming difficult.

This factor explains the proper name/common name retrieval difference without corollary assumptions about the nature of proper and common names. If we assume that access to the phonology of words is a probabilistic process that fails occasionally, then concepts for which there is more than one label will have a lower rate of recall failure. Brédart's (1993) result demonstrates that the fact that typically proper names are the only correct name for the concept with which they are associated accounts for at least some of the difficulty they pose for recall.

However, further studies are still needed. Indeed, in Brédart's experiments the two names relevant to naming a given face belonged to two different people. Indiana Jones and Harrison Ford have separate identities: the former is an unmarried adventurous archaeologist who hates snakes, while the latter is an actor who has appeared in many famous movies, for example, *Witness*, *Frantic* and *Star Wars*, and is the husband of Melissa Mathison and the father of three sons and a daughter.

Further evaluation of the hypothesis that person naming is difficult because it implies the retrieval of one specific label would require comparisons of the rates of TOTs when naming people – and not only faces – who bear two names (e.g. Norma Jean Baker and Marilyn Monroe are two names for the same person) and naming people who bear only one name.

NAMES ARE UNIQUE

Burton and Bruce (1992) proposed that the difficulty encountered when recalling proper names derives from the fact that they normally uniquely specify a person. This idea is subtly different from Brédart's (1993) unique label hypothesis. The key in Burton and Bruce's idea is that names are (typically) not shared by many people. In other words, there is only one Paul Gascoigne. For Brédart's hypothesis, it does not matter whether or not a name is shared by others, but whether the person has more than one name by which they are known.

A simulation run on Burton et al.'s (1990) model showed that indeed all semantic information units that were connected to only one person identity node (PIN) reached its activation asymptote less quickly than units shared by many PINs, and their asymptotes were also slightly lower.

According to this idea, not only should names be at a disadvantage because they are often unique to a person, but the same disadvantage should also be found for all semantic facts that are unique to a person. However, some neuropsychological patients who are pathologically incapable of remembering names can provide very specific information about people (Semenza and Zettin, 1988, 1989). Hanley (1993) explicitly set out to test this idea, studying an anomic patient, N.P., who was able to recall the occupations of forty-four out of fifty-two famous faces, but none of the names. Furthermore, she was able to give precise, uniquely specifying information about people from their faces, e.g. the catch-phrases of television presenters, how John F. Kennedy died and so on. On this task, she provided one out of twenty names and yet answered fifteen out of twenty of the uniquely specifying questions correctly. This would seem to contradict Burton and Bruce's hypothesis that uniqueness of names makes them more difficult to recall.

THE SET SIZE OF PLAUSIBLE PHONOLOGY

In adult life, the rate of acquisition of new common nouns slows down. Usually, adults still learn some technical words related to their jobs or hobbies but do not acquire a great many new lexical items in general usage. It is therefore mostly in the context of learning people's names that adults encounter new phonologies. For Brennen (1993), the observation that adults encounter more new people's names than new common names implies that there is a wider range of phonologies that are plausible and acceptable for people's names than for common names. This claim is at the core of the hypothesis. Imagine that you are told that a given person is called Mr Dreaner. This would not be remarkable. However, if you were told that a person works as a dreaner, you will probably think that you have not heard correctly. The reason for this is that our experience tells us that many more phonologies are plausible for people's names as compared to common names: we frequently encounter people's names that consist of unfamiliar phonologies.

The fact that the range of plausible phonologies is much wider for people's names than for common nouns has another implication: it should be easier to guess the complete phonology of a target word from incomplete phonology if that word is a common noun than if it is a person's name. In other words, partial phonology accessed during recall of a person's name is less specifying of the target than is partial phonology during recall of a common noun. If when you are told the name of somebody's occupation you fail to hear it clearly and catch just some of it, e.g. the initial syllable /ga/ and a terminal /ʌ/, you can confidently infer that this person is a gardener because it is difficult to think of another name of a profession that is compatible with such a string of phonemes, and from experience we know that it is very unlikely to be a profession which one has never heard of before. By contrast, if you are told the name of a person and you just catch the same phonemes, /ga/ and a terminal /ʌ/, it is much less evident that the word is Gardener, because the name could be completed with almost anything.

However, perhaps not all of a language's legal phonology is plausible for people's names in that language. Encountering people named 'Mr Biotechnologist' or 'Miss Brontosaurus' is highly improbable. These names are not plausible names for people. Evidence was presented in Chapter 2 that people rely on prototypical surface forms when generating names for new exemplars of different categories of items (Rubin *et al.*, 1991).

THE MECHANISM OF THE PLAUSIBLE PHONOLOGY HYPOTHESIS

On the basis of any partial phonology that is recalled, the phonology of a common name can be focused on rapidly; however, for people's names, the search for phonology has to be more diffuse. This parallels the 'Gardener' thought experiment above.

It is well established that access to the phonological lexicon can be a gradual process, as shown by partial knowledge of word targets that subjects can give when in TOTs (Brown and McNeill, 1966; Rubin, 1975). These studies provided evidence that knowledge of the initial letter of a word, the number of syllables it contains and (in English) its stress pattern, can all be available before the full phonology.

Assuming that access to a word's phonology always initially occurs by such a gradual process, then at a certain point the partial information will be sufficient to uniquely specify a word in a user's lexicon. At this point, it is hypothesised here that another parameter influences the ongoing recall of words' phonology: access to the stored phonology is assumed to continue in the same way as before the partial phonology uniquely specified the word, but this process will be accelerated for words from domains with a low new exemplar rate. The missing elements of the word's phonology will be accessed more quickly because the system's behaviour is adapted to the fact that it rarely encounters new exemplars from certain domains, which allows it to select the remaining elements of a word's phonology from the lexical store with a high level of certainty.

The problem faced when recalling people's names is that this kind of accelerated fragment completion will be less sure of producing the desired target. Even if the partial phonology that has been recalled is consistent with only one name that is stored in a particular lexicon, the nature of the phonology of people's names is such that neighbouring, unfamiliar phonologies are also plausible candidates. For this reason, the accelerated completion process will not be so reliable for people's names, and the standard unaccelerated lexical process has to be relied on to ensure that the intended phonology will be produced.

In order to specify even further the way in which set size of plausible phonology might influence word recall, it is necessary to take a closer look at what other processes influence it. In many models of the semantic system and the output lexicon, a name can be recalled if sufficient semantic activation passes to the node or unit representing it. There may also be top-down processes influencing word recall, by which is meant the influence of the context upon recall of the word. In laboratory situations it has been shown that seeing Oliver Hardy's face speeds up the naming of Stan Laurel's face (Brennen and Bruce, 1991), and that seeing a picture of an object speeds up the naming of a closely associated object (McCauley *et al.*, 1980). Top-down processes are not the focus of more discussion however, because it is assumed that they will operate equally for common and proper names.

However, the set size of plausible phonology (SSPP) constitutes another type of top-down influence that can play a role in recalling a name. A distinction will be drawn between top-down processes and top-down constraints. A top-down constraint is an element of the naming attempt that is independent of any particular attempt: it is invariant over all attempts to recall a particular name. We may, for instance, know that we are looking for a high familiarity word. That fact acts as a top-down constraint by providing important information that enables us to monitor the internal phonology accessed during the attempt to recall a name, and thus to articulate only words that satisfy the high familiarity criterion. Other top-down constraints on word recall may be, for instance, knowing that it is a foreign-sounding word, or knowing that the surname being searched for is also the name of a fruit. The SSPP is another top-down constraint.

The words for whom the SSPP constraint will be useful in specifying the phonology will be those that come from domains with low new exemplar rates. For such items, the full phoneme string can be generated from a few phonemes of partial phonology, because these first-recalled phonemes will tend to uniquely specify a member of the target word domain. This, in concert with the knowledge that there are very few new exemplars in this domain, will allow the generation of the desired phonology with a high degree of certainty.

On the other hand, words that are well learned or words that come from domains with a high new exemplar rate will benefit little from this accelerated lexical access. The phonology of well-learned items (regardless of word domain) will be specified with very little help from the SSPP top-down constraint, because the activation of the phonology by the standard lexical processes will already be rapid. For words from domains with high new exemplar rates, this top-down constraint is simply not much of a constraint: for people's names, as has already been argued, very many phonologies are plausible, and so extrapolating from some partial phonology to a particular phoneme string is less likely to result in the desired phonology being made available.

For this account to be correct, it is necessary that the domain of the word whose phonology is to be recalled be known before the phonology is specified. In fact, this is an assumption made by many current psycholinguistic models (see, for instance, Kempen and Huijbers, 1983). Thus, it is hypothesised that this knowledge influences subsequent phonological selection by allowing more or less completion of partial phonology according to whether the word's domain has a low or high acquisition rate.

Most of the hypotheses that have been discussed so far have contrasted proper names and common nouns. This is not the case for Brédart's (1993) proposal which predicts that any concept for which there is only one verbal label will be associated with more TOTs than multi-label concepts. Nor is it the case for Brennen's (1993) proposal which suggests that the differences in retrieval difficulty of words from different domains is due to the size of the universe of plausible phonologies for words in any particular domain. In fact, the plausible phonology hypothesis is more general than an explanation of the specific recall difficulties with people's names. It can be stated as follows: 'The higher the frequency of encounter of new phonologies within any category of words, the harder the recall of words from that domain will be'. Unlike previously discussed explanations, this hypothesis predicts various degrees of recall difficulties across different classes of proper names. Indeed, a number of sources of evidence suggest that all the categories of proper names are not equally prone to retrieval difficulties. Cohen and Faulkner (1986) have shown that learning the names of people (either the first name or the surname) is more difficult than learning the names of cities where these people live. Burke et al. (1991) have compared the occurrence of TOTs for five kinds of words among which are two kinds of proper names: people's names and place names. They showed that (in older subjects) TOTs to people's names were more frequent than TOTs to other kinds of words including place names; the latter did not elicit more TOTs than did common nouns. Moreover, among the cases of proper name anomia reported so far, two patients showed an impairment of production for all of the different kinds of proper names that were tested (Semenza and Zettin, 1988, 1989), while the other patients mainly showed an impairment of production of people's names (McKenna and

Warrington, 1980; Lucchelli and de Renzi, 1992; Carney and Temple, 1993; Fery *et al.*, 1995).

There are thus proper names and proper names, and it seems to be hazardous to generalise data obtained from people's names to all classes of proper names. The interesting question to be answered is probably not 'Why are proper names difficult to retrieve?' but rather 'Why are some kinds of proper names difficult to retrieve?'

Of course, further data are needed. The production of some kinds of proper names is still completely unexplored. Almost all of the data we have reported concern the production of people's names and geographical names. The retrieval of titles of musical pieces (Semenza and Zettin, 1989; Maylor, 1991) or of telephone numbers (Lucchelli and de Renzi, 1992) should receive more attention. Moreover, we know of no studies on the retrieval of the other kinds of proper names that we mentioned in Chapter 1, i.e. names of institutions and facilities, names of newspapers and magazines, titles of books and paintings, and names of other unique entities.

OVERVIEW, FUTURE DIRECTIONS AND CONCLUSION

We have reviewed current explanations of why the recall of people's names is usually more difficult than the recall of common names: names are arbitrary and/or meaningless, naming a person requires the retrieval of one specific label, and the set of the plausible phonology is larger for people's names than for common names.

These hypotheses are not necessarily seen as mutually exclusive, and in fact the relationship between the hypotheses is of interest in its own right. In particular, the claim of each hypothesis regarding the locus of the difficulty with proper name recall could be fruitfully explored. Recall that Young and Ellis (1989) claimed that McWeeny *et al.*'s (1987) 'Baker/baker' result demonstrated that the explanation of the difficulty with recalling people's names could not lie in the (lexical) items themselves (see p. 39). This was because in that important experiment, the same phonology/beikʌ/took longer to associate to unfamiliar faces when it was the person's name than when it was their profession. It was claimed that accounts in terms of low imageability or low frequency of recall of people's names were eliminated by this result.

A comment is in order, however. The results show that such item-related factors are insufficient by themselves to explain all of the proper name recall disadvantage, but not, for instance, that item-related factors do not play a role in everyday life. It is also the case that the explanations are underspecified, and so some explanations may turn out to overlap to some extent. For instance, Cohen (1990b) and Burke *et al.* (1991) both propose that names are meaningless and so are difficult to recall. Another example of overlapping ideas is provided by Morrison *et al.* (1992) and Brennen (1993). Morrison *et al.* (1992) have suggested that differences in naming latencies that are normally attributed to word frequency are due instead to age of acquisition – the earlier a word is learned, the hardier will be its representation (see Chapter 7). This idea may prove a high level equivalent of Brennen's (1993) low level SSPP idea – the accelerated mechanism of phonological recall outlined above may operate more for items learned early on in life. The moral is that there is much intricate experimental work to be done in order to determine which of these ideas provides an explanation of proper name recall difficulty.

In this chapter, we have sometimes referred to proper names in general and sometimes to people's names in particular. We have mentioned before that current cognitive psychologists' interest in the recall of proper names largely derives from the development of research on familiar face processing. It is thus to be expected that more data about people's names than about other kinds of proper names are available.

Many authors share the idea that access to proper names (or to some kinds of proper names) for production is particularly difficult, i.e. more difficult than access to common nouns. Semenza and Sgaramella (1993) and Cipolotti *et al.* (1993) demonstrate that proper names can be preserved relative to common names. Similarly, Brennen *et al.* (in press; see Chapter 3) show that people's names can be recalled in the absence of other information about the target person. The performance of these three patients seems not to have an analogue in healthy neurologically intact individuals, and it is noteworthy that at the time of testing all three of these cases had severely restricted linguistic abilities and all three were unfit to be clinically tested soon afterwards. Cipolotti *et al.*'s patient died a couple of weeks after testing, Semenza and Sgaramella's patient suffered a further debilitating stroke a few days after testing, and within months of testing, the comprehension and orientation of Brennen *et al.*'s patient was so reduced that further testing was impossible. In conclusion, the recall of proper names can be preserved but the condition may be unstable and found only in advanced states of intellectual dysfunction.

Chapter 6

Lexical access in the production of proper names

We have described Bruce and Young's (1986) model of face processing in detail in Chapter 3. This model can be distinguished from speech production models on one important point: lexical access is a single stage process in this model while most speech production models include two stages of lexical access. Considering that face naming is nothing but a particular case of speech production, Brédart and Valentine (1992) have tried to make a link between face processing models and speech production models, and have proposed a revision of Bruce and Young's model. Before describing this revision it is necessary to present a brief review of current psycholinguistic theories of lexical access.

In the Bruce and Young model biographical information is linked to names: the identity-specific semantic codes feed forward to the name codes. However, as mentioned in Chapter 5, many authors consider that proper names can be seen as labels that allow identification of their bearers but that say nothing about the properties of these bearers (Semenza and Zettin, 1988, 1989; Cohen, 1990a; Lucchelli and de Renzi, 1992). In particular, the function of people's names is simply to refer to the people so named and not to describe them by any property. This way of conceiving of people's names suggests that names are directly linked to representations of individuals – these representations being presumably simple token markers – but are not directly linked to properties describing the identity of individuals. So, another point that will be discussed in this chapter is how lexical units and descriptive properties are accessed from a 'token address' in memory. In particular, we will consider whether it is possible to conceive of a system, in which lexical units and biographical information are accessed in parallel from token markers, which leads to predictions that are consistent with available empirical data.

LEXICALIZATION IN SPEECH PRODUCTION MODELS

Psycholinguists usually consider that speech production involves three major stages. The first stage is *conceptualization*, i.e. processes specifying which concepts have to be expressed verbally. The second stage is *formulation*, i.e. processes that select appropriate words for these concepts and that build the syntactic and the phonological structure of the utterance to be produced. The final stage is *articulation*, i.e. processes that realise phonologically encoded materials into overt speech. In the formulation stage, lexical access comprises two steps: *lexical selection* and *word-form encoding*. This decomposition of processes is shared by most current serial stage models of speech production (Garrett, 1975, 1980; Kempen and Huijbers, 1983; Van Wijk and Kempen, 1987; Butterworth, 1989; Levelt, 1989, 1992; Schriefers, 1990; Roelofs, 1992) and also by some interactive activation models (Dell, 1986; Dell and O'Seaghdha, 1991).

In serial stage models of speech production lexical selection and word-form encoding are seen as two discrete, non-overlapping steps (this is not the case for interactive activation models; this point will be discussed later in the chapter). In Garrett's influential model (1975, 1980), once the speaker has constructed the conceptual content of the utterance to be produced (message level representation) a functional level representation has to be constructed. The *lexical search* is one of three operations that contribute to the construction of a functional level representation. This lexical search consists of selecting lexical items from a lexical set on the basis of the meaning of the lexical entries and of their grammatical category. The outcome of this search is a set of abstract entities not yet specified for form. The other two operations realised at this level are the creation of a predicate / argument structure (determination of functional structures) and the assignment of lexical items to roles within this structure (see Figure 6.1). At this functional level, the lexical content is not yet phonologically specified and the functional structure specifies neither the serial order of lexical items nor the precise sentential environment in which they will occur. The argument structure shown in Figure 6.1 can be expressed in different ways: for instance, *the witch gives an apple to Snow White; the witch gives Snow White an apple; an apple is given to Snow White by the witch.*

The retrieval of *word forms* takes place in a further stage of processing that allows the creation of a positional level representation. At this stage, lexical items are phonologically specified and also ordered, i.e. assigned to places in hierarchically organised frames (the constituent structures of phrases). The assignment of prosodic structure of words also takes place at this stage. These two stages in the formulation process work serially: there is no feedback from the second stage (construction of a positional level representation) to the first one (construction of a functional level of representation).

More recently, Levelt (1989) presented another influential model of speech production in which lexical access comprises two distinct and non-overlapping stages: lemma retrieval and lexeme retrieval (see Figure 6.2).

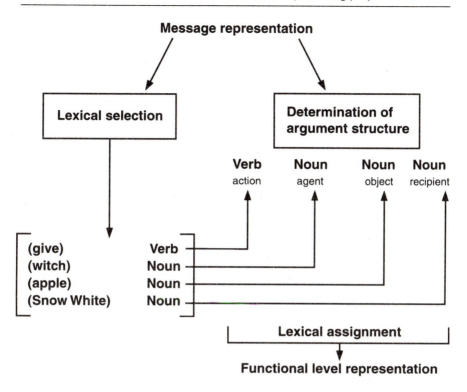

Figure 6.1 The construction of a functional level of representation

Adapted with permission from Garrett, 1980

A lemma is an abstract lexical item supplied with both syntactic and semantic features but unspecified for phonological form. For Levelt, 'the semantic information in a lemma specifies what conceptual conditions have to be fulfilled in the message for the lemma to become activated: it is the lemma meaning' (1989, p. 188). Let us look again at the example *the witch gives an apple to Snow White*. The conceptual specification for the lexical item *give* involves some actor X who causes some possession Y to go from the actor X to a recipient Z. A more formalised presentation of the conceptual specification of *give* is presented in Table 6.1. A lemma is retrieved when a match is achieved between a concept (from the conceptualisation stage) and the conceptual specification of this lemma.

The syntactic information of a lemma specifies the syntactic category of the lexical item and the grammatical functions it can assign to conceptual arguments. Syntactic information also includes a set of diacritic parameters. To go on with our example, the syntactic category of *give* is *verb*. The grammatical functions it assigns are *subject*, *direct object* and *indirect object*. This means that the lexical item *give* requires a subject, a

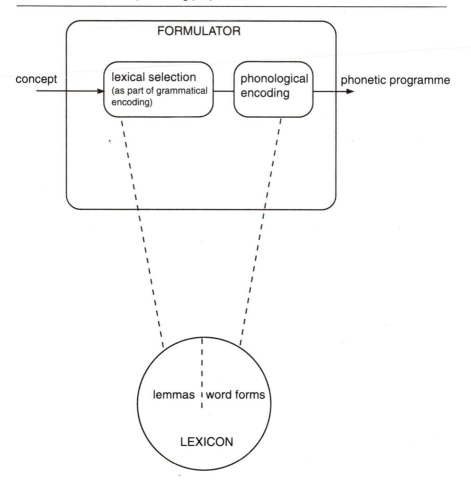

Figure 6.2 Lexical access in speech production
Reproduced with permission from Levelt, 1992

direct object and an indirect object. A specification of which conceptual
arguments is to be mapped on to which grammatical function (i.e. the
thematic mapping) is also included in the lemma. Finally, the lemma also
contains a lexical pointer, i.e. the address for the word form of the lexical
item. In fact this address corresponds to several word forms: the possible
inflections of the item (for instance, give, gives, gave, given, giving). These
word forms can be distinguished by processing values assigned to diacritic
parameters such as tense, aspect, mood, person, number or pitch accent.
This completes the content of lemmas. In short, 'a word's lemma is a
specification of the semantic, syntactic and pragmatic conditions under
which use of the word is appropriate' (Wheeldon and Monsell, 1992,

Table 6.1 Lemma for 'give'

give: conceptual specification:
CAUSE (X (GOposs (Y, (FROM/TO (X,Z))))))
conceptual arguments: (X, Y, Z)
syntactic category: V
grammatical functions: (SUBJ, DO, IO)
relations to COMP: none
lexical pointer: 713
diacritic parameters: tense
        aspect
        mood
        person
        number
        pitch accent

Reproduced with permission from Levett, 1989

p. 724). The reader will find a more extensive description of what a lemma is in Levelt (1989, Chapter 6) and in Bierwisch and Schreuder (1992).

Lemma retrieval is a part of grammatical encoding. The output of grammatical encoding is an ordered string of lemmas hierarchically organised in phrases and sub-phrases. This string may be stored in a syntactic buffer. The phonological encoding of grammatically encoded materials can then start. The retrieval of word forms or lexemes represents the second stage of lexical access. The output of phonological encoding is a phonetic plan that will be executed during a further step: articulation.

Butterworth (1989) sees lexical access as a double transcoding operation. The first transcoding device is the semantic lexicon which takes as input a semantic code and delivers as output a phonological address. The second transcoding device (the phonological lexicon) takes this address as input and delivers phonologically specified information as output. Levelt's grammatical encoding and phonological encoding stages might also be seen as transcoding operations. When Levelt states that 'Grammatical encoding takes a message as input . . . and delivers a surface structure as output', his formulation is similar to that of Butterworth, as far as this particular point is concerned.

Let us now summarise what would happen in the particular speech production task of object naming. Many authors (for instance, Seymour, 1979; Warren and Morton, 1982; Ellis and Young, 1988; Humphreys *et al.* 1988; Wheeldon and Monsell, 1992) consider that object naming involves the following sequence of processes: object identification; activation of a semantic representation; and lexicalisation (i.e. retrieval of a name). Wheeldon and Monsell (1992) recently summarised this sequence as follows:

Successful object identification enables activation of the corresponding 'semantic' representation, that is retrieval of information about the object's functional properties (e.g. what it is for, or what it can do) and its relational properties (e.g. category, associates). To generate a name, contact must now be made with the language system.

(p. 724)

Immediately after the object has been first recognised and then categorised (in other words after the concept to be expressed has been activated) there is a 'semantically driven activation of a set of lemmas' (Levelt *et al.*, 1991). This set of meaning-related items that receives activation from the input concept is called the *semantic cohort*. Only one of these lemmas survives the selection process (the target lemma). The second stage of lexical access starts only when the lemma selection process has terminated. At this stage, only the target lemma is phonologically encoded. Finally a phonetic plan is built for this target item only. Figure 6.3 illustrates this discrete two-stage theory.

We have mentioned earlier that some interactive activation models include the same decomposition of processes described above. This is the case for Dell's model (Dell, 1986; see also Dell, 1989, 1990 and Dell and O'Seaghdha, 1991, 1992). However, this model does not assume that lemma access and phonological encoding are non-overlapping stages of processing. This model conceives of lexical access in more continuous terms: 'Activation is predominantly semantic during lemma access, and activation is predominantly phonological during phonological access, but there is some activation of phonological information during lemma access and some activation of semantic information during phonological access' (Dell and O'Seaghdha, 1992, p. 289). Dell's model consists of a connectionist network. The lexical network structure includes three levels (see Figure 6.4): semantic features, lexical nodes or lemmas, and phonological segment nodes. Connections allow for a bi-directional spread of activation between units at adjacent levels. Let us consider the course of lexical access in an object naming task. In this network, the semantic units which represent the concept to be expressed receive external inputs. Activation subsequently spreads continuously and bi-directionally throughout the network. The most highly activated lexical node is selected. Upon selection, this unit is supplied with a triggering jolt of activation and then receives post-selection inhibition, setting the activation of that node to zero. Because of the extra activation of the selected lemma preceding the post-selection inhibition, the appropriate phonological nodes are selected and linked to a phonological word shape frame. One sees that in this kind of model lexical access is interactive: lemma selection is affected by phonological information (feedback influences) and phonological encoding receives feedforward influences from lexical nodes.

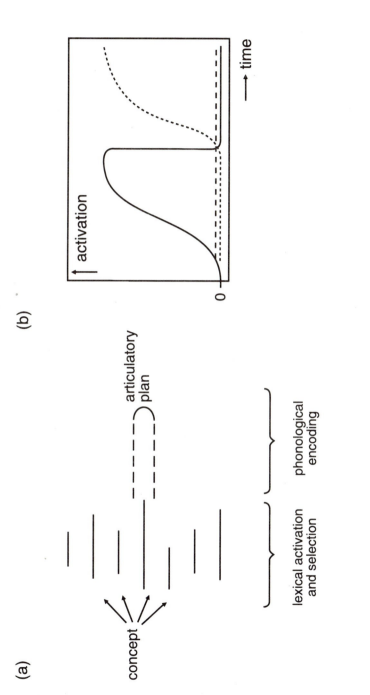

(a)

(b)

Figure 6.3 The discrete two-stage theory of lexical access: (a) Stages of lexical activation-selection and of phonological encoding; (b) Schematic diagram of the time-course of semantic (solid rule) and phonological (dotted rule) activation of target and of phonological activation of semantic alternatives (dashed rule)

Reproduced with permission from Levelt *et al.*, 1991

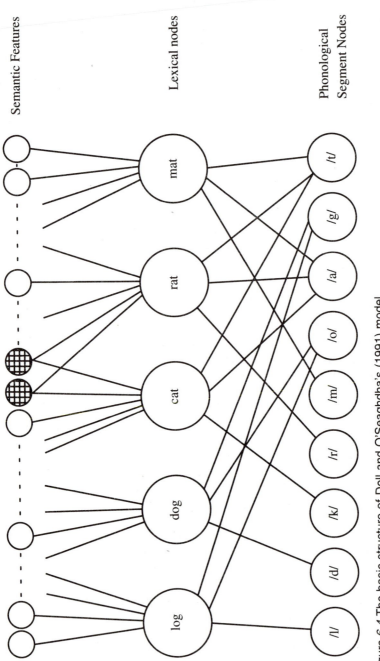

Semantic Features

Lexical nodes

Phonological
Segment Nodes

mat rat cat dog log

/t/ /g/ /a/ /o/ /m/ /r/ /k/ /d/ /l/

Figure 6.4 The basic structure of Dell and O'Seaghdha's (1991) model
Reproduced with permission

The notion that lexical access is not a purely serial process but rather an interactive process has been advocated by other authors (e.g. Stemberger, 1983, 1985; Harley, 1984, 1993; Martin *et al.*, 1989). It is still very difficult to choose between the purely serial account and the interactive account of lexical access on empirical grounds. On one side, the assumption of a backward spreading of activation explains in a simple and parsimonious way characteristics of speech errors such as the lexical bias effect, i.e. phonological speech errors result in real words more often than expected by chance (Baars *et al.*, 1975; Dell and Reich, 1981; Stemberger, 1985), and the combined similarity effect or mixed errors bias, i.e. speech errors, are more often both semantically and phonologically related to their target words than expected by chance (Dell and Reich, 1981; Stemberger, 1983; Harley, 1984; Martin *et al.*, 1989; Brédart and Valentine, 1992). In contrast, purely serial models were at first unable to account for these effects. However, independent serial stage models could eventually manage to account for the combined similarity effect by incorporating a pre-articulatory editing component in the system. The non-independence of phonological and semantic factors on error occurrence was then explained by the fact that errors which are both semantically and phonologically related to their targets are more likely to be missed by an editor than errors that are only either semantically or phonologically related to their targets (Levelt, 1989; Schriefers *et al.*, 1990). This explanation of the mixed error bias in terms of a failure of a post-lexical mechanism is tenable but is less parsimonious than that provided by interactive models.

However, independent serial stage models more recently gained support from studies of the time course of lexical access in speech production. First, Schriefers *et al.* (1990) investigated the time-course of lexical access in naming tasks by using an interference paradigm where a subject's task was to name pictures while distracter words were presented auditorily. These distracter words were to be ignored. Schriefers *et al.* (1990) found that semantic distractors (e.g. *goat* when the target to be named was *sheep*) affected naming latencies only when they were presented shortly before the picture was shown. By contrast, phonological distractors (e.g. *sheet* when the target word was *sheep*) influenced naming latencies when presented simultaneously with the picture or shortly after the picture appeared. The absence of semantic interference at positive stimulus onset asynchronies is more consistent with a serial stage view than with an interactive activation view. Indeed, a late rebound of semantic activation would be expected from the interactive activation models since these models involve backward spreading of activation from phonological nodes to lexical nodes. No trace of such a rebound was obtained.

Serial models prescribe that phonological activation follows the selection of the target lexical item and is restricted to that lexical item. In contrast, interactive activation models predict some phonological activation of semantically related non-selected items. Levelt *et al.* (1991) have proposed a method to investigate the course of semantic and phonological activation of semantic alternatives of the target. The subject's main task was to name pictures. Words or non-words were auditorily presented after the display of the picture but before the naming response. The subject's secondary task was to give a manual lexical decision to these auditorily presented stimuli. Levelt *et al.*'s assumption was that the semantic activation of the target item (the word for the picture) would affect lexical decision RT for a semantically related word and that phonological activation of the target would affect lexical decision RT for a phonologically related word. They indeed observed interference of the naming task on lexical decision RT to semantically as well as to phonologically related words. Levelt *et al.* argued that if non-target lexical items are phonologically activated to some extent then one should also obtain an interference effect of naming a target (e.g. *sheep*) on lexical decision words that are phonologically related to semantic associates (*wool*) of the target or same-category semantic alternatives (*goat*). For instance, naming the picture of a sheep should interfere with lexical decisions to words like *wood* or *goal* which are phonologically related respectively to *wool* and to *goat*. However, Levelt *et al.* found no trace of such interference when the lexical decision was to be taken on words that were phonologically related, not to the target, but to words semantically related to the target. This absence of an effect seems to indicate that non-selected items are not phonologically activated. Again, this result fits the serial stage approach better than the interactive activation approach.

In summary, lexical access is conceived of as two stages: lexical selection (as a part of grammatical encoding), and phonological encoding. This kind of distinction is present in most current serial as well as interactive models of speech production. The question of whether these two stages are discrete or interactive is still being debated (see Dell and O'Seaghdha, 1991), even though recent data on the time-course of lexical access seem to be more consistent with the serial view than with the interactive view.

NAMING INDIVIDUALS

Recently, Brédart and Valentine (1992) have proposed a revision of Bruce and Young's (1986) model. This revision is presented in Figure 6.5. Bruce and Young's model has been adapted on one point: in the original model the identity-specific semantic codes feed forward directly to a name code box whereas two stages of lexical access have been preferred in Brédart and Valentine's model, i.e. access to lemmas followed by access to lexemes. Note that a more complete version of this model also includes perceptual pre-articulatory and post-articulatory loops which were

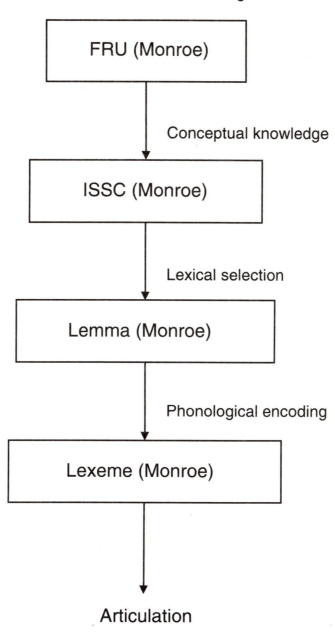

Face recognition

FRU (Monroe)

Conceptual knowledge

ISSC (Monroe)

Lexical selection

Lemma (Monroe)

Phonological encoding

Lexeme (Monroe)

Articulation

Figure 6.5 A simplified version of Brédart and Valentine's (1992) model of face naming

assumed to allow the monitoring of face naming. The question of error detection and error repair will not be addressed in this chapter (see Chapter 8).

The decomposition of processes that was proposed in this model closely corresponds to that specified in most models of speech production. However, further specification of the content of the conceptual processing stage as well as of the content of the proper name lemma is necessary. We will consider that in naming a seen person, conceptual processing involves both access to a token address in memory from a recognition unit, and access to descriptive properties that define the person's identity from this token address. In addition, following Levelt (1989), we will consider that a proper noun lemma simply specifies a conceptual token. The conceptual specification of a proper noun lemma is 'a pointer to the token's address in memory' (Levelt, 1989, p. 196). The architecture shown in Figure 6.6 represents a more detailed version of Brédart and Valentine's (1992) model.

This architecture is consistent with Semenza and Zettin's (1988, 1989) proposal that proper names are pure referring expressions and that they are directly linked to the individual they designate without intervening representations of biographical information. Yet we have previously noted that the assumption of such a direct link is controversial. Indeed, some authors argued that available empirical data support the notion of a mediation of biographical information known about individuals (e.g. Flude *et al.*, 1989; see also Chapter 3, this volume). The question is whether the empirical data which are interpreted as support for access to names being dependent on access to identity-specific semantic information really contradict the notion of a direct individual name link. Indeed, it might be the case that an architecture including parallel access to a name and to biographical information can account for available data. The relative superiority of recall of biographical information over the recall of names might be due to some factor other than the fact that identity-specific semantic codes constitute a necessary pathway to lexical access. Burton and Bruce (1992, 1993) have addressed this question.

PARALLEL ACCESS TO DESCRIPTIVE PROPERTIES AND TO NAMES: PUTTING NAMES ALONGSIDE BIOGRAPHICAL INFORMATION

Burton and Bruce's (1992) model assumes a parallel access to names and to properties defining an individual and yet it is able to account for the fact that names are more difficult to retrieve than descriptive properties of individuals. According to this model, a crucial property of names is their *uniqueness*: names represent unique or little shared characteristics. Finding two people who bear exactly the same name is not impossible

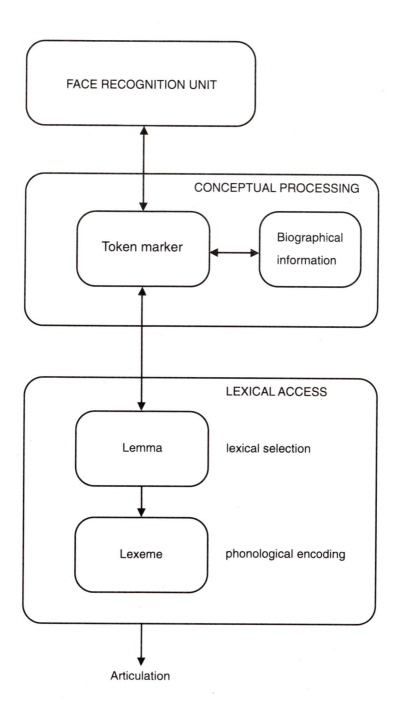

Figure 6.6 An architecture of face naming

(e.g. the authors know two people called 'Janet Jackson') but it is far less frequent than encountering people who share a characteristic like nationality, occupation, marital status and so on. Burton and Bruce showed that uniqueness may explain why names are more difficult to retrieve than descriptive properties. They used the IAC framework developed by Burton *et al.* (1990) (see Chapter 2 for details of this model) and they added name units. In fact, Burton and Bruce included name units within the pool of semantic information units (SIUs: see Figure 6.7). In other words, names were represented alongside conceptual information defining the identity of individuals.

Using this architecture, Burton and Bruce (1992) were able to show in a computer simulation that 'It is always the case that names rise to their maximum activation slowest, and that their maximum activation is the smallest of any SIU' (p. 52). In other words, the results of this simulation were quite consistent with available empirical data, in particular that decisions about semantic properties of individuals are faster than decisions about names. The important point is that this model produced such results despite names and descriptive properties being accessed in parallel from token markers.

However, Burton and Bruce's model can be criticised on two points at least. First, Burton and Bruce's model of name retrieval does not draw upon the theoretical concepts that are currently used in the literature on speech production. One consequence of this is that the exact status of names is not clear in Burton and Bruce's (1992) model: are names conceptual units or lexical units? In a more recent paper, Burton and Bruce (1993) added 'name lexical output' units in the network. These units are responsible for the production of names as opposed to the retrieval of names (which is apparently ensured by the name units included in the pool of SIUs). If we try to make a link with object naming models, two solutions seem to be possible. The first is that lexical output units correspond to lexemes, i.e. word form retrieval or phonological encoding, while name units included in the pool of SIUs correspond to lemmas. The difficulty is then to justify why lemmas, which are lexical units, are stored alongside prelinguistic conceptual information. The second solution would be that name lexical output units stand for the whole lexicalisation stage (i.e. lemmas + lexemes). This would mean that name units included in the pool of SIUs represent non-lexical, prelinguistic information. Then, the problem is that it is difficult to work out what such prelinguistic information about names could be. Our position is that names are by definition labels, i.e. lexical units.

The second criticism is probably more important. Burton and Bruce's (1992) model leads to the prediction that the more properties that are known about an individual the more difficult that person's name is to retrieve. This prediction arises because name units will receive inhibition

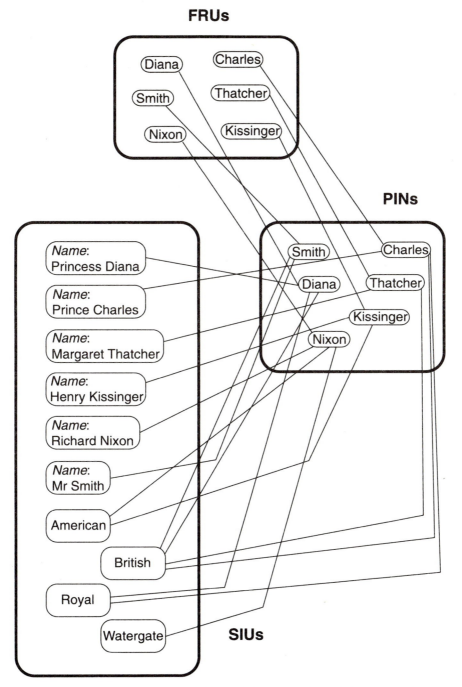

Figure 6.7 Burton and Bruce's (1992) interactive activation model of face naming
Adapted with permission

from other activated SIUs which represent descriptive properties of the individual and are included in the same pool of units. The more descriptive properties (facts) that you know about an individual, the greater will be the inhibition within the SIU pool and the more slowly activation of the name unit will rise. These authors considered that their prediction was supported by empirical data, especially by the 'fan effect' and by the 'reversed frequency effect'.

Anderson and his co-workers investigated the effect of a 'propositional fan' on memory for lists of propositions. In these studies, the subject's task was to learn a number of facts of the form 'The hippie is in the park'. The number of propositions which referred to a given entity (e.g. the hippie) was manipulated. These studies showed that a subject's response time to confirm that a particular proposition had been presented before was slower if three propositions about a given entity were learned than they were if a single proposition about this entity was learned (Anderson, 1974, 1976; see also King and Anderson, 1976; Lewis and Anderson, 1976; Cohen, 1990b). However, these empirical data relate to recently learnt material, whereas Burton and Bruce's IAC model was intended to simulate the steady state of representations of familiar individuals. Another point which should make us cautious about relating these data to a prediction from Burton and Bruce's simulation is that the fan effect is not observed if the material to be learned can be thematically integrated, for instance, by using real world knowledge (Smith *et al.*, 1978; Myers *et al.*, 1984). In this case, a negative fan effect may even be found (i.e. better performance with a greater propositional fan). In fact, such data suggest that the fan effect might not be fully applicable to the retrieval of real world knowledge.

We mentioned earlier that Burton and Bruce considered that their prediction was also empirically supported by the reversed frequency effect, i.e. the fact that 'retrieval failures are reported much more often for names that are rated as familiar than for names that are rated as not very well known' (Cohen, 1990b, p.195). This effect would support Burton and Bruce's prediction if it is assumed that more facts are known about people who are most familiar. However, this reversed frequency effect which has been observed in diary studies (Reason and Lucas, 1984; Cohen and Faulkner, 1986) might simply reflect the relative frequency of recall attempts. Names of frequently encountered people are likely to be recalled more often than names of infrequently encountered people. Therefore, all other factors being equal, the number of blocks to very familiar people's names should be higher than the number of blocks to less familiar people. But the number of recall attempts was not controlled in diary studies which reported a reversed frequency effect. It is thus impossible to estimate what the ratio of number of blocks to number of recall attempts was in these studies. Recently, Brédart (1993) tested the relationship between people's familiarity and name retrieval failures in an experimental setting in which the number of retrieval attempts was controlled. Data from two experiments showed a direct frequency effect rather than a reversed frequency effect: the more familiar a person, the less this person's name elicited retrieval failures. These data do not fit Burton and Bruce's prediction.

However, looking at frequency or familiarity effects does not allow a direct test of a prediction on the relationship between the number of properties known about a person and the ease of retrieval of that person's name. Indeed, although frequency of encounter or familiarity and the number of known pieces of biographical information are presumably highly correlated, they are nevertheless different factors. Recently, Brédart *et al.* (1995) manipulated these factors in order to evaluate more directly the relation between the number of properties known about people and the retrieval of their names. They compared latencies in naming famous faces about whom few biographical details were known with latencies in naming equally famous faces about whom people know many characteristics. Face familiarity was an estimate of the frequency of encounter of a face. For instance, people (the Belgian subjects involved in the reported study at least) know many pieces of biographical information about Gérard Depardieu (e.g. titles of films in which he starred, family information, anecdotes, etc.). By contrast, people generally know few properties about Peter Falk, apart from the fact that he plays Columbo, although Peter Falk's face is as familiar as that of Gérard Depardieu. The comparison of naming latencies showed that naming faces of people about whom many pieces of information were known was faster than naming faces of people about whom few pieces of information were known, although the two sets of faces were equated for familiarity. These results are not consistent with Burton and Bruce's model which predicted the opposite effect.

PARALLEL ACCESS TO BIOGRAPHICAL INFORMATION AND TO NAMES: CLUSTERING BIOGRAPHICAL INFORMATION

Burton and Bruce's (1992) prediction about the relationship between the ease of name retrieval and the amount of biographical information known about the person bearing that name comes from the fact that they used one single pool of SIUs including all descriptive properties and names. Given that units included in the same pool are connected by inhibitory links, the inhibitory load on one target unit (for instance, a name) increases each time a new semantic property is included in the system.

Another IAC model relevant to the study of person naming is available in literature. This is the famous 'Jets and Sharks' demonstration designed by McClelland (1981). This architecture also includes a set of token markers whose role is equivalent to Burton and Bruce's PINs. Another similarity between the two models lies in the fact that names and descriptive properties are accessed in parallel from the token markers. But there are two major differences between McClelland's network and Burton and Bruce's model. The first is that names and descriptive properties are not stored in the same pool of units. The second is that biographical information is clustered into semantic sub-domains (see Figure 6.8).

Recently, Brédart et al. (1995) designed a network based on McClelland's Jets and Sharks architecture in order to study the framework shown in Figure 6.6. This network included one pool of token markers, one pool of names, and several pools of semantic properties such as occupation, nationality or political opinion (see Figure 6.9). At this stage, it is important to point out that Brédart et al. considered that names are by definition lexical units.

Brédart et al. (1995) evaluated the nature of the relationship between speed of retrieval of a person's name and the number of properties known about that person in their network. A simulation showed that the more descriptive properties that were associated with a token marker, the higher the level of activation reached by the name associated with that token marker. (It is always the case that a unit which reaches a higher asymptote also reaches the threshold of activation faster.) The result of this simulation is consistent with the empirical result that knowledge of many facts about a person is associated with faster naming latency. Moreover, in another simulation, the authors showed that the network was able to exhibit properties consistent with mental chronometry data (described in Chapter 3) as effectively as Burton and Bruce's model: it was never the case that a name associated with a given individual reached the threshold activation before the SIUs representing biographical information associated with that individual. In addition, the maximum activation reached by names was never higher than that reached by semantic information units. Note that this network also produced Burton and Bruce's result that the course of activation of unique descriptive properties is identical to that of names.

In summary, Brédart et al.'s network was able to replicate the interesting properties of Burton and Bruce's model and to produce results that are consistent with empirical data concerning the relationship between the ease of name retrieval and the amount of known biographical information. Yet a potential problem remains with this architecture. The attenuation or the disconnection of the links between the token marker and the descriptive properties, while the link between the token marker and the name is left intact, might lead to an impairment of access to descriptive properties in the context of a preserved lexical access.

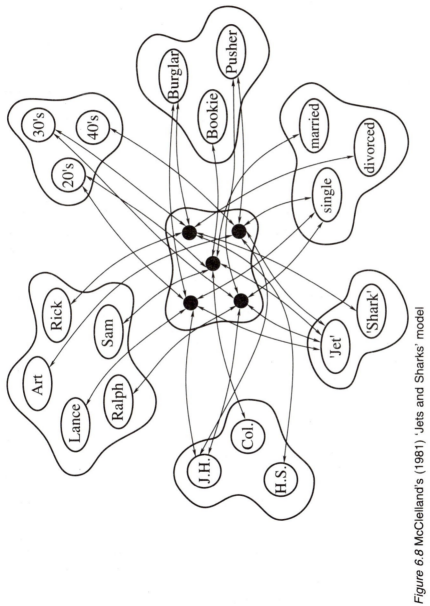

Figure 6.8 McClelland's (1981) 'Jets and Sharks' model

Reproduced with permission

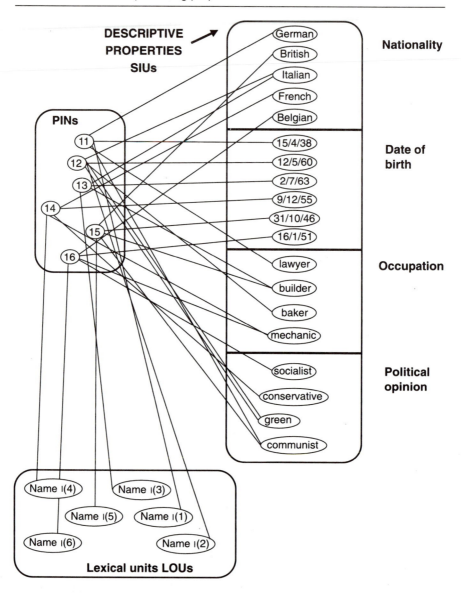

Figure 6.9 Brédart *et al.*'s (1995) interactive activation network

Reproduced with permission

However, this pattern of impairment has never been reported, either in diary studies (Young *et al.*, 1985; Schweich *et al.*, 1992) or in the neuropsychological literature (McKenna and Warrington, 1980; Flude *et al.*, 1989; Semenza and Zettin, 1988; 1989; Lucchelli and de Renzi, 1992; Shallice and Kartsounis, 1993), although see Brennen *et al.* (submitted) and the discussion of this issue in Chapter 5. It is important to appreciate that the pattern of impairment which has never been reported is a preserved ability to name a person in the absence of retrieval of *any* identity-specific semantic information. However, people are sometimes able to name someone while being unable to retrieve one or other characteristic of that person. That is, it is possible to name a person without accessing *all* information about them.

It was therefore crucial to establish:

1 what the effect of attenuating or disconnecting a PIN-name link on the level of activation of semantic information units associated with that PIN would be; and
2 what the effect of attenuating or disconnecting *all* the links connecting semantic information units to a PIN on the level of activation of the name associated with that PIN would be.

The attenuation of the PIN-name connection weight was assumed to simulate impaired lexical access, whereas the attenuation of the PIN-SIUs links was assumed to simulate impaired access to any descriptive property. The critical test was to check whether or not a name still reached a threshold activation when all PIN-SIUs links associated with the target PIN are attenuated or disconnected.

The results of the simulation were as follows. Attenuating the PIN-name links to 50 per cent of their normal weight did not prevent SIUs from reaching their threshold value. The same result was obtained even when the PIN-name links were disconnected completely. By contrast, no name reached the threshold value when the corresponding PIN-SIUs links were disconnected or their connecting strength was attenuated by 50 per cent. In short, this simulation showed that impaired lexical access does not prevent semantic information units from reaching the threshold activation but impairing access to all descriptive properties does prevent lexical access. Thus this set of simulations shows that the architecture presented in Figure 6.6, in which descriptive properties and names are accessed in parallel, does not produce a preserved ability to name in the absence of the retrieval of any semantic information.

The IAC network employed in these simulations produced other interesting results. We noted earlier that when all connections were left intact the course of activation of unique or semantic properties was the same as that of names. However when the PIN-name links were lesioned, unique descriptive properties behaved like other descriptive properties rather than like names. Such preserved access to unique biographical information in the context of an impaired naming ability has been previously reported in neuropsychological literature. Semenza and Zettin (1988) have described an Italian patient who was unable to name any of the faces of celebrities that were presented to him but who was able to recall precise biographical information about these celebrities. In some cases these biographical details consisted of unique properties. For instance, he defined Mr Craxi as 'Prime minister, he is the first socialist holding this position in our country'.

The architecture presented in Figure 6.6 is the base of the integrated model that will be developed in Chapter 8. The main assumptions of this architecture are as follows:

1　Access to descriptive properties and access to names from recognition units is made through token markers which are simple cross-domain and cross-modality gateways.
2　Descriptive properties and names are accessed in parallel from token markers. These first two assumptions are shared with the Burton and Bruce (1992, 1993) model. The other assumption departs from their model.
3　Biographical information is clustered. This assumption is not without precedent. In fact, this idea is closely related to the notion of 'focused memory search' developed by several authors including Anderson and Paulson (1978) and McCloskey and Bigler (1980). The latter authors resorted to the notion of clustered conceptual information in order to understand the paradox of the fan effect. From the observation that experts (i.e. people who know a large number of facts about a given topic) do not show particular difficulty in retrieving facts in their areas of expertise, McCloskey and Bigler (1980) hypothesised that facts stored with a concept are organised into clusters, and that fact retrieval involves a focused search of relevant clusters rather than an unfocused search of all facts stored about a concept.

The implementation of the model in Figure 6.6 in the form of an interactive activation and competition network gave results that are consistent with the empirical data. In particular, this implementation showed that the model can account for the fact that the retrieval of names is harder than the retrieval of descriptive properties, and showed that the model does not necessarily lead to the prediction of a preserved naming ability in the absence of retrieval of any semantic information, although it assumes that names and descriptive properties are accessed in parallel. By running these simulations, Brédart et al.'s (1995) aim was to explore whether it was possible to conceive of an architecture that produces results consistent with empirical data while it assumes a parallel access to names and to conceptual information that defines the identity of known people without including name units and semantic information units in a single pool. Thus the presented IAC network is not to be considered as a model *per se*. It was simply used as a tool to evaluate the framework presented in Figure 6.6. This framework will be extended in Chapter 8.

At the beginning of the present chapter, we mentioned that in most models of speech production words are explicitly represented by a lexical unit (for instance, a lemma or a lexical node) whose fundamental role is to link the level of conceptual features to the level of phonological features. We have followed this position. We do not deny the interest of another way of conceiving of the mapping between the conceptual domain and the phonological domain that has been proposed by some connectionist modellers (Seidenberg and McClelland, 1989; Hinton and Shallice, 1991). Words are not explicitly represented in these models. Rather, word-specific associations between meaning features and phonological features are represented through superimposed patterns of connections. However, our approach essentially remains a classical functional one. In this kind of approach the trilogy *conceptual processing–lexical selection and grammatical encoding–phonological encoding'* appears a reasonable way of conceiving of naming.

Further issues on lexical access to proper names are addressed in Chapter 7.

SUMMARY

In this chapter, we have briefly sketched current psycholinguistic views of lexical access in speech production. We then presented a functional architecture of face naming which is compatible both with these current views of lexical access and with the notion that proper names are pure referring expressions. One important feature of this architecture is that it does not assume that identity-specific semantic information constitutes a necessary pathway to names. Simulations using an interactive activation version of this model produced results consistent with the fact that names are more difficult to retrieve than identity-specific semantic information.

Chapter 7

Comparisons between lexical access for proper names and common names

INTRODUCTION

Models of lexical access for proper names, especially people's names, were discussed in Chapter 6. Specifically, data from studies of speech production were evaluated and concepts from models of speech production incorporated into our functional framework for face naming. An important conclusion from this analysis was that lexical access to both common and proper names should be regarded as a two-stage process in which selection of a lexical item can be distinguished from access to its phonology. In this chapter we shall compare the effects of word or name frequency and age of acquisition on speed of production of common names and proper names. We will then consider whether production of common and proper names involves access to an output lexicon via a common pathway. Finally, the hypothesis that the output lexicon can be accessed directly from word and name recognition units is evaluated.

FREQUENCY SENSITIVITY OF PROPER NAME RETRIEVAL

In Chapter 4 we discussed experiments in which the consequences of surname frequency on processing of seen or heard names was explored (Valentine *et al.*, 1991). This work begs the question of whether *production* of proper names is sensitive to surname frequency. Would subjects be quicker to articulate a high frequency surname in response to seeing a familiar face than they would to produce a low frequency surname or vice versa?

By comparison to the literature on production of common names it might be expected that high frequency surnames would be produced more rapidly than low frequency surnames. Pictures of objects with high frequency names are named more quickly than objects with low frequency names (Oldfield and Wingfield, 1965; Huttenlocher and Kubieck, 1983; Humphreys *et al.*, 1988). However, there are some reasons for caution.

First, naming an object requires production of a common name. When this act is demonstrated to be frequency sensitive, it is affected by the *word* frequency of the name. Naming a familiar face requires production of a proper name. We wish to address the question of whether proper name production is sensitive to *surname* frequency (i.e. an estimate of the number of people in the population who share the surname). As we have seen in Chapter 3, word frequency is analogous to the combined effects of surname frequency and name familiarity rather than surname frequency *per se*. Name familiarity refers to the rated familiarity of an individual's name; for example, the name of a celebrity.

A second reason for caution is that Humphreys *et al.* (1988) found that the effect of word frequency on picture naming was restricted to objects drawn from an object class which has structurally distinct exemplars (e.g. items of furniture). There was no effect of word frequency on naming latency for objects drawn from a structurally similar category (e.g. fruits). In fact, there was a non-significant trend for object names of low word frequency to be produced faster. By any standard, faces constitute a structurally similar category. Humphreys *et al.* interpret their results as evidence for cascade processing in picture naming. That is, activation is being passed from visual processing to lexical processing continuously; visual processing does *not* have to be complete before activation of lexical representations can begin. The effect of word frequency can only be detected when the visual processing is relatively easy (i.e. the objects to be named are structurally dissimilar). If the task requires fine visual discrimination, the effect of word frequency on lexical access is obscured by the time required to complete the visual identification of the object.

The final reason for caution is that Morrison *et al.* (1992) have recently reported evidence that picture naming is not affected by the word frequency of the name at all; instead, the effects are attributable to difference in age of acquisition of the object names. We shall leave this issue aside for the present and discuss age of acquisition in more detail below (see p. 150). Let us first examine the evidence for an effect of surname frequency on RT to name familiar faces.

Naming familiar faces in an experimental setting is a much more difficult task than naming objects; reaction times are variable and lengthy and the proportion of naming errors is high. (Mean RTs are typically in the range 1100ms–1600ms or longer.) Famous faces have to be extremely familiar before they can be named accurately and speedily by a majority of subjects. In order to examine the effect of *surname* frequency it is necessary to instruct subjects to produce the surname only. Although this may be quite natural for some classes of famous faces (e.g. politicians), it is highly artificial for others (e.g. pop stars). Subjects would often produce part of the first name in error.

Brédart and Valentine (1992, Experiment 3) examined the effect of surname frequency on RT to name famous faces. In an attempt to collect suitable data, subjects named all of the faces in the experiment twice before any reaction times were collected. No effect of surname frequency on naming latency was found. This null result is not convincing evidence that there is no effect of surname frequency on proper name production, as Brédart and Valentine acknowledge. It is possible that the need to repeat stimuli would have reduced any effect of surname frequency. It is known that repetition reduces the effect of word frequency on lexical decision time (Scarborough et al., 1977; Norris, 1984). Brédart and Valentine's study was primarily concerned with monitoring of face naming errors. The naming latency experiment was carried out as a check of whether frequency sensitivity of name production could account for results obtained in a different experiment (see Chapter 8). A more powerful design might have been possible had the stimuli originally been selected for this purpose.

The practical difficulties in collecting reliable naming latency data for famous faces led us to employ a strategy of teaching subjects surnames of unfamiliar faces (Valentine and Moore, in press). Subjects were presented with a set of thirty-two unfamiliar female faces and taught a surname only of each face. The faces were divided into a set of typical faces and a set of distinctive faces on the basis of subjective ratings of distinctiveness obtained from different subjects. Half of the surnames taught were extremely high frequency surnames (at least one occurrence in every 500 entries in the telephone directory) and the remaining surnames were of low frequency (less than one occurrence for every 50,000 entries). High and low frequency surnames were matched on their initial phoneme and word length. The assignment of surnames to faces was counter-balanced so that chance face–name pairings would not produce anomalous results. After having learned to name all of the faces to a criterion of naming the entire set of thirty-two faces correctly on two successive trials, naming latency was measured using a voice key to record naming latency to slides of faces presented by a projection tachistoscope. The inclusion of distinctiveness and surname frequency as factors makes the experimental design analogous to Humphreys et al.'s (1988) study of the effects of structural similarity and word frequency on object naming. The entire procedure was repeated on three successive days to ensure that the subjects would be highly practised in naming the faces.

Two dependent variables were measured: (1) the number of trials to criterion to learn the face–name associations, and (2) naming latency in the confrontation naming task. Both measures yielded remarkably similar results. Subjects learned the names of distinctive faces in fewer trials than they learned the names of typical faces. They also named distinctive faces more quickly than typical faces. Subjects learned high frequency surnames in fewer trials than they took to learn low frequency names. They also produced high frequency surnames more quickly than low frequency surnames. The effects of face distinctiveness and surname frequency were clearly additive in both measures. Naming latency was faster on each successive day, but the effects of distinctiveness and surname frequency on naming latency were undiminished by repeated testing; there was no interaction between these effects and the day of testing. The effects of both distinctiveness and surname frequency on the number of trials required to reach the criterion of learning was absent on the second and third days. However, this interaction with day is due to a ceiling effect. On the second and third days, subjects needed little, if any, further training to reach the criterion of naming all of the faces correctly twice in succession.

Teaching surnames of unfamiliar faces has demonstrated an effect of surname frequency on the latency to name faces and therefore on production of proper names. The use of a learning strategy has enabled extraneous variables to be controlled and a powerful manipulation of surname frequency to be employed. This experiment also extends evidence of the effect of distinctiveness on familiar face recognition to a naming task. The results obtained are directly analogous to Humphreys *et al.*'s (1988) study of object naming in which they found that objects with high frequency names were named more quickly than objects with low frequency names. However, in the case of naming faces the effect of surname frequency was additive with a manipulation of the ease of visual identification (facial distinctiveness). Humphreys *et al.*, however, found the effect of word frequency interacted with the effect of the structural similarity of objects. This result could be interpreted as evidence that the processing stages in naming faces are strictly sequential but the analogous processes in object naming operate in cascade.

Use of a paradigm in which subjects learned surnames of unfamiliar faces allowed precise control over the familiarity of the faces and frequency of the surname. However, the procedure rather lacks ecological validity. Would subjects name familiar faces of people with high frequency surnames more quickly, if the names and identity-specific semantics of the people had been acquired in everyday life? Valentine and Moore (in press) addressed this issue by exploring the effect of surname frequency on the latency to name famous faces. This experiment produced some surprising results.

Forty-eight famous faces were selected on the basis of subjective ratings of distinctiveness, familiarity and subjects' ability to name them. Faces were assigned to distinctive or typical groups with high or low frequency surnames. The twelve faces in each group were matched on their mean subjective familiarity ratings and number of letters in the surname. Surnames which are also words or have irregular pronunciation were avoided. The balance of males and females and the occupational categories from which the celebrities were drawn were approximately matched across conditions.

Subjects first read through a list of the full names of all of the celebrities included in the experiment in order to acquaint themselves with the set of famous faces used and to screen out any subjects who were not familiar with any of the celebrities. Subjects then named each face as quickly as possible producing the surname only. Digitised photographs of the faces were presented on a computer screen. Naming latencies were recorded by the computer using a throat microphone. The experimenter judged whether the naming response was adequate and 'cancelled' any inadequate response logged. If an acceptable naming response was not made to the face on the first attempt it was included again at the end of the block. Four blocks were presented and one acceptable naming response was recorded from each subject for each face in each block.

The effects of distinctiveness and surname frequency were consistent across all four blocks. There was no evidence that either effect diminished with repetition. Distinctive faces were named more quickly than were typical faces. This result was the same as that obtained for production of learned surnames to previously unfamiliar faces. However, low frequency surnames were produced faster than high frequency surnames. This effect is the opposite to that which had been obtained in the learning experiment. A further difference was that when subjects named famous faces, the effects of distinctiveness and surname frequency were interactive. The effect of surname frequency was found for distinctive faces but not for typical faces; and the effect of distinctiveness was found for faces with low frequency surnames but not for faces with high frequency surnames.

As famous faces had been used in this experiment it had not been possible to match the initial phoneme of the surnames for the sets of low and high frequency surnames. It is possible therefore that the differences in naming latency obtained could be attributed to differences in articulation or measurement of the naming latency. For example, a throat microphone was used so if the initial phoneme was unvoiced there could be a short delay in the response of the microphone. In order to check for this possibility the subjects took part in a delayed naming experiment immediately after the face naming experiment, in which the surnames of the celebrities used in the previous experiment served as stimuli. The subjects saw a surname on the computer screen and were instructed to prepare to say it aloud as quickly as possible. The subject pressed a space bar to indicate when they were ready and after an unpredictable delay of between one and three seconds, a 'go' signal was presented on the screen and the subject said the surname aloud as quickly as possible. If the sets of names did not differ in the time required to initiate articulation, as measured by the equipment, no effects should be found. The subjects were given as much time as was required to prepare for articulation, so that if lexical access is the stage that gives rise to frequency effects no effect should be found in this task. However, statistically significant effects were found in this experiment.

The data obtained in the face naming experiment were re-analysed using the difference between the face naming and the delayed surname reading latency for each condition. Thus face naming latencies were corrected for any differences in articulation speed between the items in the conditions of the experiment. However, the results of the face naming experiment were essentially the same as those found using the 'uncorrected' data. Distinctive faces with low frequency surnames were named faster than distinctive faces with high frequency surnames, but no effect of surname frequency was found on naming latency of typical faces. The effect of distinctiveness was only observed for faces with low frequency surnames. These data are shown in Figure 7.1.

It was confirmed that the locus of the effect of surname frequency was subsequent to the stage of visual identification of the face by using the same famous faces in a face familiarity decision task. The faces were presented mixed at random with forty-eight unfamiliar faces. Subjects had to decide whether each face was familiar. As would be expected, familiarity decisions to distinctive faces were faster than familiarity decisions to typical faces, but there was no effect of surname frequency. In summary, the effect of surname frequency was observed in a naming task but not in a task that did not require access to the celebrities' names.

At this point, let us take stock of the comparison between object naming and face naming studies. Broadly, the effects of distinctiveness were as expected: names were associated with distinctive unfamiliar faces in fewer trials than they were to typical faces; distinctive faces were recognised more quickly than typical faces, regardless of whether they were famous or previously unfamiliar faces. This effect is analogous to the effect of structural similarity in the object naming task (Humphreys et al., 1988), in which subjects were faster to name objects drawn from a structurally distinct category.

The comparison between word frequency and surname frequency is less straightforward. The latency to name previously unfamiliar faces was faster if the surname was of high name frequency than if the surname was of low frequency. This effect would have been expected by analogy to object naming tasks in which names of high word frequency are produced more quickly than object names of low word frequency. One difference is that the effects of surname frequency and face distinctiveness in naming unfamiliar faces were additive but the effects of structural similarity and word frequency in object naming were interactive (Humphreys et al., 1988). A rather artificial aspect of learning names of

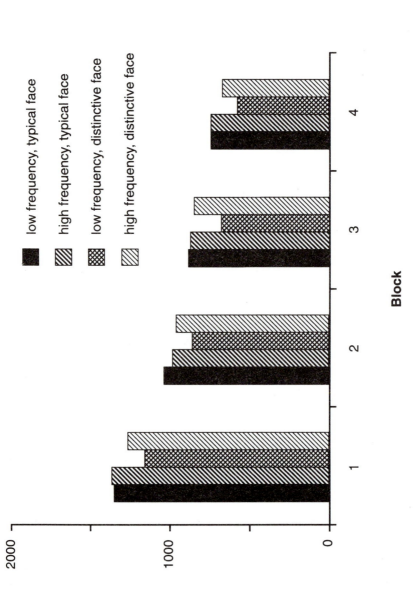

Figure 7.1 Mean naming latency of famous faces minus mean latency to articulate surnames as a function of facial distinctiveness, surname frequency and experimental block

previously unfamiliar faces is that the faces did not have any identity-specific semantic information (or at least shared the same semantic information of 'A face in the face name learning experiment'). This may make the nature of the processing rather atypical of face naming in everyday life; however, it is not clear whether this aspect of the task would affect the interaction between visual and lexical processing. A further possibility is that the task is processed as a paired associate learning task and is not processed by the person recognition system at all.

When the naming latency of famous faces was measured, the effects of surname frequency and distinctiveness were interactive. The nature of the interaction was the same as that found between the effects of word frequency and structural similarity by Humphreys *et al.* (1988). This result is consistent with the suggestion that the results obtained in the face name learning experiment may be unusual. However, it was found that subjects were faster to name celebrities with low frequency surnames than they were to name celebrities with high frequency surnames. This effect of surname frequency is the opposite of that which would be expected on the basis of the face name learning experiment and an analogy with the effect of word frequency on object naming. The result begs the questions of how the differences in the effect of surname frequency on face naming in the two experiments can be explained and which effect is more representative of face naming in everyday life.

Valentine and Moore (in press) suggest that an explanation for the apparent contradiction of the results of these two experiments may lie in a failure to match name familiarity in the learning task. Subjects are far more likely to have encountered people with the high frequency surnames than they are to have encountered people with the low frequency surnames. Therefore, the high frequency surnames will be familiar lexical items, represented by word recognition units, but low frequency surnames are much less likely to be represented by a word recognition unit. As Brennen (1993) has pointed out, learning an unfamiliar surname requires both learning the phonology and learning the association between the name and face. Therefore, a comparison between associating high and low frequency surnames to faces is similar to comparing learning of an association between a word and a face with an association between a non-word and a face. It is not surprising that there is an advantage for familiar items.

Let us assume that name familiarity is negatively related to naming latency, but surname frequency *per se* (i.e. the number of familiar people with the same surname) is positively related to naming latency. That is, the more familiar a surname, the faster it can be accessed in the output lexicon and the faster a new association to a previously unfamiliar face can be learned. But the more individuals who share that surname, the slower it can be accessed and the more difficult it is to form a new association. When associations are learned between unfamiliar faces and surnames, the advantage for low frequency surnames may be swamped by a larger effect of surname familiarity because the low frequency surnames are more likely to be entirely unfamiliar than common surnames. In short, in the learning task, confounding of surname frequency with the familiarity of known individuals who may share a surname gave an apparent advantage for high frequency names when surname-unfamiliar face associations were taught during the experiment. However, in the experiment which required famous faces to be named, name familiarity *per se* was much better matched (familiarity of the celebrities was matched) and the true effect of surname frequency was revealed as an advantage for low frequency surnames (i.e. surnames more likely to be unique to an individual).

In order to test this interpretation of the face–name learning experiment it is necessary to teach high or low frequency surnames which are matched in their familiarity. It is impossible for high frequency surnames to be unfamiliar, so low frequency surnames which are already familiar must be used to achieve the required match. In a further experiment, Valentine and Moore (in press) used the surnames of celebrities whose pictures were used in their experiment on famous face naming and taught these surnames to the unfamiliar faces used in the face–name learning task. The familiarity of celebrities who have these surnames was matched across sets of high and low frequency surnames. In this experiment the expected effects of distinctiveness were found. Surnames of distinctive faces were learned in fewer trials and then produced on confrontation more quickly than surnames of typical faces. However, there was no effect of surname frequency on either learning or naming latency.

At first sight, faster naming latency for low frequency surnames might have been expected, as was found when naming famous faces. However, in the learning task there is a highly familiar celebrity who shares each of the surnames learned. Thus even the low frequency surnames are likely to act like high frequency surnames. In other words, having matched familiarity, the effect of surname frequency would have been very much weakened. Valentine and Moore conclude that it is impossible to select surname stimuli to demonstrate an advantage in naming latency for low frequency surnames in a learning task. However, they point out that all their data are consistent with this conclusion. They interpret the data on latency to name famous faces as being more representative of face naming in everyday life than face–name learning tasks.

The results of these face naming experiments provide a challenge to current models of face naming. Why should there be an advantage in the speed of production of object names of high word frequency but an advantage for people's surnames of low frequency in the population? There is no a priori basis to predict an advantage for low frequency surnames from the Valentine *et al.* (1991) framework. The model proposed by Burke *et al.* (1991) seems to be the best candidate to provide an a priori theoretical account of the effects of surname frequency on production latency reported by Valentine and Moore. This model was discussed in Chapter 5.

AN ACCOUNT OF FREQUENCY SENSITIVITY OF LEXICAL ACCESS IN TERMS OF NODE STRUCTURE THEORY

Burke *et al.* (1991) make a comparison between production of common nouns and proper names in terms of node structure theory (NST). The architecture for lexical access to a common noun is illustrated in Figure 5.1a and for a proper name in Figure 5.1b (see p. 106). According to NST, priming is passed along the links from node to node. Priming received at a node from many links will summate. Equally, priming can dissipate via links connected to inactive nodes. The spread of priming is sub-threshold activation in the network. The node which has most priming among nodes within a level (e.g. lexical nodes) will be selected for activation. In the case of lexical nodes the activated node will select the word for articulation and in turn priming will be passed to the syllable nodes in the phonological system.

Burke *et al.* (1991) used NST to explain why proper names are particularly vulnerable to tip-of-the-tongue (TOT) states. When a common noun is to be produced, for example when naming a picture of a bush (Figure 5.1a), the associated semantic nodes receive priming. Each semantic node passes priming to the lexical level which summates at the lexical node for 'bush'. The fan-in of links from semantic nodes to lexical nodes makes retrieval of common nouns robust. If any one semantic–lexical link were to suffer temporary transmission deficit (e.g. due to infrequent use) priming would be passed by several other links. Note also that on each occasion when a bush is named, the same lexical node is activated (i.e. lexical nodes for common nouns are of types, not tokens). Therefore, frequent access to the word 'bush' will lead to a strengthening of the links between the appropriate semantic nodes and lexical node. The strengthening of connections with frequent use can account for the advantage for object names of high word frequency on latency of object naming.

When naming a famous face the appropriate identity-specific semantic nodes pass priming to a proper noun phrase node. The proper noun phrase nodes are connected to separate lexical nodes representing the initial and family surnames. There is a single link from a proper noun phrase node to a lexical node representing the surname. In the case of proper names, therefore, there is no summation of priming at the lexical nodes. Any transmission deficit on the single proper noun phrase node/family proper name node link will result in a TOT state or other failure to recall the name. In the case of surnames for which more than one individual is known, rather than having a fan-in of connections to the lexical node, there is a fan-out of connections to proper noun phrase nodes for other familiar individuals. In the situation illustrated in Figure 5.1b, priming at the lexical node representing the family proper name Bush will pass to the proper noun phrase node for Kate Bush. Lexical nodes representing high frequency surnames are likely to have a fan-out connected to more proper name phrase nodes than are lexical nodes representing low frequency surnames. Therefore, the fan-out at the lexical nodes could account for the advantage for low frequency surnames observed in naming famous faces. Node structure theory would account for the effect in terms of dissipation of priming; however, an interactive activation and competition model might produce a similar effect (cf. Burton *et al.*, 1990). A possible mechanism in an interactive activation model would be that the fan-out at the lexical node would activate competing proper noun phrase nodes, which would in turn inhibit the activation of the proper noun phrase node for the target name via inhibitory connections between nodes in the same functional pool. For example, if George Bush's face was seen, activation of the proper noun phrase node for Kate Bush would inhibit activation of the proper noun phrase node for George Bush.

AGE OF ACQUISITION AND PROPER NAME PROCESSING

In a recent paper, Morrison *et al.* (1992) argue that object naming is *not* influenced by word frequency. Instead, the effect which has been attributed to word frequency in previous studies can, in fact, be better accounted for by the age of acquisition of the object name. In a re-analysis of the data from Oldfield and Wingfield's (1965) study, Morrison *et al.* (1992) demonstrated that there was no independent effect of word frequency on object naming latency when the effect of age of acquisition has been taken into account. This view was supported by a new study of object naming latency. They also show that no effect of age of acquisition or word frequency is found in a task which requires subjects to classify objects as natural or man-made, which supports their conclusion that the effect of age of acquisition arises from the requirement to produce an object's name.

Generally, age of acquisition is highly correlated with word frequency. The estimates of age of acquisition used by Morrison *et al.* were based on subjective ratings. The estimates of word frequency were based on samples of written English. Therefore, neither the measures of age of acquisition nor word frequency are ideal. The high correlation between the two factors makes separation of the two effects even more problematic. The effects of word frequency in a wide variety of tasks have been studied in a great many investigations. However, age of acquisition is *not* one of the factors usually controlled. Therefore, the possibility exists that the effects attributed to word frequency in studies of word recognition and naming tasks, as well as object naming tasks, are in reality effects of age of acquisition. Such a possibility has important implications for studies of word recognition, speech production, aphasia and cognitive models (including connectionist models) of language processing. Much of the theoretical work and models in these areas have been developed to account for the established effects of word frequency. Little attention has been paid to modelling the effects of age of acquisition.

Given that the studies of name frequency described above were inspired by an analogy with word frequency, Morrison *et al.*'s (1992) data begs the question of the status of the observed effects of surname frequency on both name processing (reviewed in Chapter 4) and name production. In terms of the relationship between frequency and age of acquisition, proper names are an extremely interesting class of stimuli. In the case of common nouns (e.g. object names), high frequency words tend to be acquired earlier than low frequency words. Names of common objects are acquired relatively early in life. However, we continue to acquire proper names throughout our lives. Therefore, many proper names will be acquired a lot later in life. For example, most people will have acquired the surnames Yeltsin and Clinton more recently than the names Monroe and Presley, even though these are all low frequency surnames by our definition.

As we continue to encounter new proper names more frequently in adult life than new words, studies of the effect of surname frequency are less likely to be confounded with age of acquisition than studies of the effect of word frequency. Having said this, it is of course likely that high frequency surnames will on average be encountered earlier than low frequency surnames. Simply because more people have high frequency surnames, an individual is likely to encounter any given high frequency surname early than any given low frequency surname. Can the effects of surname frequency reported by Valentine *et al.* (1991) and Valentine and Moore (in press) be explained by confounding with age of acquisition of surnames?

For tasks involving the naming of famous faces or a familiarity decision to written or spoken names, the results are unlikely to be attributable to age of acquisition. In these tasks subjects were faster to respond to or produce *low* frequency surnames. The expected correlation between surname frequency and age of acquisition of surnames would lead to the opposite apparent effect of surname frequency in these tasks. The remaining tasks studied (nationality decision to names, naming latency of surnames and naming latency of faces for which surnames had been learned) all showed slower reaction time only for processing or retrieval of low frequency surnames which were unfamiliar in the sense that they were not necessarily the names of a celebrity. Although we have interpreted these results in terms of surname frequency and familiarity, the effect could be described as one of age of acquisition. Some of these surnames could be novel to some or all of the subjects or at least acquired later. Therefore, low frequency, unfamiliar surnames could be described as surnames with a late age of acquisition. However, this really only amounts to a re-description rather than a reinterpretation of the effect.

Given the ease with which surname frequency and age of acquisition of surnames can be separated, proper name processing is an ideal area in which to explore the effects of age of acquisition. First, age of acquisition may not affect proper name processing in the same way as it affects production of common nouns. This in itself would be a very interesting result, as it would demonstrate psychological reality for the linguistic and philosophical distinctions between common nouns and proper names. On the other hand, if age of acquisition does have a similar effect on production of proper names as it does on production of common nouns, some rather counter-intuitive predictions can be made. Would subjects be faster to name, say, a cartoon character known from early childhood than they would be to name a current world leader (assuming that factors such as face distinctiveness and familiarity can be controlled)? Future research in this area could make a valuable contribution to our understanding of differences and similarities between processing of proper names and common names.

ARE COMMON PATHWAYS INVOLVED IN THE PRODUCTION OF PROPER NAMES AND PRODUCTION OF COMMON NAMES?

In Chapter 4 we discussed experiments in which words which also occur as surnames were used to explore the relationship between proper name and common name processing (Valentine *et al.*, 1993). It was found that lexical decision to a word primed familiarity decision to the name of a celebrity which included the same word as their surname (e.g. bush–George Bush). Repetition priming was also found if the order of the tasks was reversed. This pattern of results was interpreted as evidence that processing of proper names and common names automatically activate representations of the alternative meaning of the stimulus. That is to say that seeing a word which can serve as a surname automatically activates representations of the names of people who have that surname and, conversely, seeing the name of somebody whose surname is a word will automatically activate the semantics of the word.

Valentine *et al.* (1995) used exactly the same logic to explore the relationship between production of proper names and common names. Does access to the lexical representation of 'bush' when reading aloud the written word require access to the same lexical representation, via the same pathway, as that required to name a picture of the previous president of the USA?

Valentine *et al.* (1995) carried out a series of repetition priming experiments. In all of these the test phase was identical. Subjects were required to name a series of famous faces by articulating their surname only as quickly and as accurately as possible. Naming latency was recorded by use of a voice key. Within the list were two sets of twelve famous faces matched for familiarity and distinctiveness of their faces and the length, word frequency and name frequency of their surname. All these celebrities had surnames which were also English words (e.g. wood, sleep, fish). The surnames of one of the matched set of items were included in the prime task. The task during the prime phase differed between experiments.

In the first experiment, subjects read aloud English words as quickly as possible during the prime task. Thus, subjects had to articulate common names during the prime phase and proper names (surnames) during the test phase although, for the primed items, the same vocal response was produced in both phases. No effect of repetition priming was found. Thus, seeing the word 'bush' and reading it aloud did not prime the latency to say 'Bush' in response to George Bush's face.

In subsequent experiments, subjects were told that all the words that they would see during the prime phase occurred as surnames (as indeed they did, although some were very low frequency as surnames). However, even after having had their attention drawn to the presence of surnames in the prime phase, no statistically significant effect of repetition priming was found. Similarly, no effect of repetition priming was observed if subjects had produced the same responses during the prime phase in response to completing an incomplete sentence. Thus it appears that forcing subjects to process the stimulus word to a semantic level did not induce repetition priming.

These experiments appear to indicate that there is no effect of repetition priming from production of a common name on to production of a proper name, even when the tasks require the same naming response. This result contrasts with the effect of repetition priming found between recognition of common names and proper names (Valentine *et al.*, 1993). However, in order to justify this conclusion it is necessary to establish that the production of a proper name during the prime phase would prime naming a face in the test phase.

In a further experiment the prime task was the same as in the first experiment described, except that full names of celebrities were presented. For example, instead of seeing the word 'bush' and saying 'bush' during the prime task, subjects saw 'George Bush' and said 'Bush'. During the test the same task of naming faces was used. In this case, a significant effect of repetition priming was observed. Subsequent experiments showed that a naming response during the prime phase was not required to produce an effect of repetition priming on face naming latency. Effects of repetition priming were observed from classification of names of celebrities according to their occupational category (indicated by a vocal response; for example, 'politician') and from name familiarity decision during the prime phase. Although the absolute size of the repetition priming effect suggested that a greater effect was obtained when the names had been read aloud during the prime phase, statistical analysis showed there was no difference in the degree of priming found between tasks in which a full name was presented during the prime phase.

As it appears that a naming response during the prime phase is not necessary to produce a repetition priming effect, the question arises: is a naming response during the test phase necessary? In other words, is lexical access the stage of face naming which is being primed or is the facilitation occurring at some early stage of person recognition? Relevant data have been reported in two previous studies. First, Bruce and Valentine (1985) found that reading a full name aloud *did* prime the perceptual threshold required to subsequently name the face of the celebrity, but the same prime task *did not* prime a familiarity decision to the face of the celebrity at test. These data suggest that a naming response is required at test if reading a name is to prime face naming. Data reported by Ellis *et al.* (1987) support a similar conclusion. They found that classifying names of celebrities according to their occupation did not prime subsequent familiarity decision to the celebrities' faces.

The data reported by Bruce and Valentine (1985) and Ellis *et al.* (1987) show that familiarity decision to a face at test is not primed by prior exposure to the celebrity's name. But the data from Valentine *et al.* (1995) and Bruce and Valentine (1985) show that a naming response at test *is* primed by prior exposure to the name. These data leave open the question of whether a semantic classification would be primed at test. In order to answer this question, Valentine *et al.* carried out a further experiment in which subjects articulated the surname of a visually presented full name during the prime phase and classified faces of celebrities according to their occupation by a vocal response during the test phase. No effect of repetition priming was observed. Taken together, these data indicate that the effects of repetition priming from seeing a full name on to face naming are located at, or subsequent to, the stage of lexical access for the name. On the other hand, the effects cannot be attributed to the stage of articulation of the phonology of the surname as no effect of repetition priming was observed when the same phonology was produced in response to reading a common name.

The framework for processing people's names proposed by Valentine *et al.* (1991) was discussed at length in Chapter 4 (see Figure 4.1, p. 60). It was concluded that the framework was able to account for the available experimental and neuropsychological data on the comprehension of seen and heard names of people. Can the framework also account for the pattern of repetition priming between processing names or words and naming famous faces reviewed above?

Following Burton *et al.* (1990) and the view that we adopted in Chapter 4, we shall assume that repetition priming results from an increase in the weight of links, which are in turn increased following simultaneous activation of nodes (or units) connected by the link. The Valentine *et al.* (1991) framework can account for the lack of repetition priming from reading a word to naming a face, even when the same phonology is produced because entirely separate pathways are activated by the two tasks up to the point of accessing the output lexicon. Reading a word will pass activation via word recognition units (WRUs)–semantics–output lexicon (or via a direct route bypassing semantics). In naming a face, activation is passed from an active face recognition unit (FRU) via the person identity node (PIN) to the output lexicon. The important point is that the output lexicon is accessed via *different* links in the two tasks. Therefore, there is no mechanism whereby an increased weight on a link can produce repetition priming.

If a name is read aloud, activation of the appropriate word recognition units will pass activation via a name recognition unit to the person identity node and then access the output lexicon via the link from the PIN. This is the same link that must be used to access the output lexicon when a face is named, so an increase in the weight of the link between the PIN and the output lexicon provides a mechanism for repetition priming from reading aloud a name to naming a face. Alternatively, when reading aloud a name the output lexicon could be accessed direct from the NRU. In this case the PIN would also have been activated by the NRU. The appropriate PIN and the corresponding unit in the output lexicon would be simultaneously active, resulting in an increase in the weight on the link from the PIN to the output lexicon. Therefore, repetition priming would be observed whether the output lexicon was accessed via the PIN or direct from the NRU.

The experimental data reviewed above showed that a naming response during the prime phase was not necessary to obtain an effect of repetition priming. This aspect of the data could be accounted for if it is argued that access to the output lexicon is mandatory and automatic when a name recognition unit is activated. A great deal of evidence suggests that this assumption may not be justified in the case of recognition of faces. We will often know that a face is familiar without being able to retrieve the name. However, in the Valentine *et al.* (1991) framework the output lexicon can be accessed direct from name recognition units but not from face recognition units. There is thus a functional difference in the access to the output lexicon from names and faces. In view of this direct route it is reasonable to assume mandatory access from names but not faces. In the experiments in which a familiarity decision or occupational decision, rather than a naming response, is made during the prime phase the NRU and PIN must be activated. (Burton *et al.* (1990) assume that familiarity decisions are based on the level of activation at the PIN.) The active NRU will pass activation to the output lexicon via the direct link. As the name represented in the output lexicon and the PIN will be simultaneously active, the weight of the appropriate PIN–output lexicon will be increased giving rise to repetition priming, even though the PIN–output lexicon may not have been the sole source of activation in the output lexicon.

It would be possible to test directly whether activation of the output lexicon by a route other than the PIN (e.g. a direct route from the name recognition units) during the prime phase of a repetition priming experiment is necessary to observe a priming effect. As has been pointed out, there is assumed to be no direct access to the output lexicon from face recognition units. If access to the output lexicon is not mandatory once the PIN has been activated, a familiarity decision to a celebrity's face should not prime RT to read their surname aloud if their full name is subsequently presented. However, articulating the surname during the prime phase should produce a repetition priming effect. These predictions provide a means of testing our interpretation of the repetition priming experiments described above.

Recall that no repetition priming was observed when the prime task involved reading a single word *even when the subjects were informed that the words were surnames*. The account of repetition priming offered makes a prediction of a clear limitation to this effect. If the single word is sufficient to unambiguously activate a single NRU, repetition priming should be observed. 'Thatcher' is a good example of a single surname that might be interpreted as having a single referent by many people and which is also a word. Thus repetition priming would be more likely to be found under these conditions for low frequency surnames. Valentine *et al.* (1995) did not manipulate the frequency of surnames (other than matching it across sets of items). Therefore, an interaction between surname frequency and repetition priming in such an experiment is a further prediction derived from the framework that remains to be tested.

One issue which the experiments reported by Valentine *et al.* (1995) does not address directly is that of whether common and proper names which share the same phonology are represented by the same unit or node in the output lexicon. In Chapter 6 we argued that the output lexicon can be subdivided into a semantic lexicon and a phonological lexicon. A proper name and a common name require separate units in the semantic lexicon since they need different syntactic markers (i.e. proper name phrase versus common noun). However, there could be a common representation in the phonological lexicon. The finding that production of a common name does not prime production of a proper name with the same phonology is consistent with separate representations in the output lexicon(s). If a single representation is shared in either the phonological lexicon or in both lexicons, the common pathways subsequent to the single unit or node cannot be the primary source of repetition priming observed in the experiments reviewed above.

The Valentine *et al.* framework assumes that the output lexicon can be accessed direct from word recognition units and name recognition units. The latter link played a key role in accounting for the repetition priming of face naming. In the following section we evaluate evidence against direct links from word and name recognition units, and consider whether a sub-lexical route could play the role assigned to a direct route in the account of repetition priming described above.

IS THERE A DIRECT LINK FROM RECOGNITION UNITS TO LEXICAL OUTPUT CODES FOR WORDS AND PROPER NAMES?

It has been widely believed that there is a direct, non-semantic, lexical route for reading or repeating spoken words. That is to say that lexical output codes can be accessed directly from visual or auditory word recognition units or logogens without mediation via the semantic system. (See, for example, models of reading proposed by Morton and Patterson, 1980; Ellis and Young, 1988.) However, direct access to lexical output codes is not believed to exist for object or face processing (e.g. Bruce and Young, 1986). Thus names of objects and faces can only be retrieved by access via the semantic system.

Is there a direct link from word recognition units to lexical output codes?

The main line of evidence to support the existence of a direct lexical route for reading comes from neuropsychological investigations of patients who, despite severe impairment in their ability to understand written words, can nevertheless read them aloud. If these patients were applying orthography–phonology conversion strategies to read aloud words that were apparently non-words, they would make regularisation errors in reading aloud irregular words. For example, the correct pronunciation of 'leopard' or 'yacht' could not be derived from orthography–phonology conversion strategies. However, some patients have been reported who can correctly read aloud irregular words which they cannot understand adequately (e.g. Schwartz *et al.*, 1980; Bub *et al.*, 1985). It has been argued that as irregular words cannot be read correctly using orthography–phonology conversion strategies and these patients show severe impairment in their ability to understand the meaning of these words, these cases provide evidence of a non-semantic, lexical route.

Ellis and Young (1988) point out that, although the suggestion of a direct link from the visual input lexicon to the output lexicon has been widely accepted, it is possible that reading aloud in these cases is mediated by a semantic route. The semantic system could mediate the flow of information from the input lexicon to the output lexicon, although the results of semantic processing may not become available to the patient to respond appropriately in a classification or other semantic task. Hillis and Caramazza (1991) argue that, although the possibility of a direct route cannot be excluded by the available neuropsychological evidence, a case study that they report and a reinterpretation of the cases previously reported in the literature do not *require* that a direct route be postulated. Instead they suggest that the case studies are better interpreted as evidence for reading that is mediated by partial preservation of some semantic knowledge and partial cues to pronunciation obtained from orthography–phonology conversion strategies.

Hillis and Caramazza (1991) proposed a 'summation hypothesis' of the normal reading process. It is assumed that representations in the output lexicon which are semantically related to the stimulus word receive activation passed via the semantic system in proportion to the degree of their semantic relation with the stimulus. In parallel, orthography–phonology conversion strategies activate representations in the output lexicon in proportion to their phonological similarity to the possible pronunciation of a stimulus word. The activation from these two sources is summed in the output lexicon and the item passed for articulation would be the first item to reach its activation threshold. For example, the stimulus word 'girl' would activate the features represented in the semantic system corresponding to 'young', 'human' and 'female'. The semantic feature of 'young' would activate to some extent the lexical output codes for 'girl', 'boy', 'lamb', 'fawn', etc. The semantic feature of 'female' might activate the lexical output codes for 'woman', 'girl', 'daughter', 'ewe', 'doe', etc., and the semantic feature of 'human' would pass activation to output codes for 'woman', 'man', 'girl', 'boy', etc. As the lexical output code for 'girl' is receiving activation from all three of these semantic features it will become the most highly activated representation in the output lexicon and will reach its threshold activation faster than the competitor items and be passed to the later stages of speech production. In the normal undamaged system, activation via the semantic system alone, with no contribution from orthography–phonology conversion strategies, will be sufficiently precise for the correct response to be selected.

Hillis and Caramazza (1991) apply their 'summation hypothesis' to the case of patients who are unable to comprehend written words which they are able to read aloud. As was noted above, the existence of patients who can correctly read aloud irregularly pronounced words that they cannot understand provides critical evidence for the existence of a direct, lexical route for reading. According to the summation hypothesis reading ability might exceed comprehension ability, even in the case of irregular words, if there is some preserved semantic processing, but it is insufficient to respond appropriately in a semantic classification task. To take the example used above, a patient might know that 'girl' specifies the property 'human', but be unable to choose between a picture of a boy and a girl in a test of comprehension. However, the representation of 'girl' in the output lexicon would receive some activation via the semantic route along with other entries connected to the semantic property 'human'. The representation of 'girl' would also receive some activation from orthography–phonology conversion strategies. Even if the phonetic specification was also incomplete, partial information about the initial and final phoneme, for example, would be sufficient to allow 'girl' to be selected for articulation. This process would also work for irregular words. For example, Hillis and Caramazza report a case study of a patient, JJ, who could only describe a sword as a weapon but could read 'sword' aloud correctly.

Hillis and Caramazza (1991) report a detailed investigation of JJ's reading and comprehension abilities. In one task, JJ was asked to read aloud a word and then choose a synonym from an array which included a semantically related foil. If JJ had pronounced a word correctly, he always selected either the correct synonym or a semantically related foil (e.g. 'blossom' for 'nectar' and 'nap' for 'lullaby'). In a further task, JJ defined each word and then read it aloud. JJ pronounced correctly all the words for which his definition revealed at least partial comprehension, including irregular words (e.g. have, sword). JJ also pronounced correctly half of the words for which he could provide no semantic information at all. Analysis of these words showed that he could correctly pronounce words for which orthographic–phonology conversion procedures might be expected to give the correct pronunciation, although this did include three regular words with inconsistently pronounced rhymes (e.g. loom). In contrast, JJ could not correctly pronounce any exception words for which he could not give any definition at all.

Hillis and Caramazza (1991) conclude that the pattern of comprehension and reading deficits shown by JJ are consistent with the summation hypothesis. This hypothesis predicts that exception words can only be read aloud correctly if there is at least partial comprehension, but regular words can be pronounced without any activation being passed by a semantic route. Hillis and Caramazza point out that postulation of a direct, non-semantic lexical route for reading does not explain why pronunciation of exception words should be less accurate than pronunciation of regular words, as found in JJ's case. If pronunciation is being mediated by direct access to the output lexicon, reading ability should not be affected by the regularity of a word's spelling. Therefore, the summation hypothesis makes a prediction which has been confirmed, and which the direct route hypothesis can only explain in a *post-hoc* manner. Hillis and Caramazza go on to analyse the case studies of other patients reported in the literature who show superior abilities of pronunciation to comprehension of irregular words. They claim that, in each case, the possibility that there is some preservation of semantic mediation of access to the output lexicon cannot be excluded. In conclusion, Hillis and Caramazza pose a strong challenge, and propose an appealing alternative to the non-semantic, lexical route for reading.

Is there a direct link from name recognition units to lexical output codes?

Valentine *et al.* (1991) showed a direct link from name recognition units to lexical output codes in their model of word, name and face processing. Two reasons were given for including this route. First, the link is analogous to the direct route from word recognition units to the output lexicon commonly included in models of word recognition. However, as discussed above, the evidence for this link is itself somewhat dubious. Second, Young *et al.* (1986a, 1988a) present evidence for parallel access from written names to semantic information and name output codes. Young *et al.* (1988a) found that when presented with the faces of two celebrities, subjects were slower to decide that they had the same first name than they were to decide that they had the same occupation. When written surnames were presented, there was no difference in RT to make decisions about first names or occupation. Young *et al.* (1986a) found that subjects could categorise a famous face (according to their occupation) faster than they could name the face. However, written names could be named faster than they could be categorised. Young *et al.* interpret these results as evidence that names can only be accessed from faces sequentially after access to identity-semantic information. They also report an experiment in which they found that names of celebrities can be read aloud faster than unfamiliar names composed of the first name of one celebrity and the surname of another. For example, subjects read aloud 'Dean Martin' and 'Jack Nicholson' faster than 'Jack Martin' and 'Dean Nicholson'. Young *et al.* argue that this result demonstrates that the relatively faster naming of names cannot be explained by sub-lexical orthography to phonology conversion procedures. The use of such procedures could not explain why famous first and surname combinations are named faster than unfamiliar names.

Hillis and Caramazza's (1991) summation hypothesis can provide an alternative interpretation of these data on categorisation and naming of faces and names. Parallel access to semantics and output name codes from written names could be mediated by orthography–phonology conversion strategies. The summation hypothesis assumes that lexical output codes can be accessed from orthography–phonology conversion strategies. Written names can be named faster than they can be categorised by occupation because pronunciation can be assembled for a written name. Therefore, partial activation spread via the semantic route and via orthography–phonology conversion strategies would be sufficient to specify pronunciation of the name; however, selection of the appropriate occupational category will only receive activation via the semantic route. Although the correct pronunciation could not be assembled in the case of irregularly pronounced names, partial activation passed via the semantic route and the orthography–phonology conversion strategies will sum in the output lexicon. Even in the case of irregular names, orthography–phonology conversion strategies would pass activation to the output representation of the target name which would lead to a faster rise in activation than if passed via the semantic route alone. However, if a face is presented activation can only be passed via the person identity node. Therefore, summation of activation in the output lexicon via a semantic route and orthography–phonology conversion strategies can account for access to a name output code from a written name not requiring a longer processing time than access to identity-specific semantics as required from a face. The account of the experimental data is essentially the same as that offered by Young *et al.* (1986a, 1988a), except that parallel access to output codes is provided by orthography–phonology conversion strategies rather than by a direct lexical route.

The summation hypothesis predicts that famous names can be read aloud faster than unfamiliar names which are a composite of different celebrities' first and surnames without the need to postulate that different routes are used. If a name is of a famous person, activation passed via the person recognition system, the word recognition system and orthography–phonology conversion strategies will sum in the output lexicon. However, if the name is unfamiliar no activation will be passed via the person recognition system. Therefore, lexical access will take longer as it has to rely on activation passed by the word recognition system and orthography–phonology conversion strategies alone. The summation hypothesis quite naturally predicts that names of familiar individuals will be accessed faster than unfamiliar names.

A direct route from name recognition units to the output lexicon was implicated to account for data on repetition priming from name processing tasks to naming familiar faces (Valentine *et al.*, 1995). The direct route was required to assure that the lexical output code and person identity node were simultaneously active even in the event of difficulty accessing the output lexicon from the PIN alone. Therefore, there is a need for 'parallel' access to the output lexicon. However, if the word recognition system and sub-lexical orthography–phonology conversion strategies can pass activation to the output lexicon, these routes rather than a direct lexical route from name recognition units could provide the required parallel access.

To conclude, we take the position that, in light of the summation hypothesis, there is no evidence that requires the postulation of direct access to the output lexicon from either word recognition units or name recognition units.

SUMMARY AND CONCLUSIONS

We began the comparison between lexical access to proper and common names by contrasting the effects of frequency on lexical access. Access to object names is speeded by high word frequency, but access to people's surnames is slower if many people share the same surname. The node structure theory proposed by Burke *et al.* (1991) provides a suitable framework to account for these effects. Access to lexical nodes representing common names is achieved by many links that converge on the lexical nodes. Each time a common name is produced it requires access to the same lexical node even if different exemplars of, for example, an object, are named. These aspects make access to common names robust and strengthened by frequent use. However, access to lexical nodes of proper names is achieved via single links from nodes representing the full name of the person. Lexical nodes representing a common surname have a fan-out of links to the proper name phrase nodes for each individual. Therefore, production of a proper name proceeds via different links for each individual and nodes of 'competitor' individuals will be triggered by activation in the lexical node representing a common surname. Therefore, access to proper names is vulnerable, as a single link must pass activation, and a common surname is subjected to additional competing activation which might further inhibit lexical access.

Recent research suggests that age of acquisition and *not* word frequency affects the latency to name objects. Confounding with age of acquisition of people's names appears to be unlikely to account for the effects of surname frequency on face naming latency which were reviewed. However, proper names provide an excellent domain in which to explore the effects of age of acquisition. We continue to acquire proper names throughout our lives and so it is easier to dissociate frequency effects from age of acquisition effects for proper names than it is for object names. This is an area of current research.

Experiments have demonstrated that production of a common name does not prime production of the same response as the surname of a famous face. However, processing a celebrity's full name does prime naming their face even if the prime task did not require production of the name. These results are consistent with the framework proposed by Valentine *et al.* (1991) in which people's names and common names are accessed in the output lexicon by separate pathways. The account of repetition priming of name production offered utilised a direct link from name recognition units to the output lexicon. In the light of evidence and analysis presented by Hillis and Caramazza (1991), we take the view that models of face, name and word recognition need to be modified to exclude a direct, non-semantic, lexical route to the output lexicon but to include access to the output lexicon from sub-lexical orthography–phonology conversion strategies. We outline a revised framework of face, name and word processing which takes account of this and other issues raised in the preceding chapters in Chapter 8.

Chapter 8

Integrating the issues
A framework for name, face, word and object recognition

By taking account of the issues raised in this book, our aim is to propose an information-processing framework that is compatible with data drawn from a wide variety of approaches and traditions. The aim is to produce a single framework which includes a model of face recognition that takes account of the literature on speech production; that provides a model of word recognition which is compatible with recent developments in the neuropsychology; that accounts for recent neuropsychological and experimental evidence of the relationship between proper name and common name processing; and that incorporates recognition of both visually and auditorily presented words and names.

The framework we propose here can account for issues which are not addressed by contemporary models of face and name recognition (Bruce and Young, 1986; Burton *et al.*, 1990). We do not regard our framework as a competitor to these earlier models but as a development of them; our approach draws directly on both of these models. Our aim is to describe a framework in the hope that it will aid future research by generating some testable predictions and drawing in research from speech production in particular, and which has not previously been seen to be relevant to models of face naming by the majority of researchers.

As we have seen, especially in Chapter 6, computer simulation of proposed cognitive architectures is often required to establish whether hypothesised effects do indeed occur (e.g. Brédart *et al.*'s (1995) simulations of parallel access to names and identity-specific semantics), and whether hypothesised mechanisms can account for the data (e.g. Burton *et al.*'s 1990 simulation of semantic and repetition priming). The framework described in this chapter has not been implemented in its entirety and there are key ideas that need to be tested in this way. We do not present a model in which every conceivable prediction has been tested empirically and by simulation. Instead, we believe there are sufficient empirical data to impose some important constraints on such an enterprise. We have been mindful of these constraints to produce a framework in which we have plundered the best ideas from speech production models, neuropsychology of word recognition and naming, and models of face and name recognition to produce a more complete and testable framework which we believe will handle the available data.

In the second part of the chapter we consider the various types of meanings which proper names can have, and the implications of the meaning of proper names in comparing functional models of processing common names and proper names. One limitation of the framework we propose is that it only addresses people's names and does not provide a general cognitive approach to proper names. We then reflect on how the framework we propose for a functional model of processing people's names might be extended into a more general approach to the cognitive psychology of proper names.

AN INTEGRATED FRAMEWORK FOR NAME, FACE, WORD AND OBJECT RECOGNITION

We shall take as our starting point the framework proposed by Valentine *et al.* (1991). For convenience the model is reproduced in Figure 8.1. This framework draws heavily on the work of Bruce and Young (1986), but has the advantage that it makes explicit the relationship that name recognition has with face recognition on the one hand and word recognition on the other. Although this framework handles adequately most of the neuropsychological and experimental data of the relationship between processing of common names and people's names (see chapters 4 and 7), a number of issues were discussed in the preceding chapters which would require modification to the framework. The following is a brief résumé of these issues:

- Person identity nodes (PINs) should function as token markers with parallel access to identity-specific semantic information and names (see Chapter 6).
- Identity-specific semantic information to be included in a general semantic system (Burton and Bruce, 1993; and see Chapter 4, this volume).
- A non-semantically mediated, direct route from word and name recognition units to the output lexicon should be removed. Access from sub-lexical orthography–phonology conversion strategies to the output lexicon should be added (Hillis and Caramazza, 1991; and see Chapter 7, this volume).
- The output lexicon should be decomposed into a semantic lexicon (or lemmas) and a phonological lexicon (or lexemes) (see Chapter 6).
- Following the decomposition of the output lexicon, it is logical to decompose word recognition into two stages. The first involves recognition of the modality-specific word form (its phonology or

orthography) followed by access to its lemma (which includes identification of its syntactic status).

- The issue of separate lexicons for speech perception and speech production versus a common lexicon for input and output must be resolved. We follow Roelofs' (1992) proposal of separate phonological lexicons but a common semantic lexicon (see below).
- Brédart and Valentine (1992) proposed that familiar face naming can be self-monitored via a perceptual loop (cf. Levelt, 1989).
- In order to incorporate self-monitoring it will be necessary to show explicitly separate input routes for visually and auditorily presented words and names.
- A route for visual recognition of objects should be included.

These points will be discussed and incorporated into the information-processing framework. Figures 8.2 and 8.3 show intermediate steps in which the framework shown in Figure 8.1 will be progressively modified to incorporate the features listed above. The final architecture is shown in Figure 8.4. However, there are some important features of the new architecture which are not made explicit in Figure 8.4. These include the following:

- Identity-specific semantic information should be organised into separate pools of units in order to account for the data reported in Chapter 6, in which it was shown that names of individuals about whom a number of facts are known can be accessed faster than names of equally familiar individuals about whom few facts are known.
- The mechanism by which people's names are more difficult to recall than common names and by which people's names are more difficult to recall than identity-specific semantic information such as occupation must be made explicit.

These issues are addressed by the more detailed architecture of the semantic system and the semantic lexicon shown in Figure 8.5.

FIRST STEPS

The framework as proposed by Valentine *et al.* (1991) followed Bruce and Young (1986) in not separating person identity nodes (PINs) from identity-specific semantic codes. However, Burton *et al.* (1990) identified person identity nodes as multi-modal entry nodes to the semantic system. Identity-specific semantic information is now represented by semantic information units (SIUs) in a separate pool. The separation of PINs from SIUs was required for the account of semantic priming proposed by Burton *et al.* in which activation is spread to related PINs via the links to shared SIUs. Therefore, the first change to the framework required is to

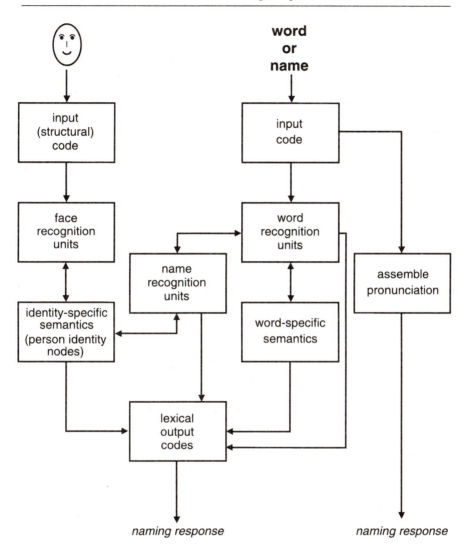

Figure 8.1 The framework for face, name and word recognition proposed by Valentine *et al.* (1991)

separate explicitly identity-specific semantic information and PINs. We have followed Burton and Bruce's (1993) implementation of the Valentine *et al.* framework in which identity-specific semantic information is included in the general semantic system. We have shown a partition in the semantic system to emphasise the different role that semantic memory plays in comprehending words and faces and names (see Figure 8.2). Word recognition units are connected to nodes representing the meanings of the relevant words, but names and faces access information about individual people. Of course these two types of semantic information are strongly related, and nodes representing 'general semantic' and 'identity-specific semantics' must be highly interconnected. No doubt general semantic features of politicians can be accessed by recognising the face of a famous politician. To classify the occupation of a celebrity requires access to semantic information which is not in itself unique to a specific individual (e.g. pop star, politician).

The framework shown in Figure 8.2 has also been amended to take account of Hillis and Caramazza's (1991) summation hypothesis described in Chapter 7. We are persuaded by Hillis and Caramazza's argument that the evidence available does not require that a direct, non-semantic lexical route to the output lexicon from word recognition units be postulated. Therefore, the direct routes from word recognition units and name recognition units to the output lexicon, which were included by Valentine *et al.*, have been removed in Figure 8.2. In line with Hillis and Caramazza's summation hypothesis the output lexicon receives activation via a route from sub-lexical orthography–phonology conversion strategies. For a full discussion of the summation hypothesis see Chapter 7 (pp. 157–162).

Two further changes to the framework affecting the output lexicon are included in Figure 8.3. First, the single output lexicon has been split into a semantic lexicon and a phonological lexicon as suggested by Brédart and Valentine (1992). Second, the semantic lexicon is shared by both input and output. Name recognition units have been replaced by lemmas in the semantic lexicon representing proper names. Orthography–phonology conversion strategies access the phonological lexicon but not the semantic lexicon. The evidence for the proposed structure of the input and output lexicons and the detailed structure of the proper name lemmas are discussed in more detail later in the chapter.

Before proceeding we need to comment on a contradiction between two of the changes made. On the one hand, following Hillis and Caramazza's (1991) argument that a lexical, non-semantic route need not be postulated, we have removed direct links from name recognition units (NRUs) and word recognition units (WRUs) to the output lexicon. However, we argue below that word or name recognition requires access to both a recognition unit of the modality-specific word form (WRU) and a semantic lexicon. We propose that a common semantic lexicon mediates both recognition and production of words, and that in the case of proper name processing the semantic lexicon takes the role of name recognition units. If there is a single semantic lexicon, there is a direct route from WRUs to the output lexicon which does not involve access to the semantic system. In short, there is a direct non-semantic route for reading aloud known words and names.

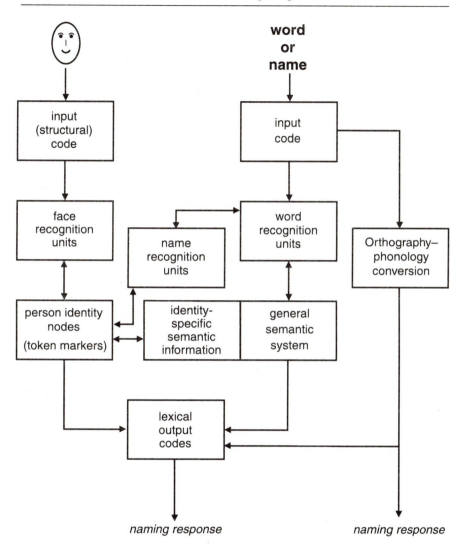

Figure 8.2 In the framework illustrated here, identity-specific semantics have been separated from PINs and included within the semantic system. Direct routes from name and word recognition units have been removed and access to the output lexicon from orthography–phonology strategies has been included

The proposed framework appears to conflict with Hillis and Caramazza's summation hypothesis. How can the two approaches be resolved? First, it is important to note that Hillis and Caramazza did not present any evidence *against* a direct route for reading aloud. First, they noted that the evidence did not require postulation of a direct route. Therefore, if there are other reasons to postulate a direct route (or common

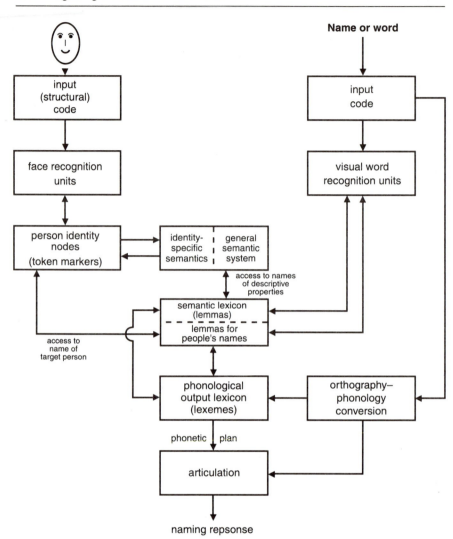

Figure 8.3 In the framework illustrated here, the output lexicon has been split into separate semantic and phonological lexicons. The semantic lexicon is common to speech production and reading. Name recognition units have been replaced by lemmas for proper names in the semantic lexicon

lexicon) the existence of a direct route does not conflict with the summation hypothesis. Second, Hillis and Caramazza noted that a direct route alone did not account for all aspects of the available data. Principally, there is no a priori reason why there should be any effect of regularity on naming latency or accuracy if a direct lexical route is used to read aloud by either normal subjects or patients who show better naming than comprehension performance. Hillis and Caramazza postulate that sub-lexical orthography–phonology conversion strategies can access the output lexicon. This is the critical aspect of the summation hypothesis which we have incorporated into the proposed framework. Therefore, the framework can be compatible with the summation hypothesis and have a semantic lexicon common to input and output.

Hillis and Caramazza pointed out that in all cases of patients whose ability to read aloud irregular words exceeded their comprehension of those words, there was none the less some residue of comprehension. Therefore, Hillis and Caramazza concluded that reading is occurring via a semantic route. In the framework shown in Figure 8.3, a pathway through the semantic system is not required to read aloud a written word. Therefore, naming could theoretically be possible in the absence of any comprehension of the word. However, there will be a very high degree of interconnectivity between lemmas for common names and the semantic system. Common name lemmas will be connected to every semantic node which represents a semantic feature of the word (e.g. the lemma for 'girl' will be connected to semantic nodes for 'young', 'female', 'human', etc. See the account of the summation hypothesis in Chapter 7, p. 158). Also, nodes in the semantic system will be connected to each lemma representing a concept which shares that feature; for example, the semantic node for 'young' will be connected to the lemmas for 'baby', 'child', 'fawn', 'lamb', 'calf', etc. The high degree of interconnectivity between semantics and lemmas contrasts with the one-to-one mapping between lemmas and lexemes. This situation is analogous to the connectivity between person identity nodes (PINs) and identity-specific semantics on the one hand (one-to-many and many-to-one), and between PINs and name codes on the other (one-to-one). Brédart et al. (1995) showed in a simulation using an interactive activation model that names did not reach their threshold activation if all of the links from PINs to identity-specific semantic nodes are attenuated (see Chapter 6, p. 137). The effect arises because attenuation of links to all identity-specific semantic information has a very substantial effect of attenuating activation of the PIN and because it is not supported by the interaction of activation passed between PINs and semantic units via the rich interconnectivity. An analogous effect would occur in an interactive activation implementation of the proposed framework for word naming and comprehension. It might be very unlikely that a lexeme will be retrieved and articulated in the absence of activation of any semantic information whatsoever. Therefore, an interactive activation model of the framework would be entirely consistent with Hillis and Caramazza's observation, although a non-semantic, lexical route for reading aloud does exist in the framework.

The final framework which we propose is shown in Figure 8.4. This framework does not differ in substance from that shown in Figure 8.3 but

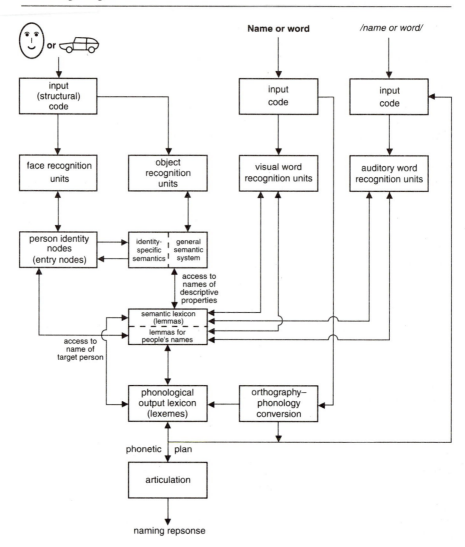

Figure 8.4 The completed architecture of the framework proposed in this chapter. Separate recognition units for auditorily and visually presented words are included. Object recognition units and self-monitoring via a perceptual loop have also been added. More details of the architecture of the semantic system and the semantic lexicon are shown in Figure 8.5

includes a number of additions. Two aspects of the changes in this figure are merely additions to show pathways and representations which have been previously proposed. First, object recognition units are included. Recognition units for objects have been proposed in previous theories of object recognition (e.g. Seymour, 1979; Warren and Morton, 1982; Bruce and Young, 1986). The assumption is merely of a set of units which store structural descriptions of familiar objects in an analogous manner to face recognition units. Object recognition units therefore allow access to semantic information about objects from a visual structural code. Second, separate routes and recognition units have been included for visual and auditory recognition of words. This does not represent any departure from the previous framework, as separate pathways had been assumed. A single set of word recognition units had been shown for convenience, as nearly all the relevant experimental data contrasted visual word or name recognition with face recognition. It has been necessary to include a separate route for auditory word recognition to make explicit the monitoring of face naming via a perceptual loop. This feature, which is based on Levelt's (1989) theory of the perceptual loop for self-monitoring of speech production, was applied to face naming by Brédart and Valentine (1992). The central idea is that subjects can monitor their naming of familiar faces by listening to their own speech. If an incorrect name is produced in error, the self-monitored speech would result in activation of a different person identity node from that activated to produce the name. A naming error will therefore be detected by the mismatch in the activated PINs. Evidence to support the application of the perceptual loop to monitor face naming is described later in the chapter.

A COMMON SEMANTIC LEXICON FOR PERCEPTION AND PRODUCTION OF LANGUAGE

Consideration of the empirical data on speech production has led us to conclude that lexical access in face naming involves two stages: access to the meaning and syntactic properties of the word (specified by a lemma), followed by retrieval of the phonological word form (a lexeme). In line with this literature we will assume that representations in the semantic system (including identity-specific semantics) are non-lexical representations of concepts and their associations. The semantic lexicon represents the meaning and syntactic class of words. Therefore, the mapping between the semantic system and the semantic lexicon represents a mapping from non-lexical conceptual knowledge on to representations of lexical items. The mapping from the semantic lexicon to the phonological lexicon represents the mapping from lexical items to their phonology. Most theories of speech production assume that common semantic and phonological lexicons can mediate speech perception and production (e.g. MacKay, 1987; Levelt, 1989). However, models of face and name processing have been derived principally from models of visual word recognition. This has had two consequences. First, the models have assumed separate input and output lexicons. This is due to the fact that visual word recognition requires a mapping from orthography to semantics but speech production requires a mapping from semantics to phonology. Clearly, in this case, different tasks are required for input and output. However, in the case of auditory word recognition or speech perception, it is not clear whether or not a single mental lexicon (comprising a semantic and phonological lexicon) could provide the required mappings between phonology and meaning. A second consequence of the development from models of word recognition is that the focus has been on recognition of single words rather than speech. It is easier to overlook the need for a semantic lexicon in theories of the perception and production of single words. The roles of the semantic lexicon are to specify the meaning and the syntactic status of a word. The semantic system is assumed to represent non-lexical conceptual knowledge. (Although the 'semantic system' in information-processing models of face, name and word recognition could perhaps be equated with a semantic lexicon rather than non-lexical conceptual knowledge.) Equally, the role of the semantic lexicon (as distinct from non-lexical conceptual knowledge) has been overlooked in some models of picture naming (e.g. Humphreys *et al.*, 1988). However, specification of syntax is required to understand and produce fluent speech or to understand text.

We have argued that models of face and name processing have much to gain from influence from the speech production literature. Brédart and Valentine (1992) have incorporated this literature into a model of face naming. However, to complete the process we also need to make models of the comprehension of proper names consistent with theories of speech perception. Two issues have to be addressed to achieve this. First, a semantic lexicon must be involved in speech perception. If the semantic system is assumed to represent non-lexical conceptual knowledge, as we have argued, a semantic lexicon is required for comprehension of written and spoken language as the level at which word meaning and syntactic class is accessed. We therefore need to decompose the lexicon into a semantic and phonological lexicon for perception as well as production of language. Second, we have to address the issue of whether the semantic lexicon and phonological lexicon are common to speech production and perception, or whether separate lexicons are used for perception and production.

The general consensus is that there is insufficient evidence to make a definitive choice between common or separate lexicons (Monsell, 1987; Ellis and Young, 1988; Shallice, 1988). The problem is that it is difficult to distinguish a single lexicon used for both production and perception from separate lexicons which have direct connections between them. We have already seen that the empirical data on priming of face naming by common and proper written names can be explained either by a common semantic lexicon or by direct links from name recognition units to the output lexicon (see chapter 7, p. 152). Three possible models can be distinguished.

- There are separate semantic lexicons and separate phonological lexicons for production and perception of speech.
- The semantic lexicon is common to speech perception and production but the phonological lexicons are separate.
- Both the semantic and phonological lexicon are common to speech production and speech perception.

The framework we propose here has a semantic lexicon which is common to speech perception and production but separate from phonological lexicons. The choice of separate phonological lexicons is the position tentatively supported by Shallice (1988) and Ellis and Young (1988). These authors cite the evidence provided by 'deep dysphasic' patients who show an auditory analogue of deep dyslexia (e.g. Michel, 1979; Morton, 1980; Michel and Andreewsky, 1983). This patient made semantic errors when asked to repeat spoken words (e.g. repeating 'balloon' as 'kite') but he did not make semantic errors when reading aloud or in writing down the names of pictures. This impairment can be interpreted as faulty access to the semantic lexicon (representations of word meaning and syntax) from the phonological input lexicon coupled with a disconnection of a direct link from the input phonological lexicon to the output phonological lexicon. It is difficult to explain in a single phonological lexicon model why activation of the single phonological representation of a word is not sufficient to mediate repetition of spoken words.

The model we propose has separate input and output phonological lexicons but no direct link between them (cf. Hillis and Caramazza's (1991) summation hypothesis of naming written words). Repetition of spoken words could be achieved either via the semantic lexicon or a non-lexical route. If there is an impairment of access to the semantic lexicon from auditory word recognition units (Figure 8.4), spoken word repetition could be supported by a non-lexical route. However, deep dysphasic patients are also impaired in non-word repetition. In the proposed model this would be a necessary condition for deep dysphasia to occur.

Monsell (1987) also tentatively supported the position of separate phonological lexicons for speech perception and production but based his conclusions on evidence of priming and dual task studies in normal subjects. Monsell identified a number of possible models. If it is assumed that Monsell's 'conceptual/functional attributes' ('semantic properties, syntactic class, usage conventions') equate to the semantic lexicon, our model is a case of his Model 3, without a lexical route from input phonology to output phonology which has an interactive pathway from conceptual/functional attributes to output phonology (cf. Stemberger, 1985; Dell, 1986). Monsell concluded that the balance of evidence supported the architecture of this model. He also pointed out that in the absence of a lexical but non-semantic pathway from the input phonological lexicon to the output phonological lexicon, interactive processing between the semantic and phonological output lexicons must be assumed in order to account for the facilitation of picture naming by phonetic cueing in both normals and anomic patients, and the advantage in repetition of words over non-words in patients with speech repetition difficulties.

In conclusion, the empirical evidence in favour of separate phonological lexicons for speech perception and production is not overwhelming but evidence from a number of sources appears to be converging in favour of separate input and output pathways. In the case of the semantic lexicon there is little evidence to distinguish accounts based on a semantic lexicon shared by input and output mechanisms or even across modalities from separate semantic lexicons (but see Funnell and Allport, 1987). Therefore, on the grounds of parsimony we assume a single semantic lexicon common to written and auditory input and speech production (our model does not extend to written output). The priming data reported by Valentine *et al.* (1995) requires that if there is a semantic lexicon used only for the perception of people's names (e.g. name recognition units) there must be mandatory activation of the output lexicon. However, Hillis and Caramazza (1991) have argued that other evidence does not require postulation of a direct route. A single semantic lexicon for perception and production provides a parsimonious resolution to these issues.

DETECTING AND EDITING FACE NAMING ERRORS

It is an empirical fact that people may detect and repair face naming errors. In order to account for this fact, the presented architecture includes feedback loops from the speech production system to the speech comprehension system. This represents an application of Levelt's (1983, 1989) perceptual loop theory of speech monitoring to the particular problem of face naming. The perceptual loop hypothesis assumes that the speech comprehension system plays a central role in the detection of production errors. This detection requires feedback, through the comprehension system, to the conceptual system where a comparison between what was said or ready to be said and what is intended is performed. Following Levelt, two perceptual loops are included in the model: a pre-articulatory loop (from the phonetic plan to auditory analysis) and a post-articulatory loop (from overt speech to auditory analysis).

Brédart and Valentine (1992) tested the hypothesis of an intervention of a perceptual loop in editing face naming errors. Recall that Valentine *et al.* (1991) showed that low frequency names are categorised faster than high frequency names in a familiarity decision task and in a semantic categorisation task (see Chapter 4, p. 65). This effect was obtained when initials and surnames were presented but not when full names were presented. It was assumed that including a first name would reduce or eliminate the difference in the spread of activation across name recognition units (NRUs) generated by high and low frequency surnames. According to Brédart and Valentine, if the perceptual loop hypothesis account of the monitoring of face naming is correct, then surname frequency should affect the occurrence of errors in a task that requires the production of surnames only. Indeed, access to the PINs from the NRUs (or lemmas for people's names) should be slower for high frequency surnames than for low frequency surnames. Then, assuming that all other factors are equal, the comparison processes responsible for error detection (which were assumed to operate at the PIN level) would be initiated later for high frequency surnames than for low frequency surnames. Such a delay is likely to result in more frequent production of erroneous high frequency surnames before the monitoring process allowed error detection. In other words, the perceptual loop theory predicts that the feedback obtained via the speech comprehension system will be slower for phonetically planned or uttered high frequency surnames than for low frequency surnames. This delay in the feedback obtained through the speech comprehension system should increase the probability that articulation of an erroneous surname has started before the error is detected.

Two predictions followed this reasoning. A first prediction was that naming errors in which a (correct) rare surname is erroneously replaced by a common surname should occur more frequently than the reverse substitution. This was called the 'error asymmetry effect'. More precisely, it was predicted that given a pair of surnames x and y in which x is substantially more frequent than y, errors where x substitutes for y should be more common than errors where y substitutes for x. The analysis of a corpus of face naming errors showed this error asymmetry effect.

Another explanation of this error asymmetry effect would be that erroneous high frequency surnames substitute more often than low-frequency names because the former are accessed faster or more easily in speech production than the latter. Then, the effect would be due to frequency sensitivity of lexical access in the speech production system. There are however two main arguments against such an interpretation of the error asymmetry effect. First, the proportion of production incidents such as hesitations and blocking states was no different in production of low frequency surnames and in production of high frequency surnames. Second, Brédart and Valentine obtained the asymmetry effect although a control experiment using the same faces showed that naming latencies to faces with high frequency names were not faster than naming latencies to faces with low frequency names. Subsequently, Valentine and Moore (in press) have shown the *opposite* effect of surname frequency on production of people's surnames: subjects were *slower* to produce high frequency surnames than they were to produce low frequency surnames when naming famous faces. Therefore, frequency sensitivity of lexical access for people's surnames cannot explain the error asymmetry effect. (See Chapter 7 for a discussion of frequency sensitivity in the production of proper names.)

The second prediction from the perceptual loop hypothesis was that the relative speed in the initiation of speech monitoring should influence the proportion of errors which are repaired after articulation has started. The proportion of errors produced because of a delayed initiation of monitoring rather than because of a failure to detect the problem should be higher when the erroneous surname articulated is high frequency than when erroneous low frequency surnames are produced. Thus, it was predicted that repairs of high frequency erroneous surnames should be proportionately more common than repairs of low frequency erroneous surnames (the error repairing effect). This prediction was also supported by Brédart and Valentine's data.

The preceding paragraphs suggest that the application of the perceptual loop theory of speech monitoring can account for the available data on face naming error detection and repair. However, we do not claim that the perceptual loop theory is sufficient to account for all speech monitoring data. Recent work suggests that postulating other monitoring processes (operating in the speech production system itself) might be necessary to account for the timing of error repairs (see, for instance, Blackmer and Mitton, 1992).

FRACTIONATING THE SEMANTIC LEXICON AND THE SEMANTIC SYSTEM

In order to account for some of the available data it is necessary to specify some parts of the framework in greater detail than shown in Figure 8.4. In particular, the internal structure of the semantic system and the semantic lexicon which are shown as having 'partitions' needs to be specified. Let us first consider the semantic lexicon. Any model of name and word processing must account for the relatively greater difficulty of lexical access to proper names than to common names. Proper names are the class of words that are most likely to provoke a tip-of-the-tongue state. In Chapter 4 we described Burke et al.'s (1991) application of node structure theory to this problem (see Figure 5.1, p. 106). Burke et al. proposed a structure in which people's names were represented by 'proper name phrase nodes' and nodes representing the constituent parts of people's full names. An internal structure to the semantic lexicon is shown in Figure 8.5. Thin lines denote a one-to-one mapping from a node for a specific entity to a node at a different functional level for the same entity (e.g. links from face recognition units to person identity nodes or from visual word recognition units to lemmas). Bold lines represent connectivity which is not one-to-one. For example, each lemma may be connected to many nodes in the semantic system and vice versa.

Essentially, we have adopted the structure proposed by Burke *et al.* (1991). First names and surnames are shown in separate pools as it is assumed that first names will inhibit each other but not surnames and vice versa. First names and surnames associated with a particular individual will activate each other via excitatory links to a shared 'proper name phrase lemma'. Thus the architecture of the proposed framework provides a further mechanism by which names of famous people can be articulated more quickly than jumbled names (Young *et al.*, 1986a). For example, subjects read aloud 'Jack Nicholson' (actor) faster than they do 'Dean Nicholson' (unfamiliar name). This effect could occur because activation from the first name node for 'Dean' activates the surname node for 'Martin' (actor) via the proper name phrase node for 'Dean Martin'. The activation of the surname node will inhibit the rise of activation via within-pool inhibitory connections when reading the inappropriate surname 'Nicholson'. In contrast, when the name of a familiar person is read aloud activation spread via the proper name phrase node will prime activation of the appropriate node. See Chapter 7 for an account of this data in terms of Hillis and Caramazza's summation hypothesis.

Which units in our framework are analogous to Burke *et al.*'s (1991) visual concept nodes depend on whether the stimulus is a face or an object. Burke *et al.* did not consider perception of words or names as they were concerned with accounting for tip-of-the-tongue states which clearly do not occur if the sought-for lexical item is presented! For faces, the structure differs from Burke *et al.* in that the proper name phrase nodes do not connect directly to the identity-specific semantic system but only via a person identity node. The PIN is a pre-lexical node which represents an individual. It is a gateway for access to all information about the person (identity-specific semantics, name information stored in the form of lemmas). PINs are similar to Burke *et al.*'s visual concept nodes except that PINs are multi-modal representations. In the case of objects, the visual concept node is equivalent to an object recognition unit, but there is no direct link from the visual concept node to the lemma, given as a dotted line in Burke *et al.*'s model (see Figure 5.1).

Retrieval of common names is more robust than retrieval of proper names because multiple links from the semantic system converge on lemmas for common names. In contrast, links from identity-specific semantics converge on PINs which are connected by only a one-to-one mapping to lemmas for proper name phrases. The single links from PINs to proper name phrase lemmas make retrieval of proper names relatively vulnerable to transmission deficit. The situation is made worse by the mapping from proper name phrase nodes to first names and surnames. Relatively few first names and surnames are shared by many people. If,

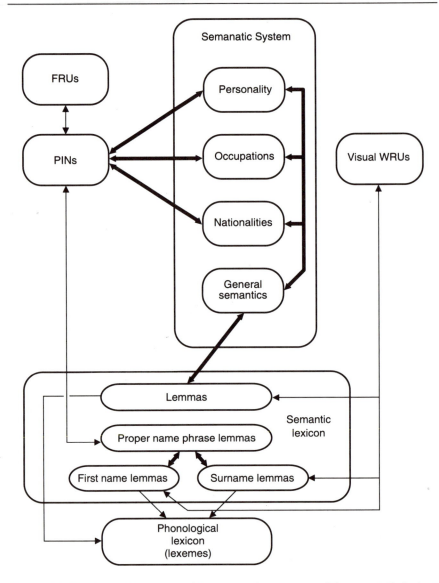

Figure 8.5 The internal structure of the semantic system and the semantic lexicon for the framework shown in Figure 8.4

within an interactive activation model, a common surname receives activation from one proper name phrase node, activation will be passed to competing name phrase nodes which share the same surname. Activation of the competitor nodes will inhibit the activation of the intended proper name phrase node. The connectivity between proper name phrase nodes and the constituent names have the disadvantage of a many-to-one mapping but not the advantage of a one-to-many mapping, in which many nodes feed back activation to sustain activation of a single node in the level initially activated. Such connectivity will result in rare or low frequency names being articulated faster than common or high frequency names. This effect was observed in the latency required to produce the surnames of famous faces by Valentine and Moore (in press; and see Chapter 7, this volume).

A further aspect of the data for which any model of face and name processing must account is the evidence that it is more difficult to access people's names than it is to access identity-specific semantic information. This is reflected in diary studies of everyday errors and neuropsychological case studies in which retrieval of identity-specific semantic information in the absence of naming is not uncommon but subjects or patients never name faces without being able retrieve some identity-specific semantics. (One exception to this is a case reported by Brennen *et al.* (in press) which is discussed in more detail below.) Subjects are also slower to access information about people's names than they are to access identity-specific semantic information (Young *et al.*, 1988a; Johnston and Bruce, 1990). Burton and Bruce (1992) explain these data by suggesting that names are represented alongside identity-specific semantic information in a large pool of units. They point out that names are usually unique and therefore there will be one-to-one mappings between nodes which represent names and PINs. Activation of nodes unique to one PIN will always rise more slowly and be more vulnerable to attenuation than nodes that are more highly interconnected.

The framework we present here relies on the same basic idea that names are usually unique to explain why access to names is slower than access to identity-specific semantic information. However, we have separated identity-specific semantic information into separate pools of competing nodes (see Chapter 6). For example, there is a pool of occupations, a pool of nationalities, etc. However, there is no inhibition between pools (i.e. an occupation node does not inhibit a nationality node). This architecture has a number of advantages: (1) It allows for a selective impairment to access to names accompanied by unimpaired access to unique identity-specific semantic information. This pattern of impairment is not possible within the model proposed by Burton and Bruce (1992). Hanley (1995) has shown that it occurs. (2) The present framework correctly predicts that subjects are faster to name people about whom they know many facts than they are to name equally familiar people about whom they know few facts (Brédart *et al.*, 1995; and see Chapter 6, this volume). Burton and Bruce's (1992) model makes the opposite prediction: that subjects would be faster to name people about whom fewer facts are known. (3) The architecture allows names to be represented by nodes which have a different functional status from identity-specific semantic nodes. In order to make the architecture compatible with current models of speech production, it is necessary that people's names are represented by lexical nodes and identity-specific semantic information is represented by non-lexical nodes.

In Figure 8.5 excitatory links between pools of identity-specific semantic information and 'general semantics' are shown. Our intention is not to suggest that identity-specific semantics are organised differently from the rest of the semantic system or that all semantics other than that about people are organised in a single pool with inhibitory links between all nodes. Use of a single pool for general semantics is merely expedient to keep the architecture tractable. The simulation reported by Brédart *et al.* (1995) shows that separate pools with no links between them provides a better model of identity-specific semantics than a single pool with inhibitory links between all nodes. However, identity-specific semantics must be closely interconnected with the general semantics. Therefore, some excitatory links must exist between pools. We take the view that nodes representing competing pieces of information will generally inhibit each other. Thus one occupation will inhibit activation of other occupations, but we see no reason to postulate that it must inhibit all other semantic information. Brédart *et al.* (1995) present strong evidence against a large build-up of inhibition created by availability of many facts about people. However, recalling that a person is a teacher can no doubt bring to mind general semantic information about the teaching profession. Therefore, there must be links between identity-specific semantics and more general semantic information. We would subscribe to the view that associated semantic information nodes will pass activation to each other via excitatory links. We know of no simulations of face recognition in which the semantic system includes inhibition of competing nodes and excitation of associated nodes. Clearly more simulation work is required. However, such work requires a model of human semantic memory and as such is beyond the scope of the simulations we have reviewed and of this book. We readily acknowledge the shortcomings of an interactive activation (IAC) model of human cognition in general and semantic memory in particular. Such models can be useful to evaluate theories of the macro-structure of the cognitive architecture; for example, the relationship between proper name and common name processing. However, IAC models are by no means complete. There is no theory of how nodes can represent 'content' or of learning.

CAN THE FRAMEWORK ACCOUNT FOR THE AVAILABLE DATA?

We have described how the proposed framework can account for the main empirical points of concern to us in this book (e.g. easier access to common names than to proper names, easier access to identity-specific semantics than to names, frequency-sensitivity of naming latency for famous faces). In this section we shall briefly summarise how our framework can account for the many findings from the experimental and neuropsychological literature that impose constraints upon any functional model of face, name and word recognition. In many cases the mechanisms are the same as those proposed in earlier models, and have been discussed elsewhere in the book. In such cases we will merely note the original source of the relevant account.

Following Burton *et al.* (1990), we will assume that familiarity decisions to faces and people's names are taken at the level of the person identity node. The effects of repetition priming and semantic priming can be accounted for in the manner proposed by Burton *et al.* Repetition priming is assumed to reflect an increase of the weight of links due to recent use. For example, repetition priming of a familiarity decision to a famous face would reflect an increase in the relevant link from a face recognition unit to a person identity node. Semantic priming reflects activation spread to PINs of related people via shared nodes representing identity-specific semantic information. Covert recognition in prosopagnosic patients can be explained by sub-threshold activity in PINs (see Burton *et al.*, 1991; Diamond *et al.*, 1994).

The effects of surname frequency on various tasks involving the comprehension of people's names were reviewed in Chapter 4. These effects are accounted for by the present framework in the manner suggested by Valentine *et al.* (1991), except that lemmas now assume the role of name recognition units. For example, name familiarity decisions to the initial and surnames of celebrities with common surnames are slower because competing lemmas of familiar people who share the surname slow down the unique identification of the 'target' lemma.

Lexical decisions to common names have been shown to prime recognition of people's names whose surnames shared the same orthography as the common name (Valentine *et al.*, 1993). The present framework would account for the repetition priming between recognition of common names and proper names in the same way as Valentine *et al.* (1991), by assuming that both lemmas for proper names and common names are automatically triggered by activation of a word recognition unit connected to both types of lemma. Repetition priming occurs because the weights on both links are increased as a result of the activation.

When production of names is considered, a different pattern of repetition priming between common names and proper names is observed (see Chapter 7). Valentine *et al.* (1995) found that a prime task which involved reading or producing a common name did not prime reaction time to produce the same phonology as the surname of a famous face. However, making a familiarity decision or occupation decision or reading aloud the surname of a visually presented full name of a celebrity does prime the latency to produce the surname of the celebrity on seeing their face. Valentine *et al.* interpreted these data by proposing that activation of a name recognition unit by seeing a celebrity's full name automatically activates a lexical output code and the person identity node for the celebrity concerned. As both the lexical output code and the PIN are simultaneously active the weight of the link between the units is increased. It is the increase in weight of the PIN to the lexical output code that produces an effect of priming subsequent face naming latency. As it was necessary to postulate that name recognition units automatically activated the corresponding lexical output units in order to account for the effects of repetition priming of production of people's names, these data are entirely consistent with our proposal that name recognition units and lexical output codes for people's names can be amalgamated into a single functional level – lemmas for people's names.

There is mounting evidence from the study of naming disorders in Alzheimer's disease that naming can be selectively preserved relative to comprehension (see, for example, Bayles and Trosset, 1992; Shuren *et al.*, 1993). The clearest demonstration of a patient naming without semantics is the case study reported by Brennen *et al.* (in press). The patient would occasionally name objects and faces, and yet be unable to provide any further information about them, even denying knowledge of them. This ability to name without *at the same time* being unable to provide any further information about the person is difficult to explain in the terms of a strictly sequential information-processing model.

These observations appear to rule out a strict sequential dependency as in the Bruce and Young model, but ironically may be accounted for in *computer* models that are essentially sequential. If, for instance, access to the different modules was probabilistic (but weighted highly against access to the lemmas for people's names), then normally people's names would be harder to recall than other words, but occasionally one would correctly name a face without knowing any other identity-specific information about it. This is the case of Brennen *et al.*'s patient. However, such a model would predict that normals should also name without semantics from time to time yet, as pointed out above, this does not seem to be the case.

Another possible explanation derives from the observation in Chapter 5 that the three patients with preserved recall of proper names (that we know about) do not appear to remain in this state for a long time. In each case, at the time of testing, the patients were intellectually restricted, and became untestable within a matter of months. This suggests a speculative hypothesis that proper name preservation occurs when the semantic system is in an unstable, highly degraded state. In computational terms this may mean that as semantic units are lost, the advantage of common name lemmas over proper name lemmas is also lost, because the convergence of many nodes in the general semantic system on to one common name lemma would no longer be the case.

PREDICTIONS FROM THE FRAMEWORK

So far in this chapter we have outlined a revised framework for face, name and word recognition designed to make a model of face naming and processing of people's names which is compatible with models of speech production. We have described how the framework retains mechanisms required to account for a variety of empirical data from earlier models of face processing and production of proper names (e.g. Burton *et al.*, 1990; Burke *et al.*, 1991). We have also considered how the framework could account for the data which have been discussed in detail in earlier chapters of this book. We have outlined a number of theoretical reasons why the framework should be preferred to earlier models (e.g. Valentine *et al.*, 1991). For example, it is consistent with models of speech production (e.g. Roelofs, 1992), with Hillis and Caramazza's (1991) summation hypothesis, with Brédart *et al.*'s (1995) experiment on the effect of the number of facts known about famous people on naming latency, and with a report of a patient who cannot name famous faces being able to produce unique identity-specific semantic information (Hanley, 1995). No other model of face and name processing has all of these features.

Although there are strong theoretical reasons to prefer the framework we propose here over previous models, ultimately the success of any functional model can be judged by its ability to produce predictions which differ from other models and can be tested empirically. What predictions can be derived to test the proposed model?

Some of the theoretical advantages of the framework listed above are backed by empirical data. The summation hypothesis is supported by neuropsycholological data (see Chapter 7). Speech production models which incorporate two stages in lexical access are reviewed in Chapter 6. It is extremely unparsimonious to assume that face naming, which is an act of speech production, should require a different means of lexical access in the absence of any evidence requiring such a distinction.

One feature of the framework is the fractionation of the semantic system into separate competing pools of units for separate semantic features. This model is supported by experimental data (see Chapter 6). In addition it is possible to derive some new predictions from this view of the semantic system. Brédart (1993) has shown that people with two names (e.g. actors long associated with one character) can be named more successfully than people who are known by only one name, if subjects are required to produce either name. Brédart explains the effect by suggesting that two names allowed subjects a larger degree of freedom in retrieving a relevant lexical item to name the target face. If one name is temporarily unavailable, subjects have the possibility of producing the other name. The effect of a choice of two names is perhaps enhanced because usually both names of a celebrity will not necessarily be equally available initially. Subjects can choose to produce the most available name. For example, a subject may be more familiar with the name of the character 'Columbo' than the name of the actor who portrays the detective on screen (Peter Falk). If a celebrity has two names *and they are equally available,* the framework would predict that in such circumstances the celebrity would be named more slowly than a celebrity who has only one name. If lexical name codes are stored in a separate pool from identity-specific semantic information and a celebrity has only one name, there should be little or no competition between units in the name pool. However, people with two names would take longer to name because both names would be activated and would inhibit each other. In everyday life, one name may be (temporarily) more available through recent or frequent use so there would be little inhibition because one name would rapidly win the competition. However, if subjects were given a lot of practice at producing both actor and character names to equate availability through repetition priming effects, the framework would predict that celebrities with two names who subjects had practised naming would be slower to be named than celebrities who have only one name, even if subjects are allowed to produce either name at test. This prediction remains to be tested. The Burton and Bruce (1992) model would not make a clear prediction in this experiment, as access to the name for all celebrities will be inhibited by activation of a host of identity-specific semantic information. Therefore, it is not clear that inhibition from a single unit representing an alternative name would have a detectable effect as this unit has a status which is no different from any other semantic information unit.

The other major feature of the framework is the proposal that a semantic lexicon is common to recognition and production of people's names. The assumption that a familiarity decision is based on activation of the person identity node (from Burton *et al.*, 1990) coupled with a semantic lexicon common to recognition and production makes some strong predictions possible. As both auditorily and visually presented names access the same lemma and therefore access the PIN, cross-modality repetition priming should be found from familiarity decision to auditorily presented names on to latency of familiarity decision to written names. Both tasks require activation of the PIN from the lemma; therefore an increase in the weight on this link will produce a cross-modality effect of repetition of the same name. This prediction contrasts with repetition priming of familiarity decision to faces. No effect of priming of the latency to make a familiarity decision to a famous face is observed from a prior familiarity decision to the celebrity's name is observed (Bruce and Valentine, 1985). As familiarity decision to a face does not require activation of the PIN–lemma link there is no common pathway to deciding that a name is familiar and deciding that a face is familiar. However, face *naming* does require activation of the PIN–lemma link and repetition priming from a familiarity decision to a celebrity's name on to the latency required to name their face is observed, as would be expected (Valentine *et al.*, 1995). The prediction that the effect of repetition priming on familiarity decision to names should cross modality also contrasts with little, if any cross-modality effects of repetition in lexical decision (Morton, 1979). These data can be accommodated within the present framework if it is assumed that a lexical decision can be made on the basis of activity of the modality-specific word recognition units and therefore the decision is based on activation prior to any multi-model pathways.

Alternatively, if it is assumed that access to semantic information is required for a lexical decision to be made, as we have argued previously (see Chapter 4), it could be argued that links involving one-to-many and many-to-one mappings do not support as large effects of repetition priming, possibly due to the many parallel pathways to pass activation rapidly in the absence of repetition priming.

EXTENDING CURRENT INFORMATION PROCESSING MODELS TO OTHER TYPES OF PROPER NAME

How, in terms of the information processing models, are different categories of proper names represented? Valentine *et al.*'s (1991) model of name, word and face recognition is based on an analogy with words and faces and, in principle, it could be extended to other names easily enough. It comprises three stages of long-term memory – the input recognition units, the semantic store and the lexicon.

First, input recognition units will be considered. The neuropsychological literature is rich with case studies of dissociations between face, object and word recognition, and all three domains show double dissociations from each other, which at first glance seems to imply three independent processing routes. However, Farah (1991) reviewed ninety-nine cases of agnosia (essentially the entire agnosia literature in French and English since 1966 plus a few other cases), and showed that (1) agnosia for objects always co-occurred with either prosopagnosia or alexia or both, and (2) prosopagnosia and alexia did not occur without at least some degree of object agnosia. This dependence of object recognition deficits upon other types of recognition deficits is inconsistent with the notion of a processing route dedicated to object recognition.

Rather, Farah argues that the data are consistent with the idea that normal recognition draws upon two, rather than three, types of representational capacity: one for representing the parts of objects themselves including complicated parts that may even be an object which cannot be decomposed in sub-parts, the second capacity for representing multiple parts. Face recognition is deemed to draw almost exclusively on the first type of representation, because it depends upon recognition of the stimulus as a whole, and not upon recognition of any of its constituent parts. Reading, on the other hand, is an example of a recognition task that relies almost exclusively on the capacity to represent multiple parts, and so will be disrupted to the degree that this capacity is impaired. The recognition of most other types of object, according to Farah, does not rely so heavily upon one type of representational capacity, but poses demands on both types to a greater or lesser degree. For example, we may conjecture that the recognition of animals may be holistic and so depend more on the representation of parts, and that the recognition of a lawn-mower and other machines would depend more on the representation of multiple parts.

This theory is more parsimonious than the multiple parallel routes theory. A problem with the latter approach is that faces and words have a route each, as does the extremely heterogeneous category of objects. For instance, are cars and animals recognised via the same route as tools and the outlines of countries? Farah (1991) offers a plausible, more elegant alternative. However, it needs to be fleshed out to explain exactly how the representational capacities operate and also to specify the demands that different objects pose for the two capacities.

Farah's hypothesis rests on the claim that there have been no un-ambiguous reports of two patterns of impairments to word, object and face recognition which according to her analysis should not exist. However, one of these patterns has been reported recently. Rumiati et al. (1995) have reported a case of an agnosic patient who is impaired in object recognition, but does not suffer from either prosopagnosia or alexia. Given that, according to Farah, object recognition deficits reflect either impairment to the ability to represent parts (and undecomposable objects) or impairment to the ability to represent multiple parts, visual agnosia should always be accompanied by either prosopagnosia or alexia or both. Rumialti et al.'s patient appears to falsify Farah's hypothesis.

The Bruce and Young (1986) framework and similar information-processing models predict that the damage giving rise to a failure to recog-nise familiar faces could be located at the structural encoding stage in which case faces will appear distorted, or at the FRU level in which case patients will be unable to recognise familiar faces but perception will be normal. Farah, on the other hand, argues that perception and representation of faces cannot be separated and that distorted perception of faces is just a more severe case of prosopagnosia. (For example, this situation could arise from distributed representation of faces in a neural network.

Lesioning the network could affect both perception of unfamiliar faces and representation of familiar faces.)

Previously, Farah (1988) argued that imagery requires access to the representations utilised for perception. Therefore, her stance makes some clear predictions about the relationship between the severity of prosopagnosia and the ability to form mental images of faces.

Suppose that a prosopagnosic patient is asked about the visual appearance of a celebrity whose face he or she cannot recognise. The information-processing models predict that if the problem is at the level of structural encoding, imagery should be unimpaired as intact FRUs can be accessed from PINs. If perception of faces is unimpaired, but the problem is due to damaged FRUs or disconnection of FRUs from PINs, then the patient should not be able to access visual information from the celebrity's name.

What consequences does Farah's hypothesis have for the ability of prosopagnosic patients to form images of familiar faces? Farah's hypothesis leads to the prediction that if damage is bad enough to cause impaired perception, imagery must also be impaired.

Young *et al.* (1994) tested the ability of two patients who have been extensively reported in the literature to answer questions about the visual appearance of celebrities whom they could not recognise. HJA is a visual agnosic who has some impairment to his visual perception (Humphreys and Riddoch, 1987). HJA could answer questions about the visual appearance of celebrities; for example, he could say that Bjorn Borg has longer hair than Jimmy Connors and John McEnroe. However, HJA could not answer questions which required processing of configural information, but this is the ability that is believed to be impaired; for example, he could not say whether Elizabeth Taylor looks more like Joan Collins or Barbara Windsor. In contrast, PH (who is not agnosic but is impaired on within-category recognition, for example, cars, as well as face recognition) could not perform any imagery task. Young *et al.* concluded that these patients' ability to form mental images of familiar faces is better predicted by the information-processing models which separate structural encoding from face recognition units than by Farah's hypothesis.

PH shows evidence of covert recognition of famous faces which he does not overtly recognise. One source of evidence for this covert recognition is that he can learn true famous face–name pairings more easily than he can learn untrue pairings (de Haan *et al.*, 1987). Such effects of covert recognition have been interpreted as evidence that PH's impairment arises because his FRUs (and identity-specific semantic information) are intact, but that they are disconnected from 'consciousness'. It is therefore possible that his failure to answer questions about the appearance of a person's face is due to the same problem: access to intact FRUs is disconnected from consciousness. This possibility raises the question of whether he would show savings for correct pairings on a facial feature–name learning task compared to incorrect pairings. For example, would he take longer to learn that Björn Borg has short hair and John McEnroe has long hair than he would to learn the correct visual features? If PH does not show any benefit in learning correct visual information–name associations it would be difficult to account for his impairment in face processing in terms of Farah's hypothesis, where perception and imagery are subserved by the same mechanisms.

It is too early to judge the success of Farah's approach but there is at least good reason to doubt it. One alternative is to postulate a proliferation of recognition units for famous buildings, outlines of countries, the location of cities on maps, pieces of music, etc. This approach seems clumsy and implies almost endless patterns of dissociations to be sought! Perhaps such unique referents are represented within pools of more general recognition units for the appropriate modality (e.g. object recognition units). Even if there are parallel routes for face, word and object recognition, Farah's hypothesis might account for differential recognition abilities observed in patients for different classes of objects (e.g. animate versus inanimate object). Extending the hypothesis to faces and words could be thought of as an extreme of an approach that might avoid a need for categorical organisation of object recognition units or the semantic system.

One important aspect of proper names that we have identified is that they generally have a unique referent (but see Chapter 1). In theories of person recognition this is instantiated by access to semantic information being mediated via a token marker or person identity node. Perhaps visual representations of unique objects differ from common objects in that access to semantic information is mediated via a token marker. This would require that token markers for all referents of proper names must be postulated. It is in just this manner that recognition of written and auditorily presented proper names differs from recognition of common names in the proposed model. This distinction allows one to account for preservation of recognition of proper names in global aphasics by postulating that the impairment is to the semantic system, access to it or even possibly restricted to the semantic lexicon for common names.

There are neuropsychological dissociations that impinge on the production of names, with patients showing uneven naming of different categories of proper names. For instance, as discussed in Chapter 5, Lucchelli and de Renzi (1992) and Fery et al. (1995) have showed that the naming of people's names can be more impaired than that of other categories of proper names, e.g. cities, countries, etc. McKenna and Warrington (1980) also briefly reported a similar patient.

Dissociations between categories of proper names could be accounted for by postulating a categorically organised lexicon. So, the lexical representations of people's names could be separate from the representations of cities, rivers and countries. This is unappealing on grounds of parsimony and is only a redescription of the data. An alternative has been offered by Brennen (1993), who argues that the neuropsychological data are consistent with the plausible phonology hypothesis. This predicts that names in categories constantly being replenished with new exemplars should be most difficult to access. There is no need to postulate categorically separated lexical representations. The plausible phonology hypothesis offers a reason for the special difficulty posed by the recall of people's names. The hypothesis is testable; for example, it leads to the prediction that people's names will always be the category of proper names that will pose the greatest naming difficulty. (Many new people are frequently encountered both in person and via the media.) Intact recall of people's names in the context of a deficit for another category of proper names would falsify the plausible phonology hypothesis, but it remains to be tested in detail. Other functional differences between categories of proper names also exist that might account for differences between the recall of categories of proper names. These differences, for example, the raw number of exemplars known or age of acquisition, need to be ruled out before it is concluded that the lexicon is categorically organised.

To sum up, the same basic box model framework can account for the identity processing of referents of proper names. A proliferation of pools of recognition units for all referents of proper names may be unnecessary (e.g. famous building recognition units, country outline recognition units, etc.). Such entities may be represented within a more general pool of recognition units connecting to appropriate token markers. Differential abilities to comprehend stimuli drawn from the various categories of referents of proper names may be explicable in terms of the different demands such stimuli make on the processing system (cf. Farah, 1991). For example, the outline of countries may be processed as a whole but recognition of famous buildings may require representation of several defining parts. If Farah's hypothesis is correct, this analysis would predict certain patterns of association and dissociation of comprehension of the referents of proper names with prosopagnosia and alexia. For example, a deficit in recognition of country outlines may be likely to co-occur with prosopagnosia, if faces and country outlines require holistic processing. Impairment to the ability to recognise famous buildings and alexia may be likely to be associated.

It is difficult to see how proper name processing can be accounted for without postulating a token marker for each entity which carries a proper name (e.g. people, famous buildings, pets, etc.). However, there is no evidence at present to suggest that such token markers are categorically organised. Such a conclusion would require that subjects would show double dissociations between different classes of proper names. If token markers are themselves destroyed, subjects should show category-specific deficits for a single class of proper names which affects comprehension of the referent (i.e. a picture), visual and auditory comprehension of the proper name and the ability to name the referent from a definition.

It may be possible to avoid postulation of categorical organisation within lemmas for proper names by incorporating Brennen's (1993) plausible phonology hypothesis.

SO WHY *ARE* PROPER NAMES SO DIFFICULT TO RECALL?

We pointed out in Chapter 1 that the interest of cognitive psychologists in proper name processing has been drawn by the observation that proper names are particularly difficult to recall, and are particularly vulnerable to the effects of ageing and brain-injury. We have reviewed the evidence and explored a number of hypotheses. In conclusion, we must address the original question with which we began: why are proper names so difficult to recall?

In the time-honoured tradition of psychologists, we can conclude that there is no one single factor that make proper names difficult to recall but a number of factors are involved in the explanation! Of central importance is the fact that proper names and their referents are generally unique. This means that in order to recall a proper name, activation must be passed by a single link from a token marker to a proper name phrase node. It is this single link (as opposed to multiple pathways) that makes proper name retrieval more difficult than recall of common names or identity-specific semantics. In western cultures, people's full names are usually unique but are often composed of first names and surnames which are shared by many others. This is the worst possible situation for recall of people's names. Not only must a proper name phrase node be activated by a single link, but once first names and surnames begin to be activated, the proper name phrase node is inhibited by other nodes sharing the same first name or surname. Other factors also contribute to the difficulty of recall of proper names. There is usually no possibility of resorting to the use of another relevant name, the plausible phonology of the name to be retrieved is almost unlimited and many new exemplars of proper names are often being created and encountered throughout one's lifetime. Perhaps, as cognitive psychologists, we should be more impressed that people successfully recall proper names as often as they do, rather than focus on the occasional failure.

Bibliography

Abson, V. and Rabbitt, P. (1988) 'What do self rating questionnaires tell us about changes in competence in old age? In M.M. Gruneberg, P.E. Morris and R.N. Sykes (eds), *Practical Aspects of Memory: Current Research and Issues, Volume 2*. Chichester: Wiley & Sons.

Alford, R.D. (1988) *Naming and Identity: A Cross-cultural Study of Personal Naming Practices*. New Haven, CT: HRAF Press.

Allerton, D.J. (1990) 'Language as form and pattern'. In N.E. Collinge (ed.), *An Encyclopedia of Language*. London: Routledge.

Alspach, E.M. (1917) 'On the psychological response to unknown proper names'. *American Journal of Psychology*, 28, 436–443.

Anderson, J.R. (1974) 'Retrieval of propositional information from long-term memory'. *Cognitive Psychology*, 6, 451–474.

Anderson, J. R. (1976) *Language, Memory and Thought*. Hillsdale, NJ: Erlbaum.

Anderson, J.R; and Paulson, R. (1978) 'Interference in memory for pictorial information'. *Cognitive Psychology*, 10, 178–202.

Anonymous (1991) *Le vif/l'express*, p. 8.

Anonymous (1992) *Le vif/l'express*, p. 9.

Baars, B.J., Motley, M.T. and MacKay, D. (1975) 'Output editing for lexical status from artificially elicited slips of the tongue'. *Journal of Verbal Learning and Verbal Behavior*, 1, 382–391.

Baddeley, A. (1990) *Human Memory – Theory and Practice*. Hove: Lawrence Erlbaum.

Baggett, P. and Ehrenfeucht, A. (1982) 'How an unfamiliar thing should be called'. *Journal of Psycholinguistic Research*, 11, 437–445.

Balota, D.A. and Chumley, J.I. (1984) 'Are lexical decisions a good measure of lexical access? The role of word frequency in the neglected decision stage'. *Journal of Experimental Psychology: Human Perception and Performance*, 10, 340–357.

Balota, D.A. and Chumley, J.I. (1985) 'The locus of word frequency effects in the pronunciation task: Lexical access and/or production'. *Journal of Memory and Language*, 24, 89–106.

Bayles, K.A. and Trosset, M.W. (1992) 'Confrontation naming in Alzheimer's patients: Relation to disease severity'. *Psychology and Aging*, 7, 197–203.

Beauvois, M.-F. and Saillant, B. (1985) 'Optic aphasia for colours and colour agnosia: A distinction between visual and visuo-verbal impairments in the processing of colours'. *Cognitive Neuropsychology*, 2, 1–48.

Benson, D.F. (1988) 'Classical syndromes of aphasia'. In F. Boller and J. Grafman (eds), *Handbook of Neuropsychology*. North Holland: Elsevier.

Bertoncini, J., Bijeljac-Babic, R., Jusczyk, P.W., Kennedy, L.J. and Mehler, J. (1988)

'An investigation of young infants' perceptual representations of speech sounds'. *Journal of Experimental Psychology: General*, 117, 21–33.

Bierwisch, M. and Schreuder, R. (1992) 'From concepts to lexical items'. *Cognition*, 42, 23–60.

Blackmer, E.R. and Mitton, J.L. (1992) 'Theories of monitoring and the timing of repairs in spontaneous speech'. *Cognition*, 39, 173–194.

Bloomfield, L. (1933) *Language*. New York: Henry Holt.

Bock, K. (1990) 'Structure in language: Creating form in language'. *American Psychologist*, 45, 1221–1236.

Bolla, K.I., Lindgren, K.N., Bonaccorsy, C. and Bleecker, M.L. (1991) 'Memory complaints in older adults, fact or fiction?' *Archives of Neurology*, 48, 61–64.

Boucaud, P. (1990) 'La nomination dans le droit comparé'. In J. Clerget (ed.), *Le nom et la nomination: Source, sens et pouvoir*. Toulouse: Erès.

Brédart, S. (1993) 'Retrieval failures in face naming'. *Memory*, 1, 351–366.

Brédart, S. and Valentine, T. (1992) 'From Monroe to Moreau. An analysis of face naming errors'. *Cognition*, 45, 187–223.

Brédart, S., Valentine, T., Calder, A. and Gassi, L. (1995) 'An interactive activation model of face naming'. *Quarterly Journal of Experimental Psychology*, 466–486.

Breen, R. (1982) 'Naming practices in Western Ireland'. *Man*, 17, 701–713.

Brennen, T. (1993) 'The difficulty with recalling people's names: The plausible phonology hypothesis'. *Memory*, 1, 409–431.

Brennen, T. and Bruce, V. (1991) 'Context effects in the processing of familiar faces'. *Psychological Research*, 53, 296–304.

Brennen, T., Baguley, T., Bright, J. and Bruce, V. (1990) 'Resolving semantically-induced tip-of-the-tongue states for proper nouns'. *Memory and Cognition*, 18, 339–347.

Brennen, T., David, D., Fluchaire, I. and Pellat, J. (in press) 'Naming faces and objects without comprehension – a case study'. *Cognitive Neuropsychology*.

Brown, A.S. (1991) 'A review of the tip-of-the-tongue experience'. *Psychological Bulletin*, 109, 204–223.

Brown, R.W. and McNeill, D. (1966) 'The "tip-of-the-tongue" phenomenon'. *Journal of Verbal Learning and Verbal Behavior*, 5, 325–337.

Brown, R.W. and Nuttall, R. (1959). 'Method in phonetic symbolism experiments'. *Journal of Abnormal and Social Psychology*, 59, 441–445.

Brown, R.W., Black, A.H. and Horowitz, A.E. (1955) 'Phonetic symbolism in natural languages'. *Journal of Abnormal and Social Psychology*, 50, 388–393.

Bruce, V. (1979) 'Searching for politicians: An information-processing approach to face recognition'. *Quarterly Journal of Experimental Psychology*, 31, 373–395.

Bruce, V. (1981) 'Visual and semantic effects in a serial word classification task'. *Current Psychological Research*, 1, 153–162.

Bruce, V. (1983) 'Recognizing faces'. *Philosophical Transactions of the Royal Society, London*, B302, 423–436.

Bruce, V. (1986) 'Influences of familiarity on the processing of faces'. *Perception*, 15, 387–397.

Bruce, V. (1988) *Recognising Faces*: London: Lawrence Erlbaum.

Bruce, V. and Valentine, T. (1985) 'Identity priming in the recognition of familiar faces'. *British Journal of Psychology*, 76, 373–383.

Bruce, V. and Valentine, T. (1986) 'Semantic priming of familiar faces'. *Quarterly Journal of Experimental Psychology*, 38A, 125–150.

Bruce, V. and Valentine, T. (1988) 'When a nod's as good as a wink: The role of dynamic information in face recognition'. In M.M. Gruneberg, P.E. Morris and R.N. Sykes (eds), *Practical Aspects of Memory: Current Research and Issues, Volume 1*. Chichester: Wiley & Sons.

Bruce, V. and Young, A. (1986) 'Understanding face recognition'. *British Journal of Psychology*, 77, 305–327.

Bruyer, R. (1987) *Les mécanismes de reconnaissance des visages*. Grenoble: Presses Universitaires de Grenoble.

Bruyer, R., Laterre, C., Seron, X., Feyereisen, P., Strypstein, E., Pierrard, E. and Rectem, D. (1983) 'A case of prosopagnosia with some covert remembrance of familiar faces'. *Brain and Cognition*, 2, 257–284.

Bruyer, R., van der Linden, M., Lodewijck, M., Nelles, B., Schils, J.-P., Schweich, M. and Brédart, S. (1992) 'Age differences in putting names and occupations to faces'. *Archives de Psychologie*, 60, 243–257.

Bub, D., Cancelliere, A. and Kertesz, A. (1985) 'Whole-word and analytic translation of spelling-to-sound in a non-semantic reader'. In K. Patterson, J.C. Marshall and M. Coltheart (eds), *Surface Dyslexia*. London: Lawrence Erlbaum.

Burke, D.M., Worthley, J. and Martin, J. (1988) 'I'll never forget what's her name: Aging and the tip of the tongue experiences in everyday life'. In M.M. Gruneberg, P.E. Morris and R.N. Sykes (eds), *Practical Aspects of Memory: Current Research and Issues, Volume 2*. Chichester: Wiley & Sons.

Burke, D.M., MacKay, D.G., Worthley, J.S. and Wade, E. (1991) 'On the tip of the tongue: What causes word finding failures in young and older adults?' *Journal of Memory and Language*, 30, 542–579.

Burton, A.M. and Bruce, V. (1992) 'I recognise your face but I can't remember your name: a simple explanation?' *British Journal of Psychology*, 83, 45–60.

Burton, A.M. and Bruce, V. (1993) 'Naming faces and naming names: Exploring an interactive activation model of name retrieval'. *Memory*, 1, 457–480.

Burton, A.M., Bruce, V. and Johnston, R.A. (1990) 'Understanding face recognition with an interactive activation model'. *British Journal of Psychology*, 81, 361–380.

Burton, A.M., Young, A.W., Bruce, V., Johnston, R.A. and Ellis, A.W. (1991) 'Understanding covert recognition'. *Cognition*, 39, 129–166.

Butterworth, B. (1980) 'Some constraints on models of language production'. In B. Butterworth (ed.), *Language Production, Volume 1: Speech and Talk*. London: Academic Press.

Butterworth, B. (1989) 'Lexical access in speech production'. In W. Marslen-Wilson (ed.), *Lexical Representation and Process*. Cambridge, MA: MIT Press.

Calder, A.J. (1993) *Self Priming in Face Recognition*. Ph.D. dissertation, University of Durham.

Carney, R. and Temple, C.M. (1993) 'Prosopanomia? A possible category-specific anomia for faces'. *Cognitive Neuropsychology*, 10, 185–195.

Carroll, J.M. (1985) *What's in a Name? An Essay in the Psychology of Reference*. New York: W.H. Freeman and Company.

Chierchia, G. and McConnell-Ginet, S. (1990) *Meaning and Grammar: An Introduction to Semantics*. Cambridge, MA: MIT Press.

Cipolotti, L., McNeil, J.E. and Warrington, E.K. (1993) 'Spared written naming of proper names: A case report'. *Memory*, 1, 289–311.

Clark, E. (1988) 'On the logic of contrast'. *Journal of Child Language*, 15, 317–335.

Clark, H.H. and Gerrig, R.J. (1983) 'Understanding old words with new meanings'. *Journal of Verbal Learning and Verbal Behavior*, 22, 591–608.

Clarke, R. and Morton, J. (1983) 'Cross modality facilitation in tachistoscopic word recognition'. *Quarterly Journal of Experimental Psychology*, 35A, 79–96.

Cohen, G. (1990a) 'Recognition and retrieval of proper names: Age differences in the fan effect'. *European Journal of Cognitive Psychology*, 2, 193–204.

Cohen, G. (1990b) 'Why is it difficult to put names to faces?' *British Journal of Psychology*, 81, 287–297.

Cohen, G. and Faulkner, D. (1984) 'Memory in old age: "Good in parts"'. *New Scientist*, 11, 49–51.

Cohen, G. and Faulkner, D. (1986) 'Memory for proper names: Age differences in retrieval'. *British Journal of Developmental Psychology*, 4, 187–197.

Collier, G.A. (1970) 'Nicknames and social structure in Zinacantan'. *American Anthropologist*, 72, 289–302.

Colman, A.M., Hargreaves, D.J. and Sluckin, W. (1981) 'Preferences for Christian names as a function of their experienced familiarity'. *British Journal of Social Psychology*, 20, 3–5.

Crystal, D. (1980) *A First Dictionary of Linguistics and Phonetics*. London: André Deutch.

Dannenbring, G.L. and Briand, K. (1982) 'Semantic priming and the word repetition effect in a lexical decision task'. *Canadian Journal of Psychology*, 36, 435–444.

Davidoff, J.B. and Ostergaard, A.L. (1984) 'Color anomia resulting from weakened short-term memory'. *Brain*, 107, 415–431.

Dawkins, R. (1989) *The Selfish Gene – New Edition*. Oxford: Oxford University Press.

de Haan, E.H.F., Young, A.W. and Newcombe, F. (1987) 'Face recognition without awareness'. *Cognitive Neuropsychology*, 4, 385–415.

de Haan, E.H.F., Young, A.W. and Newcombe, F. (1991) 'Covert and overt recognition in prosopagnosia'. *Brain*, 114, 2575–2591.

de Saussure, F. (1916) *Cours de linguistique générale*. Paris: Payot.

Dell, G.S. (1986) 'A spreading activation theory of retrieval in sentence production'. *Psychological Review*, 93, 283–321.

Dell, G.S. (1989) 'The retrieval of phonological forms in production: Tests of predictions from a connectionist model'. In W. Marslen-Wilson (ed.), *Lexical Representation and Process*. Cambridge, MA: MIT Press.

Dell, G.S. (1990) 'Effects of frequency and vocabulary type on phonological speech errors'. *Language and Cognitive Processes*, 5, 313–349.

Dell, G.S. and Reich, P.A. (1981) 'Stages in language production: An analysis of speech error data'. *Journal of Verbal Learning and Verbal Behavior*, 20, 611–629.

Dell, G.S. and O'Seaghdha, P.G. (1991) 'Mediated and convergent lexical priming in language production: A comment on Levelt *et al.* (1991)'. *Psychological Review*, 98, 604–614.

Dell, G.S. and O'Seaghdha, P.G. (1992) 'Stages of lexical access in language production'. *Cognition*, 42, 287–314.

Dennis, M. (1976) 'Dissociated naming and locating parts of the body after left anterior temporal lobe resection'. *Brain and Language*, 3, 147–163.

Devolder, P.A. and Pressley, M. (1991) 'Memory complaints in younger and older adults'. *Applied Cognitive Psychology*, 5, 443–454.

Diamond, B.J., Valentine, T., Mayes, A.R. and Sandel, M.E. (1994) 'Evidence of covert recognition in a prosopagnosic patient'. *Cortex*, 30, 377–393.

Dorian, N.C. (1970) 'A substitute name system in Scottish Highlands'. *American Anthropologist*, 72, 303–319.

Dubois, J., Giacomo, M., Guespin, L., Marcellesi, C., Marcellesi, J.-B. and Mevel, J.-P. (1973) *Dictionnaire de linguistique*. Paris: Larousse.

Ellis, A. and Beechley, R.M. (1954) 'Emotional disturbance in children with peculiar given names'. *Journal of Genetic Psychology*, 85, 337–339.

Ellis, A.W. and Young, A.W. (1988) *Human Cognitive Neuropsychology*. Hove: Lawrence Erlbaum.

Ellis, A.W., Young, A.W. and Critchley, E. M. R. (1989) 'Loss of memory for people following temporal lobe damage'. *Brain*, 112, 1469–1483.

Ellis, A.W., Young, A.W., Flude, B.M. and Hay, D.C. (1987) 'Repetition priming of face recognition'. *Quarterly Journal of Experimental Psychology*, 39A, 193–210.

Engel, P. (1990) 'Les noms propres et la théorie de la référence directe'. In J. Clerget (ed.), *Le nom et la nomination: Source, sens et pouvoir*. Toulouse: Erès.

English, G. (1916) 'On the psychological response to unknown proper names'. *American Journal of Psychology*, 27, 430–434.

Erwin, P.G. and Calev, A. (1984) 'The influence of Christian name stereotypes on the marking of children's essays'. *British Journal of Educational Psychology*, 54, 223–224.

Farah, M.J. (1988) 'Is visual imagery really visual? Overlooked evidence from neuropsychology'. *Psychological Review*, 95, 307–317.

Farah, M.J. (1991) 'Patterns of co-occurrence among the associative agnosias: Implications for visual object representation'. *Cognitive Neuropsychology*, 8, 1–19.

Fery, P., Vincent, E. and Brédart, S. (1995) 'Personal name anomia: A single case study'. *Cortex*, 31, 181–190.

Fischler, I. (1977) 'Semantic facilitation without association in a lexical decision task'. *Memory and Cognition*, 5, 335–339.

Flude, B.M., Ellis, A.W. and Kay, J. (1989) 'Face processing and name retrieval in an anomic aphasic: names are stored separately from semantic information about familiar people'. *Brain and Cognition*, 11, 60–72.

Fox, C.W. (1935) 'An experimental study of naming'. *American Journal of Psychology*, 47, 545–579.

Frege, G. (1892) 'Über Sinn und Bedeutung'. *Zeitschrift für Philosophie und Philosophische Kritik*, 100, 25–50.

Funnell, E. and Allport, A. (1987) 'Non-linguistic cognition and word meanings: Neuropsychological exploration of common mechanisms'. In A. Allport, D. Mackay, W. Prinz and E. Scheerer (eds), *Language Perception and Production: Relationships Between Listening, Speaking, Reading and Writing*. London: Academic Press.

Gailey, P. (1986) 'Supporters of La Rouche are winning local ballot spots in growing numbers'. *The New York Times*, 23 March, p. 38.

Garrett, M.F. (1975) 'The analysis of sentence production'. In G.H. Bower (ed.), *The Psychology of Learning and Motivation*. New York: Academic Press.

Garrett, M.F. (1980) 'Levels of processing in sentence production'. In B. Butterworth (ed.), *Language Production, Volume 1, Speech and Talk*. London: Academic Press.

Gelman, S.A. and Taylor, M. (1984) ' How two-year-old children interpret proper and common names for unfamiliar objects'. *Child Development*, 55, 1535–1540.

Goodenough, W.H. (1965) 'Personal names and modes of address in two Oceanic societies'. In M.E. Spiro (ed.), *Context and Meaning in Cultural Anthropology*. New York: Free Press.

Goodglass, H. and Butters, N. (1988) 'Psychobiology of cognitive processes'. In R. Atkinson, R. Hermstein, D. Luce and G. Lindzey (eds), *Stevens Handbook of Experimental Psychology, Volume 2*. New York: Wiley-Interscience.

Goodglass, H. and Wingfield, A. (1993) 'Dissociations in comprehension of body parts and geographical place names following focal brain lesions'. *Memory*, 1, 313–328.

Goodglass, H., Klein, B., Carey, P. and Jones, K.J. (1966) 'Specific semantic word categories in aphasia'. *Cortex*, 2, 74-89.

Goodglass, H., Kaplan, E., Weintraub, S. and Ackerman, N. (1976) 'The "tip-of-the-tongue" phenomenon in aphasia'. *Cortex*, 12, 145–153.

Goodglass, H., Wingfield, A., Hyde, M.R. and Theurkauf, J.C. (1986) 'Category-specific dissociations in naming and recognition by aphasic patients'. *Cortex*, 22, 87–102.

Goose, A. (1986) *Le bon usage (Grévisse)*. Gembloux: Duculot.

Grand dictionnaire encyclopédique Larousse, Volume 8 (1984) Paris: Larousse.

Hall, D. (1991) 'Acquiring proper nouns for familiar and unfamiliar animate objects: Two-year-olds' word-learning biases'. *Child Development*, 62, 1142–1154.

Hanley, J.R. (1995) 'Are names difficult to recall because they are unique? A case study of a patient with anomia'. *Quarterly Journal of Experimental Psychology*, 48A, 487–506.

Hanley, J.R. and Cowell, E.S. (1988) 'The effects of different types of retrieval cues on the recall of names of famous faces'. *Memory and Cognition*, 16, 545–555.

Hanley, J. R., Young, A. W. and Pearson, N. A. (1989) 'Defective recognition of familiar people'. *Cognitive Neuropsychology*, 6, 179–210.

Harari, H. and McDavid, J.W. (1973) 'Name stereotypes and teachers' expectations'. *Journal of Educational Psychology*, 65, 222–225.

Harley, T.A. (1984) 'A critique of top-down independent levels models of speech production: Evidence from non-plan-internal speech errors'. *Cognitive Science*, 8, 191–219.

Harley, T.A. (1993) 'Phonological activation of semantic competitors during lexical access in speech production'. *Language and Cognitive Processes*, 8, 291–309.

Harris, M.B. (1975) 'Sex role stereotypes and teacher evaluations'. *Journal of Educational Psychology*, 67, 751–756.

Hart, J., Berndt, R.S. and Caramazza, A. (1985) 'Category-specific naming deficit following cerebral infraction'. *Nature*, 316, 439–440.

Hartmann, R.R.K. and Stork, F.C. (1972) *Dictionary of Language and Linguistics*. London: Applied Science Publishers.

Hay, D.C. and Young, A.W. (1982) 'The human face'. In A.W. Ellis (ed.), *Normality and Pathology in Cognitive Functions*. London: Academic Press.

Hay, D.C., Young, A.W. and Ellis, A.W. (1991) 'Routes through the face recognition system'. *Quarterly Journal of Experimental Psychology*, 43A, 761–791.

Hensley, W. and Spencer, B. (1985) 'The effect of first names on perceptions of female attractiveness'. *Sex Roles*, 12, 723–729.

Hillis, A.E. and Caramazza, A. (1991) 'Mechanisms for accessing lexical representations for output: Evidence from a category-specific semantic deficit'. *Brain and Language*, 40, 106–144.

Hinton, G.E. and Shallice, T. (1991) 'Lesioning an attractor network: Investigations of acquired dyslexia'. *Psychological Review*, 98, 74–95.

Hoorens, V. and Todorova, E. (1988) 'The name letter effect: Attachment to self or primacy of own name writing?' *European Journal of Social Psychology*, 18, 365–368.

Hoorens, V., Nuttin, J.M., Erdelyi-Herman, I. and Pavakanun, U. (1990) 'Mastery pleasure versus mere ownership: A quasi-experimental cross-cultural and cross-alphabetical test of the name letter effect'. *European Journal of Social Psychology*, 20, 181–205.

Humphreys, G.W. and Riddoch, M.J. (1987) *To See but not to See: A Case Study of Visual Agnosia*. Hove: Lawrence Erlbaum.

Humphreys, G., Riddoch, M.J. and Quinlan, P.T. (1988) 'Cascade processes in picture identification'. *Cognitive Neuropsychology*, 5, 67–103.

Huttenlocher, J. and Kubicek, L.F. (1983) 'The source of relatedness effects on naming latency'. *Journal of Experimental Psychology: Learning, Memory and Cognition*, 9, 486–496.

Jespersen, O. (1922) *Language: Its Nature, Development and Origin*. London: Allen & Unwin.

Jespersen, O. (1965) *The Philosophy of Grammar*. New York: Norton.

Johnson-Laird, P.N. (1983) *Mental Models*. Cambridge: Cambridge University Press.

Johnston, R.A. and Bruce, V. (1990) 'Lost properties? Retrieval differences between name codes and semantic codes for familiar people'. *Psychological Research*, 52, 62–67.

Journet, O. (1990) 'La personne au risque du nom'. In J. Clerget (ed.), *Le nom et la nomination: Source, sens et pouvoir*. Toulouse: Erès.

Kamin, L.J. (1958) 'Ethnic and party affiliations of candidates as determinants of voting'. *Canadian Journal of Psychology*, 12, 205–212.

Kasof, J. (1993) 'Sex bias in the naming of stimulus persons'. *Psychological Bulletin*, 113, 140–163.

Katz, J.J. (1972) *Semantic Theory*. New York: Harper & Row.

Katz, N., Baker, E. and Macnamara, J.M. (1974) 'What's in a name? A study of how children learn common and proper names'. *Child Development*, 45, 469–473.

Kay, J. and Ellis, A.W. (1987) 'A cognitive neuropsychological case study of anomia – implications for psychological models of word retrieval'. *Brain*, 110, 613–629.

Kempen, G. and Huijbers, P. (1983) 'The lexicalisation process in sentence production and naming: Indirect election of words'. *Cognition*, 14, 185–209.

Kendall, M.B. (1980) 'Exegis and translation: Northern Yuman names as texts'. *Journal of Anthropological Research*, 36, 261–273.

King, D.R.W. and Anderson, J.R. (1976) 'Long-term memory search: An intersecting activation process'. *Journal of Verbal Learning and Verbal Behavior*, 15, 587–605.

Köhler, W. (1947) *Gestalt Psychology*. New York: Liveright Press.

Kohn, S.E. and Friedman, R.B. (1986) 'Word-meaning deafness: A phonological-semantic dissociation'. *Cognitive Neuropsychology*, 3, 291–308.

Koriat, A. and Lieblich, I. (1974) 'What does a person in a "TOT" state know that a person in a "don't know" state doesn't know?' *Memory and Cognition*, 2, 647–655.

Kripke, S. (1980) *Naming and Necessity*. Oxford: Basil Blackwell.

Lallemand, S. (1978) *Systèmes de signes*. Paris: Hermann.

Larrabee, G.J., West, R.B. and Crook, T.H. (1991) 'The association of memory complaint with computer-simulated everyday memory performance'. *Journal of Clinical and Experimental Neuropsychology*, 13, 466–478.

Lawless, H. and Engen, T. (1977) 'Associations to odors: Interference, mnemonics and verbal labeling'. *Journal of Experimental Psychology: Human Learning and Memory*, 3, 52–59.

Levelt, W.J.M. (1983) 'Monitoring and self-repair in speech'. *Cognition*, 14, 41–104.

Levelt, W.J.M. (1989) *Speaking: From Intention to Articulation*. Cambridge, MA: MIT Press.

Levelt, W.J.M. (1992) 'Accessing words in speech production: Stages, processes and representations'. *Cognition*, 42, 1–22.

Levelt, W.J.M., Schriefers, H., Vorberg, D., Meyer, A.S., Pechmann, T. and Havinga, J. (1991) 'The time course of lexical access in speech production: A study of naming'. *Psychological Review*, 98, 122–142.

Levi-Strauss, C. (1962) *La pensée sauvage*. Paris: Plon.

Lewis, C. H. and Anderson, J. R. (1976) 'Interference with real world knowledge'. *Cognitive Psychology*, 8, 311–335.

Lindauer, M.S. (1990a) 'The meanings of the physiognomic stimuli taketa and maluma'. *Bulletin of the Psychonomic Society*, 28, 47–50.

Lindauer, M.S. (1990b) 'The effects of the physiognomic stimuli taketa and maluma on the meanings of neutral stimuli'. *Bulletin of the Psychonomic Society*, 28, 151–154.

Loar, B. (1978) 'The semantic of singular terms'. *Philosophical Studies*, 36, 553–577.

Lovelace, E.A. (1987) 'Attributes that come to mind in the TOT state'. *Bulletin of the Psychonomic Society*, 25, 370–372.

Lovelace, E.A. and Twohig, P.T. (1990) 'Healthy older adults' perceptions of their memory functioning and use of mnemonics'. *Bulletin of the Psychonomic Society*, 28, 115–118.

Lucchelli, F. and de Renzi, E. (1992) 'Proper name anomia'. *Cortex*, 28, 221–230.

McCarthy, R.A. and Warrington, E.K. (1985) 'Category specificity in an agrammatic patient: The relative impairment of verb retrieval and comprehension'. *Neuropsychologia*, 23, 709–725.

McCauley, C., Parmalee, C.M., Sperber, R.D. and Carr, T.H. (1980) 'Early extraction of meaning from pictures and its relation to conscious identification'. *Journal of Experimental Psychology: Human Perception and Performance*, 6, 265–276.

McClelland, J.L. (1981) 'Retrieving general and specific information from stored knowledge of specifics'. *Proceedings of the Third Annual Conference of the Cognitive Science Society*, 170–172.

McClelland, J.L. and Rumelhart, D.L. (1981) 'An interactive activation model of context effects in letter perception: Part 1. An account of basic findings'. *Psychological Review*, 88, 375–407.

McCloskey, M. and Bigler, K. (1980) 'Focused memory search in fact retrieval'. *Memory and Cognition*, 8, 253–264.

McDavid, J.W. and Harari, H. (1966) 'Stereotyping of names and popularity in grade school children'. *Child Development*, 37, 453–459.

MacKay, D. (1987) *The Organization of Perception and Action: A Theory for Language and Other Cognitive Skills*. New York: Springer.

McKenna, P. and Warrington, E.K (1978) 'Category-specific naming preservation: A single case study'. *Journal of Neurology, Neurosurgery and Psychiatry*, 41, 571–574.

McKenna, P. and Warrington, E.K. (1980) 'Testing for nominal dysphasia'. *Journal of Neurology, Neurosurgery and Psychiatry*, 43, 781–788.

McWeeny, K.H., Young, A.W., Hay, D.C. and Ellis, A.W. (1987) 'Putting names to faces'. *British Journal of Psychology*, 78, 143–149.

Marks, L.E. (1978) *The Unity of the Senses*. London: Academic Press.

Martin, M. (1986) 'Ageing and patterns of change in everyday memory and cognition'. *Human Learning*, 5, 63–74.

Martin, R.M. (1987) *The Meaning of Language*. Cambridge, MA: MIT Press.

Martin, N., Weisberg, R.W. and Saffran, E.M. (1989) 'Variables influencing the occurrence of naming errors: Implications for models of lexical retrieval'. *Journal of Memory and Language*, 28, 462–485.

Maylor, E.A. (1990a) 'Recognizing and naming faces: Aging, memory retrieval and the tip of the tongue'. *Journal of Gerontology: Psychological Sciences*, 45, 215–226.

Maylor, E.A. (1990b) 'Age, blocking and the tip of the tongue state'. *British Journal of Psychology*, 81, 123–134.

Maylor, E.A. (1991) 'Recognizing and naming tunes: Memory impairment in the elderly'. *Journal of Gerontology: Psychological Sciences*, 46, 207–218.

Maylor, E.A. and Valentine, T. (1992) 'Linear and non-linear effects of aging on categorizing and naming faces'. *Psychology and Aging*, 7, 317–323.

Mehler, J., Jusczyk, P., Lambertz, G., Halsted, N., Bertoncini, J. and Amiel-Tison, C. (1988) 'A precursor of language acquisition in young infants'. *Cognition*, 29, 143–178.

Mehrabian, A. (1992) 'Interrelationships among name desirability, name uniqueness, emotion characteristics connoted by names, and temperament'. *Journal of Applied Social Psychology*, 22, 1797–1808.

Meyer, D.E. and Schvaneveldt, R.W. (1971) 'Facilitation in recognising pairs of words: Evidence of a dependence between retrieval operations'. *Journal of Experimental Psychology*, 90, 227–234.

Michel, F. (1979) 'Préservation du language écrit malgré un déficit majeur du language oral'. *Le Lyon Medical*, 241, 141–149.

Michel, F. and Andreewsky, E. (1983) 'Deep dysphasia: An analogue of deep dyslexia in the auditory modality'. *Brain and Language*, 18, 212–223.

Mill, J.S. (1843) *A System of Logic*. London: Longman.

Monsell, S. (1987) 'On the relation between lexical input and output pathways for speech'. In A. Allport, D. Mackay, W. Prinz and E. Scheerer (eds), *Language Perception and Production: Relationships Between Listening, Speaking, Reading and Writing*. London: Academic Press.

Monsell, S. (1991) 'The nature and locus of word frequency effects in reading'. In D. Besner and G.W. Humphreys (eds), *Basic Processes in Reading: Visual Word Recognition*. Hillsdale, NJ: Lawrence Erlbaum.

Monsell, S., Doyle, M.C. and Haggard, P.N. (1989) 'Effects of frequency on visual word recognition tasks: Where are they?' *Journal of Experimental Psychology: General*, 118, 43–71.

Monsell, S., Matthews, G.H. and Miller, D.C. (1992) 'Repetition of lexicalization across languages: A further test of the locus of priming'. *Quarterly Journal of Experimental Psychology*, 44A, 763–783.

Morrison, C.M., Ellis, A.W. and Quinlan, P.T. (1992) 'Age of acquisition, not word frequency, affects object naming not object recognition'. *Memory and Cognition*, 20, 705–714.

Morton, J. (1969) 'Interaction of information in word recognition'. *Psychological Review*, 76, 165–178.

Morton, J. (1979) 'Facilitation in word recognition: Experiments causing change in the logogen model'. In P.A. Kolers, M. Wrolstad and H. Bouma (eds), *Processing of Visible Language*. New York: Plenum.

Morton, J. (1980). 'An anologue of deep dyslexia in the auditory modality'. In M. Coltheart, K. Patterson and J.C. Marshall (eds), *Deep Dyslexia*. London: Routledge & Kegan Paul.

Morton, J. and Patterson, K. (1980) 'A new attempt at an interpretation, or, an attempt at a new interpretation'. In M. Coltheart, K. Patterson and J.C. Marshall (eds), *Deep Dyslexia*. London: Routledge & Kegan Paul.

Murrell, G.A. and Morton, J. (1974) 'Word recognition and morphemic structure'. *Journal of Experimental Psychology*, 102, 963–968.

Myers, J. L., O'Brien, E. J., Balota, D. A. and Toyofuku, M. L. (1984) 'Memory search without interference: The role of integration'. *Cognitive Psychology*, 16, 217–242.

Neely, J.H. (1976) 'Semantic priming and retrieval from lexical memory: Evidence for facilitatory and inhibitory processes'. *Memory and Cognition*, 4, 648–654.

Norris, D. (1984) 'The effects of frequency, repetition and stimulus quality in visual word recognition'. *Quarterly Journal of Experimental Psychology*, 36A, 507–518.

Nuttin, J. (1985) 'Narcissism beyond Gestalt and awareness: The name letter effect'. *European Journal of Social Psychology*, 15, 353–361.

Nuttin, J. (1987) 'Affective consequences of mere ownership: The name letter effect in twelve European languages'. *European Journal of Social Psychology*, 17, 381–402.

O'Boyle, M.W. and Tarte, R.D. (1980) 'Implications for phonetic symbolism: The relationship between pure tones and geometric figures'. *Journal of Psycholinguistic Research*, 9, 535–544.

O'Boyle, M.W., Miller, D.A. and Rahmani, F. (1987) 'Sound–meaning relationships in speakers of Urdu and English: Evidence for a cross-cultural phonetic symbolism'. *Journal of Psycholinguistic Research*, 16, 273–288.

O'Sullivan, C.S., Chen, A., Mohapatra, S., Sigelman, L. and Lewis, E. (1988) 'Voting in ignorance: The politics of smooth-sounding names'. *Journal of Applied Social Psychology*, 18, 1094–1106.

Oldfield, R.C. and Wingfield, A. (1965) 'Response latencies in naming objects'. *Journal of Experimental Psychology*, 18, 3–16.

Onifer, W. and Swinney, D.A. (1981) 'Accessing lexical ambiguities during sentence comprehension: Effects of frequency of meaning and contextual bias'. *Memory and Cognition*, 9, 225–236.

Perlmutter, M. (1978) 'What is memory aging the aging of?' *Developmental Psychology*, 14, 330–345.

Popkin, S.J., Gallagher, D., Thompson, L.W. and Moore, M. (1982) 'Memory complaint and performance in normal and depressed older adults'. *Experimental Aging Research*, 8, 141–145.

Putnam, H. (1975) 'The meaning of meaning'. In H. Putnam (ed.), *Philosophical Papers*. Cambridge: Cambridge University Press.

Quinlan, P.T. (1991) *Connectionism and Psychology: A Psychological Perspective on New Connectionist Research*. Hemel Hempstead: Harvester-Wheatsheaf.

Quirk, R., Greenbaum, S., Leech, G. and Svartvik, J. (1985) *A Comprehensive Grammar of the English Language*. London: Longman.

Rabbitt, P. (1982) 'Development of methods to measure changes in activities in daily living in the elderly'. In S. Corkin, K.L. Davis, J.H. Growdon, E. Usdin and R. Wuttman (eds), *Alzheimer's Disease: A Report of Progress in Research*. New York: Raven Press.

Read, J.D. and Bruce, D. (1982) 'Longitudinal tracking of difficult memory retrievals'. *Cognitive Psychology*, 14, 280–300.

Reason, J.T. and Lucas, D. (1984) 'Using cognitive diaries to investigate naturally occurring memory blocks'. In J.E. Harris and P.E. Morris (eds), *Everyday Memory, Actions and Absentmindedness*. London: Academic Press.

Roelofs, A. (1992) 'A spreading-activation theory of lemma retrieval in speaking'. *Cognition*, 42, 107–142.

Rubellin-Devichi, J. (1990) 'Le droit, le nom et la nomination'. In J. Clerget (ed.), *Le nom et la nomination: Source, sens et pouvoir*. Toulouse: Erès.

Rubin, D.C. (1975) 'Within word structure in the tip-of-the-tongue phenomenon'. *Journal of Verbal Learning and Verbal Behavior*, 14, 392–397.

Rubin, D.C., Stoltzfus, E.R. and Wall, K.L. (1991) 'The abstraction of form in semantic categories'. *Memory and Cognition*, 19, 1–17.

Rumiati, R., Humphreys, G.W., Riddoch, M.J. and Bateman, A. (1995) 'Visual object agnosia without prosopagnosia or alexia: Evidence for hierarchical theories of visual recognition'. *Visual Cognition*, 1, 181–225.

Russell, B. (1905) 'On denoting'. *Mind*, 14, 479–493.

Ryan, M.P., Petty, C.R. and Wennzlaff, R.M. (1982) 'Motivated remembering efforts during tip-of-the-tongue states'. *Acta Psychologica*, 51, 137–147.

Saffran, E.M., Schwartz, M.F. and Marin, O.S.M. (1976) 'Semantic mechanisms in paralexia'. *Brain and Language*, 3, 255–265.

Saffran, E.M., Bogyo, L.C., Schwartz, M.F. and Marin, O.S.M. (1980) 'Does deep dyslexia reflect right hemisphere reading?' In M. Coltheart, K. Patterson and J.C. Marshall (eds), *Deep Dyslexia*. London: Routledge & Kegan Paul.

Sapir, E. (1929) 'A study of phonetic symbolism'. *Journal of Experimental Psychology*, 12, 225–239.

Scarborough, D.L., Cortese, C. and Scarborough, H.S. (1977) 'Frequency and repetition effects in lexical memory'. *Journal of Experimental Psychology: Human Perception and Performance*, 3, 1–17.

Schloss, I. (1981) 'Chickens and pickles'. *Journal of Advertising Research*, 21, 47–49.

Schriefers, H. (1990) 'Lexical and conceptual factors in the naming of relations'. *Cognitive Psychology*, 22, 111–142.

Schriefers, H., Meyer, A.S. and Levelt, W.J.M. (1990) 'Exploring the time course of lexical access in production: Picture-word interference studies'. *Journal of Memory and Language*, 29, 86–102.

Schwartz, M.F., Saffran, E. and Marin, O.S. (1980) 'Fractionating the reading process in dementia: Evidence for word-specific print-to-sound associations'. In M. Coltheart, K. Patterson and J.C. Marshall (eds), *Deep Dyslexia*. London: Routledge & Kegan Paul.

Schweich, M., van der Linden, M., Brédart, S., Bruyer, R., Nelles, B. and Schils, J.-P. (1992) 'Daily-life difficulties in person recognition reported by young and elderly subjects'. *Applied Cognitive Psychology*, 6, 161–172.

Searle, J. (1958) 'Proper names'. *Mind*, 67, 166–173.

Seidenberg, M.S. and McClelland, J.L. (1989) 'A distributed developmental model of word recognition and naming'. *Psychological Review*, 96, 523–568.

Seidenberg, M.S., Waters, G.S. and Barnes, M.A. (1984) 'When does irregular spelling or pronunciation influence word recognition?' *Journal of Verbal Learning and Verbal Behavior*, 23, 282–404.

Seidenberg, M.S., Tanehaus, M.K., Leiman, J.M. and Bienkowski, M. (1982) 'Automatic access of the meanings of ambiguous words in context: Some limitations of knowledge-based processing'. *Cognitive Psychology*, 14, 489–537.

Semenza, C. and Sgaramella, T.M. (1993) 'Production of proper names: A clinical case study of the effects of phonemic cueing'. *Memory*, 1, 265–280.

Semenza, C. and Zettin, M. (1988) 'Generating proper names: A case of selective inability'. *Cognitive Neuropsychology*, 5, 711–721.

Semenza, C. and Zettin, M. (1989) 'Evidence from aphasia for the role of proper names as pure referring expressions'. *Nature*, 342, 678–679.

Seraydarian, L. and Busse, T.V. (1981) 'First names stereotypes and essay grading'. *Journal of Psychology*, 108, 253–257.

Severi, C. (1980) 'Le nom de lignée. Les sobriquets dans un village d'Emilie'. *L'Homme*, 20, 105–112.

Seymour, P.H.K. (1979) *Human Visual Cognition*. London: Collier Macmillan.

Shallice, T. (1988) *From Neuropsychology to Mental Structure*. Cambridge: Cambridge University Press.

Shallice, T. and Kartsounis, I.D. (1993) 'Selective impairment of retrieving people's names: A category-specific disorder?' *Cortex*, 29, 281–291.

Shuren, J., Geldmacher, D. and Heilman, K.M. (1993) 'Nonoptic aphasia: Aphasia with preserved confrontation naming in Alzheimer's disease'. *Neurology*, 43, 1900–1907.

Simpson, G.B. and Krueger, M.A. (1991) 'Selective access of homograph meanings in sentence context'. *Journal of Memory and Language*, 30, 627–643.

Smith, B.L., Macaluso, C. and Brown-Sweeney, S. (1991) 'Phonological effects shown by normal adult speakers learning new words: Implications for phonological development'. *Applied Psycholinguistics*, 12, 281–298.

Smith, E. E., Adams, N. and Schorr, D. (1978) 'Fact retrieval and the paradox of interference'. *Cognitive Psychology*, 10, 438–464.

Smith, S.M., Brown, J.M. and Balfour, S.P. (1991) 'TOTimals: A controlled experimental method for studying tip-of-the-tongue states'. *Bulletin of the Psychonomic Society*, 29, 445–447.

Soja, N.N., Carey, S. and Spelke, E.S. (1992) 'Perception, ontology and word meaning – Discussion'. *Cognition*, 45, 101–107.

Stanhope, N. and Cohen, G. (1993) 'Retrieval of proper names: Testing the models'. *British Journal of Psychology*, 84, 51–65.

Stemberger, J.P. (1983) 'Distant context effects in language production: A reply to Motley *et al*'. *Journal of Psycholinguistic Research*, 12, 555–560.

Stemberger, J.P. (1985) 'An interactive activation model of language production'. In A.W. Ellis (ed.), *Progress in the Psychology of Language, Volume 1*. London: Lawrence Erlbaum.

Strawson, P.F. (1959) *Individuals*. London: Methuen.

Sunderland, A., Watts, K., Baddeley, A. and Harris, J.E. (1986) 'Subjective memory assessment and test performance in elderly adults'. *Journal of Gerontology*, 41, 376–384.

Tanehaus, M.K., Leiman, J.M. and Seidenberg, M.K. (1979) 'Evidence for multiple stages in the processing of ambiguous words in syntactic contexts'. *Journal of Verbal Learning and Verbal Behavior*, 18, 427–440.

Tarkhov, S.A. (1992) 'From Karlo-Libknekhtovsk and New York to Propoysk and Rastyapino? How place names are changing in the former USSR'. *Post-Soviet Geography*, 33, 454–462.

Tarte, R.D. (1974) 'Phonetic symbolism in adult native speakers of Czech'. *Language and Speech*, 17, 87–94.

Tarte, R.D. (1982) 'The relationship between monosyllables and pure tones: An investigation of phonetic symbolism'. *Journal of Verbal Learning and Verbal Behavior*, 21, 352–360.

Temple, C.M. (1986) 'Anomia for animals in a child'. *Brain*, 109, 1225–1242.

Thorndyke, P.W. and Bower, G.H. (1974) 'Storage and retrieval processes in sentence memory'. *Cognitive Psychology*, 6, 515–543.

Tranel, D. and Damasio, A.R. (1985) 'Knowledge without awareness: An autonomic index of facial recognition by prosopagnosics'. *Science*, 228, 1453–1454.

Valentine, T. and Bruce, V. (1986a) 'Recognizing familiar faces: The role of distinctiveness and familiarity'. *Canadian Journal of Psychology*, 40, 300–305.

Valentine, T. and Bruce, V. (1986b) 'The effects of distinctiveness in recognising and classifying faces'. *Perception*, 15, 525–535.

Valentine, T. and Ferrara, A. (1991) 'Typicality in categorization, recognition and identification: Evidence from face recognition'. *British Journal of Psychology*, 82, 87–102.

Valentine, T. and Moore, V. (in press) 'Naming familiar faces: The effects of facial distinctiveness and surname frequency'. *Quarterly Journal of Experimental Psychology*.

Valentine, T., Moore, V. and Brédart, S. (1995) 'Priming production of people's names'. *Quarterly Journal of Experimental Psychology*, 48A, 466–486.

Valentine, T., Brédart, S., Lawson, R. and Ward, G. (1991) 'What's in a name? Access to information from people's names'. *European Journal of Cognitive Psychology*, 3, 147–176.

Valentine, T., Moore, V., Flude, B., Young, A. and Ellis, A. (1993) 'Repetition priming and proper name processing'. *Memory*, 1, 329–349.

Van Lancker, D. and Klein, K. (1990) 'Preserved recognition of familiar personal names in global aphasia'. *Brain and Language*, 39, 511–529.

Van Wijk, C. and Kempen, G. (1987) 'A dual system for producing self-repairs in spontaneous speech: Evidence from experimentally elicited corrections'. *Cognitive Psychology*, 19, 403–440.

Vernier, B. (1977) 'Emigration et déréglement du marché international'. *Actes de la Recherche en Sciences Sociales*, 31, 63–87.

Vernier, B. (1980) 'La circulation des biens, de la main d'oeuvre et des prénoms à Karpathos: du bon usage du bien et de la parenté'. *Actes de la Recherche en Sciences Sociales*, 31, 63–87.

Vitkovitch, M. and Humphreys, G.W. (1991) 'Perseverant responding in speeded naming to pictures: It's in the links'. *Journal of Experimental Psychology: Learning, Memory, and Cognition*, 8, 336–341.

Wapner, W. and Gardiner, H. (1979) 'A note on patterns of comprehension and recovery in global aphasia'. *Journal of Speech and Hearing Research*, 29, 765–772.

Warren, C. and Morton, J. (1982) 'The effects of priming on picture recognition'. *British Journal of Psychology*, 73, 117–129.

Warrington, E.K. and Clegg, F. (1993) 'Selective preservation of place names in an aphasic patient: A short report'. *Memory*, 1, 281–288.

Warrington, E.K. and McCarthy, R.A. (1987) 'Categories of knowledge. Further fractionations and an attempted integration'. *Brain*, 110, 1273–1296.

Warrington, E.K. and Shallice, T. (1979) 'Semantic access dyslexia'. *Brain*, 102, 43–63.

Webster's Third New International Dictionary of the English Language, Volume II (1976) London: Encyclopedia Britannica.

Wheeldon, L.R. and Monsell, S. (1992) 'The locus of repetition priming of spoken word production'. *Quarterly Journal of Experimental Psychology*, 44A, 723–761.

Wilde, O. (1957) *The Original Four-act Version of 'The Importance of Being Earnest'*. London: Methuen.

Williams, M. and Smith, H.V. (1954) 'Mental disturbances in tuberculous meningitis'. *Journal of Neurology, Neurosurgery, and Psychiatry*, 17, 173–182.

Williams, J.M., Little, M.M., Scates, S. and Blockman, N. (1987) 'Memory complaints and abilities among depressed older adults'. *Journal of Consulting and Clinical Psychology*, 55, 595–598.

Winnick, W.A. and Daniel, S.A. (1970) 'Two kinds of response priming in tachistoscopic recognition'. *Journal of Experimental Psychology*, 84, 74–81.

Yamadori, A. and Albert, M.L. (1973) 'Word category aphasia'. *Cortex*, 9, 112–125.

Yarmey, A.D. (1973) 'I recognize your face but I can't remember your name: Further evidence on the tip-of-the-tongue phenomenon'. *Memory and Cognition*, 1, 287–290.

Young, A.W. and de Haan, E.H.F. (1988) 'Boundaries of covert recognition in prosopagnosia'. *Cognitive Neuropsychology*, 5, 317–336.

Young, A.W. and Ellis, H.D. (1989) 'Semantic processing'. In A.W. Young and H.D. Ellis (eds), *Handbook of Research on Face Processing*. Amsterdam: North Holland.

Young, A.W., Ellis, A.W. and Flude, B.M. (1988a). 'Accessing stored information about familiar people'. *Psychological Research*, 50, 111–115.

Young, A.W., Hay, D.C. and Ellis, A.W. (1985) 'The faces that launched a thousand slips: Everyday difficulties and errors in recognizing people'. *British Journal of Psychology*, 76, 495–523.

Young, A.W., Hellawell, D.J. and de Haan, E.H.F. (1988b) 'Cross-domain semantic priming in normal subjects and a prosopagnosic patient'. *Quarterly Journal of Experimental Psychology*, 40A, 561–580.

Young, A.W., Humphreys, G.W., Riddoch, M.J., Hellawell, D. and de Haan, E.H.F. (1994) 'Recognition impairments and face imagery'. *Neuropsychologia*, 32, 693–702.

Young, A.W., Ellis, A.W., Flude, B.M., McWeeny, K.H. and Hay, D.C. (1986) 'Face–name interference'. *Journal of Experimental Psychology: Human Perception and Performance*, 12, 466–475.

Young, A.W., McWeeny, K.H., Ellis, A.W. and Hay, D.C. (1986) 'Naming and categorising faces and written names'. *Quarterly Journal of Experimental Psychology*, 38A, 297–318.

Ziff, P. (1960) *Semantic Analysis*. Ithaca: Cornell University Press.

Zonabend, F. (1977) 'Pourquoi nommer? Les noms de personnes dans un village français: Minot-en-Châtillonais'. In C. Levi-Strauss (ed.), *L'identité*. Paris: Grasset.

Zonabend, F. (1980) 'Le nom de personne'. *L'Homme*, 20, 7–23.

Zweigenhaft, R.L. (1977). 'The other side of unusual first names'. *Journal of Social Psychology*, 103, 291–302.

Name index

Subject index